# *Nothing is being suppressed*

*British poetry of the 1970s*

*Selected previous publications by Andrew Duncan*

## Poetry

*In a German Hotel*
*Cut Memories and False Commands*
*Sound Surface*
*Alien Skies*
*Switching and Main Exchange* *
*Pauper Estate* *
*Anxiety Before Entering a Room. New and selected poems*
*Surveillance and Compliance*
*Skeleton Looking at Chinese Pictures*
*The Imaginary in Geometry*
*Savage Survivals (amid modern suavity)* *
*Threads of Iron* *
*In Five Eyes* *
*On the Margins of Great Empires. Selected Poems* *

## Criticism

*The Poetry Scene in the Nineties* (internet only)
*Centre and Periphery in Modern British Poetry* **
*The Failure of Conservatism in Modern British Poetry* **
*Origins of the Underground*
*The Council of Heresy* *
*The Long 1950s* *
*A Poetry Boom 1990-2010* *
*Fulfilling the Silent Rules* *

## As editor

*Don't Start Me Talking* (with Tim Allen)
Joseph Macleod: *Cyclic Serial Zeniths from the Flux*
Joseph Macleod: *A Drinan Trilogy: The Cove / The Men of the Rocks /*
*Script from Norway* (co-edited with James Fountain)

* *original Shearsman titles*
** *revised 2nd editions from Shearsman*

# Nothing
# is being
# suppressed

*British Poetry of the 1970s*

## Andrew Duncan

Shearsman Books

First published in the United Kingdom in 2022 by
Shearsman Books Ltd
PO Box 4239
Swindon
SN3 9FN

Shearsman Books Ltd Registered Office
30–31 St. James Place, Mangotsfield, Bristol BS16 9JB
*(this address not for correspondence)*

ISBN 978-1-84861-749-0

Copyright © 2022 by Andrew Duncan.

Acknowledgements
'Twelve Vortices for Twelve Brothers' was published in *PN Review*, 2014.
Part of the piece on Paul Evans was published in *Poetry Wales*, 2010.

# Contents

"A great deal of work remains to be done, but it seems increasingly clear that we cannot now postulate four hundred years of chaos and an almost complete return to nomad conditions."
—Zel'devich

"I recall how one of my fellow students interrupted Jürgen Habermas' lecture in the university's largest auditorium to ask him whether he could express himself a little less complicatedly, for it was so difficult to understand him. One half of the audience applauded. He promised to do his best in order to be intelligible, Habermas replied, whereupon the other half of the audience started booing. To those who were now booing, Habermas replied, he could promise that his good intentions were bound to fail."
—Günter Hofmann, *quoted by* Müller-Doohm
(*Habermas. A Biography*)

"'Jeremiah,' said this personage, '**devildom first** and **poetising** afterwards.' There was an unpleasant tone of banter in this speech, which did not seem in…'"
—James Bowker, *Goblin Tales of Lancashire*

He ceasd for rivn link from link the bursting Universe explodes
All things reversd flew from their centers rattling bones
To bones join, shaking convulsd the shivering clay breathes
Each speck of dust to the Earths center nestles round & round
In pangs of an Eternal Birth in torment & awe & fear
—William Blake

# Introduction

Edward Lucie-Smith compiled, in 1970, a broad-based anthology of 86 poets. They were moving at different speeds. Mottram, four years later, by taking only the most innovative of these poets, created a magical environment in which we were hurtling into the future at an intoxicating speed. It is not too much to say that people who absorbed this environment saw a completely new world. Where elite poets were moving so fast, a comparison seemed attractive, where those who weren't moving forward seemed inferior. This insight was corrosive, even devastating, to reputation. It is hardly surprising if it was not shared by the people who were written off by it.

The rise of Jeremy Corbyn since 2015 raises the stakes for politicised poets who were born within two years of Corbyn and roughly followed his political trajectory from the white heat of 1968 onwards. The market value of cultural assets can go down as well as up. What sums up the splinter effect is that being a critic of Seventies poetry is like being Jeremy Corbyn – a startlingly wide range of people disagree with everything you say.

I am not trying to re-evaluate a period that has passed by. It was never evaluated in the first place, so this is the first run. Imposing a view from the present day would be unreasonable because poetic opinion in the present day is hopelessly divided. My interest is in presenting the Seventies through the eyes of the Seventies. The time is still here, simply overlaid by decades of later memories. The key to writing has been to forget everything that has happened since. To sink back into the horizon of 1975 and write something that suits the prejudices of the times.

There are several reasons for writing about the Seventies at this point. One is a reading of a recent collection of memories of the decade by participants (London poets, in fact). My impression was that they couldn't remember the period – too much time had gone by. They had lost all sense of differentiation and were writing about 1975 as if it was 2015. It is also possible that any attitudes of the previous time which didn't chime with current positions were being written out, consciously or unconsciously. The extent of the mismatch is of great importance, I think. This suggested that there was a real problem with memory, justifying an account based on contemporary documents. The other problem with memory is that we are living in a splinter dictatorship, a cultural phase where the forces of convergence have stacked arms and opinions are split up into small groups. How can there be a collective memory when there is no single point on which all factions agree? So how can I record collective memory? In what sense is any statement about poetry true? But this argues even more for putting facts down and increasing the area free from malicious invention. We need to think about the divergence as a phenomenon in itself, a kind of cultural gravity that guides all the watercourses. The splintering allows local freedom at most locations – what it does not allow is unifying literary opinion.

Victor Turner remarks, about a tribe in Mali: "A fascinating historical and diffusionist problem is posed by the close resemblance between Dogon myth and cosmology and those of certain neo-Platonist, Gnostic, and Kabbalistic sects and 'heresies' that throve in the understory of European religion and philosophy. One wonders whether, after the Vandal and Islamic invasions of North Africa and even before these took place, Gnostic, Manichæan and Jewish-mystical ideas and practices might have penetrated the Sahara to the Western Sudan and helped to form the Dogon *Weltbild*. The Gnostic sequences of 'archons', arrayed as binarily opposed androgynous twins, have affinities with Fon and Dogon notions. (…) It is possible that adherents of such persuasions filtered or fled through the centuries to the Niger region and as bearers of a more complex culture exercised influence on the beliefs of its inhabitants." (*Dramas, Fields, and Metaphors*, 1974, p. 161.)

It is hard, when looking at these banished and *déclassé* scholars spreading heretical doctrines among the culturally marginalised, not to think of the counter-culture – of whom Turner's book is, tacitly, the best picture. Fairly obviously, the geographical periphery (of the Mediterranean) is a stand-in for a social periphery within Western cities, the Underground. At the time, the accusation of not being alternative was enough to make someone burst into tears. The fantasy of having banned and subversive knowledge, of being the Underground which was preparing revolution, of making an exit from the institutions, of dissolving organised knowledge and breaking into a new productive intellectual framework, lifted people hundreds of feet into the air. Scepticism about the Cold War cultural consensus migrated into a creation of a hidden and suppressed and fabulous Past, left out of the records or caught in obscure texts. Thus, the Underground was a thousand years old. This story doesn't really allow the opposition to win, but suggests that the "orthodoxy", however defined, would have no power more than 50 feet outside their command posts.

I did not understand Seventies poetry as it was happening, but really picked it up in the 1990s. My career as a critic started with resentment at the false gatekeepers who denied the existence of an alternative poetry. (The phrase *Nothing is being suppressed* is a piece of dialogue from an episode of *Doomwatch*, in 1972.) This extended to the alternative scene and its internal failure to create a public account, such as reviews and anthologies. I am looking at Internet pages offering for sale *ivan12man*, by Ulli McCarthy, at £30, and the issue of *Joe DiMaggio* which includes two poems by Paul Gogarty, *How Much do Toads Eat* and *The Storm*, a snip at £50. I can't afford these, but I wish to claim that we have assimilated the Seventies, and the Seventies search project is over. This project lasted so long, it slowed up because we were enjoying it too much, it involved lavish amounts of cooperation, imagination, tenacity, and above all full-on shopping skills. I have a tremendous feeling of confidence about how far we have got, but I must admit that there are works I have never read. I do have 'Junky Tango (aka 'Stratton Elegy')', *Red Eye,* and early Hartley Williams poems, key Seventies products which were not published until forty years later. After assimilating 46 poets listed by Eric Mottram in his two statements on the British Poetry Revival, I have to reveal that there are roughly another 30, active in the decade, whom we need to esteem and read. The write-up must be incomplete because of the vast number of good poets. Obviously I have not repeated material found in my earlier books, so poets found there are not found here.

A long research programme, whose unstated goal was to disprove the thesis that poets have to use modern techniques in order to be artistically successful, was written up in my previous book, *The Long 1950s.* I am unable to use the same material again, brilliant as many mainstream poets were. If I am presenting information about the breach between the new poetics and the conservative literary world, it is in an attempt to end this breach, and this new book is written for the unpredisposed. A sector of the scene was changing at a great rate. Yet most poets wrote in traditional ways and were not stylistically self-conscious. The poetry audience did not have a progress ideology and made a limited take-up of the new style. I am sure that much in poetry was out of date and out of time, but I don't think conversation has changed all that much – and poetry is interesting in the same ways that conversation is.

The proposal that a thing X is part of progress makes a bet about how the future will turn out. This bet can be lost. If we look at the poetry scene in 2018, it is apparent that the experimental poetry scene of 1975 has not become The Future. Experimentation produces a new thing but does not whittle the future down to a single outcome path. The more the "underground" poets converged, the more the future floated away from their hands.

Discovering affinities for one's own policies among the unratified traditions of the world was gratifying, but could be an exit from history.

*Postscript*

This was completed as a draft in March 2017, when Corbyn, as Seventies Man as you can get without having a collection of *Grosseteste Review*, was at the zenith. His exit to a cell furnished and wired by his opponents represents a defeat for '70s Left culture – not the first. I am tempted to say that poetic texts from 1975 are now suffering from post-Corbyn trauma. My feeling is that the possibilities evoked in the poetry, and articulated by politicians who failed to buy into the neo-liberal consensus, remain the most enticing possibilities. The social reception of this poetry is tangled up with the reception of a social possibility by the poetry. This reception has continued post 1980 and reached a glowing intensity between about 2015 and 2019. The history of the memory of '70s culture is now worth a volume in itself – mainly a record of vandalism, malicious rewrites, deletion of stored information, and even insect damage. Of course, the poets involved have also produced a lot of new work over the last 40 years – retirement and Corbyn sometimes generating a new fertility.

# Generalisations about the Seventies

I don't propose to spend the time we have arguing so these statements are designed not to be controversial and are placed at the front as a basis.

*Revolutionary ideals*
It is 1967. Ginsberg is in London and a local talent is interviewing him about the imminent revolution of the soul. Iain Sinclair is pointing a microphone.

**Geoffrey**: It seems that Grogan and you are the only people who have any viable method for guiding & controlling the inception of mass psychosis that has to take place in order that any change of consciousness can come about.

**Ginsberg**: Is that what Laing said? I wasn't thinking in terms of inducing a mass psychosis. Of course, his definition of psychosis is: a breakthrough of the old consciousness formation & an insight into the new.

**Geoffrey**: How about spiking the water supplies of the big cities?

**Ginsberg** [says no] The whole thing is deception & hostility & force anyway.

[…]

**Ginsberg**: We all have that reservoir of awareness which has been repressed or suppressed or conditioned, but as anyone knows who has expressed a unitive experience or an LSD experience, it's there all along, the awareness. What Blake and all the visionaries have been saying for centuries is that we all have the awareness but we're not using it. It's not up to the surface, as the analysts will say.

[…]

**Geoffrey**: By what practical steps do you envisage the change of consciousness coming about? Do you envisage people setting up their own self-satisfying communities & these communities spreading, other people forming similar communities?

**Ginsberg**: Once you have a large group of people who have touched the basic ground of their own nature, or the nature of the universe, then they are mutually supportive. (*transcript printed in* Second Aeon, *14, 1971*)

The word psychosis needs to be put in the connection of an official classing of psychedelic drugs as psychotomimetic. It refers also to R.D. Laing's idea that madness was an expression of genuine stresses and contradictions, and that by travelling through it you could cure yourself and reach a non-alienated state. I don't know who Geoffrey was – probably not Geoffrey Howe.

This is the LSD-based radicalism and my point is how envious modest poets were of this and how *small-scale* art seemed which didn't offer that spiritual lift, (or trip into hyper-inflated meaninglessness, whichever it was). It is quite clear that much poetry in the Seventies was written as part of this planned change of consciousness. The urgency of vision leads on to the project for imitating Blake, which was central. We have to recall something else, the spirit of the student revolt of 68, which was another kind of radicalism but one with no roots in religion but instead a commitment to rational change through changes to laws and reform of the machinery of government, a continuation of the Enlightenment. Collective memory has merged these two currents, but on the ground their members couldn't agree on anything.

**Geoffrey**: It's like the end of the cycle. All the religions seem to have foreseen this. It's thought that every 500 years or so the doctrine was going to decline radically & at the end there would be a period when the doctrine was pretty well gone & presumably after that a new doctrine would arise & a new cycle.

This leads on to the New Age movement and in fact the term "new age" expresses the idea of a cycle closing and a new one opening. The contrast between a belief in great Time, preordaining what people feel and believe, and the individualism, stress on *my* personal spiritual path devised by *me*, is troubling but was not troubling to people who went on this journey.

1968 saw a student revolt in most universities in the West, and a good many of those in the Third World. The big media hit in Britain was the demonstrations against the Vietnamese War in Grosvenor Square. These could be televised, and met with incomprehension among people who saw the basic role of culture as reinforcing the willingness of the masses to carry out their role in the Cold War effort. The attitude of the students was so idealistic that pinning it down is equivalent to falsifying it. I can release it, therefore, by a dreamlike rhapsody.

*Society has been based on inequality but we can put a halt to this by inventing a radically equal society. All the minorities are profoundly opposed to the social order and would go out on the streets to overthrow it if not for marginalisation which means that they are forced to remain silent. Everyone silent, actually, is on our side. In history almost everyone was silent but despite that we know what they were thinking due to our terrific levels of empathy and philosophical insight. Minorities need to be allowed to express their own feelings and insights but in the meantime we can articulate all that for them. Everyone has special insight but people who have read Marx and Freud can have this insight on their behalf. The people who run society basically see life in black and white and we see it in colour. Every social institution is based on the people who make it work and will collapse as soon as they realise the fact of their oppression. The media produce false consciousness in the service of the wealthy and people are wrong to believe in society as it is. The point of knowledge is not to serve as a test of memory, preparing faithful servants of the wealthy, but to liberate people. The realm of the imaginary is a projection of social concepts into other terms but can be seized back to reflect other possibilities. Authenticity is to be found in prehistory, among non-urban tribal societies, and in the Third World in general. There is an alternative everything and it is always better. Social roles are the instrument by which a corrupt society reproduces itself and turns everyone into cells of its body, willing to reproduce it. Culture is completely dedicated to making people accept lowly roles and hard work, but as society is sick adjustment to it means adopting a state of sickness which imitates functionality. The source of neuroses is this sense of duty which grows as part of socialising and which bestows abiding frustration. The advance of technology means that in future there will be endless leisure and the main problems will be in filling that leisure. The location of social reform is no longer in the workplace but in the structure of small groups and in the pressures which people put on each other. A reform of language is needed to disentangle personal relationships. Recapturing key moments of childhood is like studying history, it recovers the stages by which our freedom was forfeited. Liberation involves endless introspection and, even better, endless talking. The new society needs leaders who will emerge spontaneously while being non-authoritarian and we are ideally qualified to fill that role.*

### Generalisations about the Scene

— there were many long poems composed in the era;

— the volume of good poetry was very large;

— there was a growth in the scale of poetic production, probably meaning a slackening of the grip of gatekeepers;

— the take-on of new poetry by critics malfunctioned and broke up;

— polarisation of the new market took place, increasing the variety of poetry being written;

— there was a political crisis and poets were happy to think about alternative forms of government;

— there were three governments, summed up as three prime ministers losing their reputation;

— poets became politicised, and those on the Right were in a minority;

— most sectors of British industry were in deep trouble, both in profitability and inability to export. The news, thus, validated attacks on "the system" every day. The pattern could be analysed either as lack of capital or as overmanning. Modernisation was either going to mean a recapitalisation or mass redundancies. But, by 1976, investing in new plant was going to mean that you could cut millions of jobs without reducing output;

— Heath had an economic plan which called for the owners of capital to invest it locally and productively. They declined, and it turned out that the "turning point" had happened, in silence, twenty or thirty years before. The owners were more willing to see their shares gradually lose value than to invest fresh money;

— the mainstream was in deep trouble in the face of many factions seeing it as obsolete and stuck in imitation;

— gurus were in decline and the skills of analysing radically new claims about human behaviour, and new fields of knowledge, were making great advances;

— there was a decline in the influence of High Street publishers and an increase in the influence of the universities and student audiences;

— the rapid growth in the number of graduates changed the rules and especially weakened the ability of authority figures to impose arbitrary positions. The base came to dominate the apex;

— while the rise of universities was the central process in the world of knowledge, poetry presented itself as an archaic folk practice, ripe for colonisation. The mediation between disentailed intelligence and subjective expression was crucial for poetry. Poetry is made of information so presumably is made out of knowledge;

— the inflationary spiral which followed the oil price hikes of 1972-4 brought a crisis in the world of poetry magazines, which were unable to raise the cover price to match the new costs of paper and printing; there was a slump in the second half of the decade which brought a hardening of lines and possibly a drop in overall activity;

— in 1974, roughly, there was a collapse in the size of audiences for live poetry;

— the student revolt, the classic moment where the base tried to sweep the apex away, became much weaker. The unifying issue of the Vietnamese War was replaced as a focus of protests by the activities of the racist National Front;

— conceptual practices were on the rise, with their target of attack being autobiographical poetry rather than (as for *visual* conceptual art) the representational picture;

— there are no poor men who own newspapers or TV companies. Evidently, what the powerful had in mind was power for themselves and degradation for everyone else. The images of fellow humans which the media give are fundamentally false and consciousness which is fed by those images is also false, a kind of toxin. Intuition could easily be a metabolism of that falsehood to make it seem like personal experience and therefore true. Yet poetry was founded on intuition. Intuition is a residue of unexamined deposits;

— new lines of inquiry opened up language as something in which every layer was significant. This coincided with the *cultural critical* line for which every element of social rules needed to be questioned. In poetry, the division between data and rules was shifted. Rules were dragged into daylight and arbitrary rules were made up. Ideally, radical poetry could open up a path into a new society. Less ideally, the reader scraps the message of the poetry and treats the poet as an object, a didactic cadaver of unreconstructed emotions;

— at the point where problems emerged with a set of rules for generating poems, you could follow the impulse into a zone of theory. Here, the presence of unlimited alternative possibilities gave a sense of weightlessness and freedom which could be the core sensation associated with reading poetry. Another fraction of opinion held that intellectuals could not write poetry and that speculation was forbidden. Poetry was to be weighty because freedom was denied in all the paths which had led up to it;

— the tempo of books was slow compared to the tempo of little magazines. The instability of magazines reached the same outcome, a final score-line, but went through many more cycles to reach it. The magazine favoured the possible over the attainable, the fragment over the finished idea, the new poet over the old one;

— a series of political disasters made the society wished-for wonderfully clear and tangible. It became sharp and poignant, enough to write about. By virtue of expressing wishes, this scene had a thousand, or a million, variants. Disliking thought about politics was allied to dislike of thinking about poetry;

— there were alternatives for focus, either on language as a serial signal or on the static data fields underlying language or perception;

— feminism rose steadily, starting to produce significant poetry in the second half of the decade; and was beginning to demand a separate market and standards of artistic value;

— while the English avant-garde was heavily in the grip of the American avant-garde of the 1950s, as the decade advanced it was becoming more normal for young poets to take local British poets as models; this arguably meant the end of the mid-century malaise;

— in Scotland and Wales, the student revolt directed itself at nationalism in the guise of decolonisation. In the outlands, the nationalists converted or silenced the Marxists, were strikingly successful at persuading the population of the worth of their cause, and made a transition into running civil society. In poetry, there is a geography of innovation;

— "magic realism" became a frequent phrase after Miguel Angel Asturias won the Nobel in 1967, and this opened up a quadrant of the non-sociological. Together with the game poetry of MacBeth and Edwin Morgan, this meant that pre-runs of what was later called post-modernism were taking place;

— following the large-scale "collective improvisation" project of the *English Intelligencer* (1966-8), involving 40 or so poets, the idea of writing about space and territory as an organising principle for knowledge was influential;

— as chronicled by Alan Sinfield, the declining arc of the Anglican Church as the voice of cultural expression in England led to a feeling of being a ship with no sea for writers from that theological direction. Imagery of emptiness and being alone was popular. Theories based on the idea that history had gone wrong had some circulation;

— there was a shared project of imitating Blake which apparently came to an end during the decade;

— there is a quadrilateral in the "underground" and at its points are the hippies, the student radicals of Sixty-Eight, the New Age line of religiosity, and people interested in using language in unusual ways. No-one could hit all four points. Reading any poet involved slipping them into where they best fit in this charged field;

— anyone in the "radical world" was liable to suspect that the patterns they were playing with were unreal or unstable, and that there was a deeper world based on ownership which still followed 19th century rules and tempos. The whole game was brought to an end by a right-wing surge in 1979. Critics have exaggerated both to what extent conservative poetry then became interesting and how far radical poetry lost its credibility.

## THREE STYLE BLOCS

There were three styles which had a claim to be the style of the 1970s. Anthony Thwaite published his classic scene-interpreting essay 'The Two Poetries' in *The Listener* early in 1974. He defines the two sides as, roughly, academic poetry based on close reading, and populist poetry of immediate reactions, written by the young (and the majority of amateur poets). Somewhat reluctantly, I have to modify his version: where he talks about "vaguely permissive gestures towards self-expression and undif-ferentiated creativity", this doesn't sit well with the poets listed by Eric Mottram, where being critical is the entry ticket, and the work is highly differentiated. In fact, when Mottram launched the idea of an alternative poetry, at that weekend in June 1974, the whole enterprise involved a third sector, and the count of poetries inevitably went up to three.

The big thing happening in the 1960s was Pop. Culture was being written in a continuous present. Because of the influence of the new media, such as records and TV, a new mode of cultural consumption arose, separating people growing up after about 1960 from older generations. It would be difficult to imagine a modern poet who was not 'sensitive'. This is the contemporary idiom. There was a new and worldwide youth culture, and if we assign to people *born in the 1940s* (crudely) a primary role in it then we can lay bare a line of deep conflict between this sentiment (youth, hedonism, consumerism, irresponsibility) and the sentiment of poets born between 1920 and 1940 (crudely) who were saying 'culture is serious and is not play' and who were massively installed in the poetry world. The idiom of the new student poetry had nothing to do with modernism, the avant-garde, or even the British Poetry Revival, but instead represents the norms developed by singer-songwriters in the first half of the '60s, which have become unconscious and universal assumptions for poetry. These norms involve the death of rhetoric, intimacy, egocentricity, informality, but also a line of warmth, emotional receptiveness, lack of *hauteur*. It is not hard to see why the most prestigious poets are ones who reject these conventions. A key concept was play: people were supposed to do only things which they enjoyed, so that alienation would disappear, creativity would solve economic problems, and people could behave authentically. Character armour would dissolve, affection would replace habit and economic compulsion within marriage. Leisure would be the dominant activity. Hedonism would prevail over moral restrictions, and social life would be spontaneous and never boring. All this was the expression of a feeling that the older generation had lost interest in their lives, a diminished sense of reality with regard to anyone not in the counter-culture. The idea of 'child centred learning' was also applied in practice, and in fact the idea of childhood had been redefined in the wider society. These new ideas never looked like applying to normal jobs. The idea that 'character armour' produced cultural sterility was especially popular with poets, and the subjective 'sense of diminished reality' was applied to tired old poets.

In 1970, Lucie-Smith remarked on Liverpool poetry that "On reflection, the 'pop' element seems to me much less important than the commitment to modern art. The alliance between modern poets and modern painters has been of special significance to modernism as a whole", and continues to point out "the appearance of a small but growing number of extreme modernist poets in Britain. [...] the sudden influence of a sensibility which was dominant in Paris and Zurich fifty years ago." (*British Poetry Since 1945*, p. 338) The key seems to be that students at art schools didn't have a problem with modernism, whereas their peers doing EngLit at university were taught by their teachers that modernism was dubious and probably right-wing; so modernism reached Seventies poetry via the art schools. What are pop songs like? The arrival of Dylan and of the mature work of Lennon and Macartney had blown a big hole in the world of teenagers and let the spectre of the avant-garde infiltrate through it. Being absolutely in the moment can cut two ways. It can represent naivety, the vividness of someone who has never been in love before or never visited a great city before, or it can represent great sophistication, the breezy wake of Breton and Prévert. Youth does not last, and there was a fundamental instability with Pop poetry, that it was either going to develop on the lines of its Surrealist or Dada models and start "the manipulation of found material" and so on, or to lose its youthfulness and sink into low-information dumbing-down. (I wrote about the new intimate or 'Pop' poetry in *The Long 1950s*, pp. 130–57.)

It is plausible that the *generation born in the 1920s* were the apical point of conservative, academic, sceptical, uninspired poetry. This would correlate with the Conservatives winning three general elections in the 1950s. In the cohort *born between 1920 and 1940* we find the highest level of interest in commitment, personal witness, avoidance of grand ideas and grand language, focus on the concrete even when it is unattractive, subordination of art to moral obligations, belief in tests and in style as a test of character. This can make for poetry which has no surface attractions and no deep attractions either. These poets were the "Mainstream". Early usage of this, as "broad central current," had a positive sound, part of a statement that eccentrics (i.e. modernists and intellectuals) could never write important poetry. The word took on a pejorative sense because of the prevalence of tedious poetry in the 1950s. Adjectives for this bloc are *academic, Christian*, and *existentialist*. A typical event is description of physical sensations and objects, with reviewers using adjectives like *tough, sensuous*, and *muscular*. In 1970, we find a large number of poets writing to this aesthetic. This group has as limiting conditions its dislike of propaganda and of popular culture. Of the Christian-academic group of the 1950s we can mention Philip Larkin, Geoffrey Hill, John Holloway, Peter Levi, Anthony Thwaite, Emyr Humphreys. The retreat to the island correlates with a belief in ethical and literary restraint: the scale of the remaining poem is out of proportion to the giant nature of the prohibitions hemming it in. A tiny area of close attentiveness is defined as the truth.

For the third bloc, we are going to rely on a description by Eric Mottram. There had always been an experimental fringe. Around 1960, a patch of the poetry scene changed radically and was the start of what Mottram called the 'British Poetry Revival'. Books like *City*, *Persephone*, *torse 3*, *Songs*, *Identities*, *The Nature of Cold Weather*, *A Domesday Book*, *A Theory of Diet* signalled the arrival of a new experimental sector. This area involved work, complexity, ideas. The incredulity of a whole bloc of readers about the local Big Figures is a key fact for what happened next. The new poetry deleted the local legacy, but had an 'elective ancestry', transfusions of poetic DNA from the original modernist poetry and from the American avant-garde of the 1950s. In his essay about the 'British Poetry Revival 1960–74' published as part of the catalogue for a conference in 1974, Mottram lists, first of all, 17 of the poets in John Matthias' 1971 anthology as:

> David Jones, Hugh MacDiarmid, Basil Bunting, Charles Tomlinson, Ted Hughes, Ian Hamilton Finlay, Christopher Logue, Gael Turnbull, Matthew Mead, Nathaniel Tarn, Roy Fisher, Christopher Middleton, Anselm Hollo, Ken Smith, Lee Harwood, Harry Guest, Tom Raworth.

He then adds 19 poets Matthias left out:

> Tom Pickard, Bob Cobbing, Stuart Montgomery, Jeff Nuttall, Allen Fisher, Dom Silvester Houédard, Jeremy Hilton, Elaine Feinstein, Michael Horovitz, David Chaloner, Andrew Crozier, Peter Redgrove, Barry MacSweeney, Jim Burns, Edwin Morgan, Chris Torrance, John James, Peter Riley, John Hall.

Mottram wrote another text for the 1977 PCL Conference. The anthology for that event added:

Peter Finch, B. Catling, Iain Sinclair, Bill Griffiths, Colin Simms, Tom Leonard, David Tipton, J.P. Ward, Eric Mottram, and John Freeman. Total: 46 poets

The additions largely cover a new generation, not visible in 1971. Actually, any historian of the Seventies is going to be filling in the negative space left around Eric's era definition, which is complete in itself.

Mottram says the centre of his document is the catalogue of small press resources, and his opening paragraphs make the focus the use of small-scale economics, the thesis that non-capitalist production is the key and that it instantly bypasses factors of repression, conformism and commodification. Thus the exit from "the business" brings about nonconformity and this brings about artistic success. He gives a much clearer picture of cultural censorship and its systematic connections than of the new art. The filtering directs the art towards comfort and ease – the opposite of resistance. It is rare to find a document which so vividly expects capitalism to dissolve just by people walking out of it. The poets in question had chosen to take great risks and write in a style which was alien, eccentric, easy to mock, uncomfortable, one-sided, taken to extremes, out of proportion (and so on). It was not imitating existing speech. With time, these styles became acceptable: as we grew to take them on. Mottram was powerfully encouraging young poets to experiment. His style is compulsively aggregative – he sets up 40 wonderful artistic assets and then rolls them up together, and rolls 30 or 40 poets up together. None of the poets had all 40 assets, in fact it is doubtful they had more than four or five, so there is a gap between the position statement and the poems themselves. Stylistic affinity is never claimed for his raft of poets. This makes it irrelevant to ask whether the "revival" continued after 1974, or whether someone belongs to it. No group is being identified, rather a perimeter of repression and an outlaw economy.

Strangely, Eric seems more interested in cultural critique than in the exploration of subjective feelings – the personal realm. This does not reflect a distrust of such poetry but a distrust of the public sphere. The belief in intellectuals belongs in a time when civil society was expected to solve its problems, before a time when a systematic overview only came from accountants.

I don't want to spend time on identifying the overlap between Lee Harwood and Hugh MacDiarmid, or squeezing people born before 1900 and after 1940 into one generation. I suggest that we scrap the first seven poets in the first block above, all of whom reached maturity before 1960. This gives us a generation, a cultural object we can think about. Incidentally, Mottram's wording makes it clear that he associated the *viv* part of "revival" with live as in live performance, and its boom in the Sixties, and he was not thinking of a prior "poetic death", which he never mentions. He was writing a catalogue to an exhibition open for three days only, and we need to tweak his list to make it work for us. Eric also does not talk about the impact of the cultural waves of 1967 (psychedelia) and 1968 (student revolt), although it would be surprising if this impact was nil.

So, what is the difference between the Fifties style and the BPR poets? One line is that in the new poetry the poet is allowed to draw information from anywhere and sequence it as needed to support an argument. Original blocks of experience are dissolved out to allow other patterns to be presented. It is going to be a culture-critical argument, in general.

The availability of this data points to a shift in the economics of information – data has become cheap (and the reader is expected to be flexible about dealing with rapid shifts of frames of reference). The underlying goal is to generate new information. The recombinatory power is attained by breaking down rigid connections (which may be typical of everyday speech).

The low level of predictability requires the poem to flip out of conventional bonds to a community or an ego, because those patterns are predictable. Authenticity is not a pivotal value. The response (part of it) said that the new poetry was lightweight – it was covering a vast terrain but without density. Its cargo was abstraction, speculation, theory, new analogies. It was interested in patterns rather than facts.

This poetry is made of numerous, small, independent parts and not of few, large, rigid parts. It is not focused on predictable patterns in the world we live in. Sequence of ideas has become the dominant feature, and classification of endless different forms of montage, frame-shifting, capture of frames and textures, etc., asks for attention. The leaps may be irritating because they suggest so much freedom for the poet, taken as winning by unfair means.

Without a sweep of philosophical forgetting that produces ignorance, the game of building a *new* world of knowledge cannot get under way. The project of new connections of knowledge involves the loss of the old ones. This can produce infantile language. It can be intensely annoying to those whose (old) knowledge is a form of status – and an investment.

When every individual has autonomy, the possibilities diversify out of control – this is desired as much in a transformed *society* as in the poem. This diversity disables traditional political arguments in poetry – every focus is dissipated except the attack on constraints. Coherence becomes a problem.

The poetry does not loop back to record and project a personality. Realism is less valuable than richness of patterns and their openness as a matrix in which unfamiliar analogies are created. The point of departure for this freedom is mediation through an existing text, in which the new poem hangs as if in a tree; it is not wiped from memory but is a source for patterns which are dissolved out of their bindings. The 'tree' may be a work of visual art. The double layer makes conscious what is normally the unconscious aspect of speech, a reflexivity which allows a personal signature to permeate and also allows a recognition of the history of style which is also part of cultural critique.

Along with a cheap attitude to data goes a habit of treating data as a material that can be inverted, cut to length, stretched, translated into numbers. Language becomes an object with the passivity of objects.

I like this solution, but I have to question how much of the primary data it really accounts for. If we ran through 30 patterns of change, we might get something approximating to a complete explanation. And utter exhaustion. This one does have some interesting patterns to offer. After discovering that the population being studied is not homogeneous, we have to halt. There was a generational shift but we have to build a low-res structure so as to be vague enough not to distort things. We can deduce that Ken Smith differs from many of the BPR poets and also the generalisation we have outlined. According to rumour, he disliked the poetry of all the other BPR poets except Pickard and Nuttall.

Other poets who will migrate into the underground during the decade include Tony Lopez, Michael Haslam, Michael Gibbs, Steve Sneyd, Maggie O'Sullivan, John Ash, Jeremy Reed, Denise Riley, David Chaloner, Anthony Barnett, Ralph Hawkins, Asa Benveniste, Robert Hampson, Grace Lake, Tom Lowenstein, Gavin Selerie, Nigel Wheale, John Wilkinson, Rod Mengham, Martin Thom, Paul Brown, Brian Marley, Philip Jenkins, Peter Philpott and Paul Gogarty. Biologically, this list includes a number of poets born during the 1930s and an especially dense concentration of those born during the 1940s. The dates obviously affect the development of this bloc over the ensuing thirty years. Generally speaking, the poets directly involved in the events of 1968 will join the Underground and will not sign up with any High Street firms.

The history of the decade involves the intertwined fates of these three blocs. My aim is not to pick winners, but to recover real differences which were misrepresented for partisan reasons. The direct participants recognised categories, and I am trying to make explicit the basis for those judgements of category. The free-data thing allows us to separate conventional young poets and unconventional ones, an often discussed point for the poets emerging roughly 1970-1990. Just to get perspective, around half of the 86 poets in Lucie-Smith's 1970 Penguin anthology don't fit well into these 3 blocs. You could make them fit, with a hammer, but they aren't a good match. Poets succeed by being idiosyncratic. Plausibly, feminism provided a new and fourth bloc from 1975 on, appealing to a large market not usually interested in poetry while arguably not providing a new model for how a poem is written.

Faber published four volumes of *Poetry Introduction* in our period (dated 1969 to 1978), and these offered a list of 33 young poets who could be read as a version of what was happening in the decade:

No 1 includes Douglas Dunn, Elaine Feinstein, Ian Hamilton, David Harsent, Bartholomew Quinn, V.C. Horwell, John Cotton, John Daniel, Jeremy Hooker;

No 2: Paul Muldoon, Wes Magee, William Peskett, Alasdair Maclean, Pete Morgan, Richard Ryan, Clive Wilmer, Grevel Lindop, Dick Davis;

No 3: John Cassidy, Gillian Clarke, Valerie Gillies, Paul Groves, Ian McDonald, Andrew Motion, Tom Paulin, Jeffrey Wainwright, Kit Wright;

No 4: Anne Cluysenaar, Cal Clothier, George Szirtes, Alastair Elliot, Alan Hollinghurst, Craig Raine.

Exactly one of these names re-appears in Mottram's "top tips" of 46 names – already a sign that we are dealing with a different view of the world. Crudely, we can define this group as the continuing mainstream of the Seventies; a survey of the poems included shows a profound breach with the Movement poets and Fifties inhibition. These are early poems, and we would do better to look at 33 first books (or, even better, second books). Names which we still know forty years later are Jeremy Hooker, Craig Raine, Jeffrey Wainwright, George Szirtes and David Harsent.

Vitally, Mottram is claiming that only the rejected, only those who reject the poetic centre and write in an "anti-language", are genuinely creative. It would be surprising if all the poets favoured by "mainstream editors" were bad, and in fact that was not a true claim. It is hardly true, either, that editors did not share the tastes of most of the poetry-reading audience. His is not the only view. If you look at Lucie-Smith, he includes about half of Mottram's poets. So this was already there in the High Street. To get the decade, it is important to read also the notes in Lucie-Smith's anthology. He includes 86 poets, and generally relates each one to a microclimate of opinion which views work in that style as necessary. He breaks down the separation between wish and fulfilment. The 'impresario' who devises the style may not be the same person as the poet. Mottram perceives a gulf whereas Lucie-Smith shows us a continuous landscape, where the extreme regions are in contrast with each other. Mottram's version is more exciting but Lucie-Smith's is more convincing.


TURNING POINT?

The thirty years after the war saw steady growth in the wealth of the West. People had absorbed this rise in expectations as if it were historical law, and this euphoria was actually more overwhelming for the young than for people with longer runs of experience to offset it. In 1973, let's say, people would walk out of their jobs in the expectation that other jobs would be available as soon as they were ready to work again. The thirst for social reforms was a side-effect of a prosperous feeling which meant that the costs were not expected to cause bankruptcy and poverty. The shift from this to expecting a future of zero growth, with ever increasing problems from the scarcity of natural resources and shifts in world power and prices, was profound and irreversible. It is very hard to recover what the euphoria meant as a state of mind.

British politics were ripped in two by the oil price shocks, which catastrophically shifted the terms of trade, led to a sterling crisis which saw the government apply to the IMF for a special loan – something normally reserved for Third World countries in crisis – and then led to inflation which broke down the relations between workers and employers.

Inflation at 26% saw the impoverishment of groups who couldn't obtain equivalent wage rises, which employers were being encouraged (by shareholders, media, and government) to withhold. This switched euphoria off like a light. But I can't find clear traces of this in poetry. Dominic Sandbrook's recent book on the Seventies (about 2,000 pages, for the whole decade) says that "certainly by 1972, […] the counter-culture was effectively dead". This would locate the whole of the rest of the decade as a reaction to the end of the dream. This could involve, variously, abandoning a creative life for a safe job and a mortgage, stepping up oppositional practices into a dogma, usually Marxist, in which compromise was simply weakness, a move into single-issue politics, regrouping as a "failed elite", or a retreat into New Age spirituality. I am not convinced that 1971 was the right date, and other sources put the same event in 1974, or over a stretch 1974–76. Sandbrook cites a key counter-cultural event which took place in August 1974, contradicting himself. In any case, a loss of energy among the most influential and advanced groups was simultaneous with primary experience of the new ideas among more peripheral groups – the outwash of the initial wave. Something which was new in Berkeley in 1966 might be new in Burnley in 1974. The Counter-Culture became more and more energy-rich as it spread outwards and affected more and more people. We have to superimpose two processes – a continuing rapid change of fashions among a "youth elite" group, working in the media in a few rich cities, structurally under pressure to be ahead, and an outwash, affecting a *far larger* number of people, less fragile, more substantial, and adapted to last for longer by shedding the more illusory and unsustainable features of the original ideas complex. I suspect 18-year-olds were as idealistic in 1975 as they were in 1968. The doorway into personal gnosis could not be sealed off again.

The starting point for this book was reading recollections by 'underground' poets of the decade and noticing that they didn't record any disillusion during the decade and didn't record any phase of burning optimism and political idealism, possibly because mentioning this would have exposed the fact that they had lost it. You can't recover the Seventies without radical politics, without a terrific high of irrational expectations and an irrational crash of pessimism, despondency, emptying of shared symbolism. The exciting quality of alternative poetry in that time was that it contained, even in non-verbal form, the optimism of the poets writing it and of the people around them: the future was the essential content. This future is no longer available. However, I can't find any poets who admit to disillusion, or poetic texts which record the passage through self-doubt or the flattened, disillusioned state. My book is dedicated to recovering the euphoria.

The point of a ball, in a game, is to isolate meaningful action to a single point. Only those controlling the ball are really in play. The poetry world obviously does not work in this way, and there are hundreds of event sequences taking place at any time, unaffected by each other. If we imagine a ball in play, in this period, it would obviously be the developing movement of Sixty-Eight, or the Counter-Culture. Michael Gibbs: "The failure of the student revolts of 1968 and the privatisation of hedonism beginning in the early seventies (the shift from communal joy to the narcissism of the Me generation), followed by the deadening effects of AIDS on gay (in the general sense of the word) sensibilities, marked the exhaustion of idealism and the end of communality. The hope invested in the idea of an avant-garde has become just that: a theory divorced from practice, a loss to be mourned instead of a living presence. According to one recent account, the very discourse surrounding any discussion of the avant-garde already articulates its death. The dialectical double bind that fatally affects the avant-garde also conditions any avowal of an 'oppositional' or 'idealist' art. Perhaps the only beneficiaries of this dilemma are the theorists and art historians for whom art is already dead matter."

Gibbs was writing in 1992, a point at which the public's loss of patience with the Major administration was irrefutable proof that the New Right wave had broken and a new cycle had started. The great conceptual artist was referring really to the period 1974-1986 (especially). Economics seem to show a collapse in the audiences for live readings around 1974, and a decline in the number of poetry magazines during the period of high inflation, so the whole second half of the decade. The number of magazines recovered in the Eighties, and I can't detect any decrease in book publication.

The most celebrated form of exit from the counter-culture was through a bad acid trip. This is what happened to the foot-soldiers, and it was an inevitable accompaniment of widespread use of mind-expanding drugs. If you want to know what this felt like, it is agreed that the first four Black Sabbath albums sound like a documentary of a bad acid trip. I have not found any poetry that describes this sound. Poetry is sensitive to cultural processes, connected to them by a thousand filaments, a picture of collective psychological states – but it is selective in every way. It cannot work as a cultural record.

I can only write the history for which there is evidence. Poets were taking on new schemas in profusion, but the schemas acted as protection against new and upsetting processes in the wider society. It is more effective to write up the history of the schemas than to find slippery matches between the poems and social or political events.

# Crave That Hurting Thing

One version of what happened could be like this. Because the young were so numerous, the number of graduates or the literate growing so fast, the old system seemed bound to be washed away. You could list a hundred things wrong with the poetry world. This was especially true if you included its connections to malfunctions in society as a whole, or found fault with the minority nature of poetry as an analogical support for the domination of society by a minority. These faults could be identified with the people in the poetry world: if you eliminated the people, you would eliminate the problems. Excluding the corrupt and compromised elders could not happen within the institutions, because the elders ran those and made the rules. Instead, the incorrupt would withdraw from the central area and condemn it to withering away. Forty years later, the outcome was that the conservatives had got rid of the radicals, not that the radicals had got rid of the conservatives. The withdrawal had created a parallel world of poetry which had ineffective means of distribution and was ignored by the media and the bookshops. The history of the Alternative has largely yet to be written. But it is clear that its unity was a spiritual mood which in daily life dissolved into a hundred sub-groups and as many accusations of new-style corruption. Further, the negative qualities of elitism, imperialism, class mentality, etc. were subjectless actions: nobody consciously carried them out, and so the difference between old and new poets was visible from afar but disappeared under close examination. What seemed clear-cut in 1968 was quite blurred by 1980.

The elders could never accept that the claim was that the corruption was in them.

Their paraphrase of the claim was a total distortion. Dialogue was inhibited and they produced dozens of fictitious versions of what the younger generation were saying. These have been consecrated as history.

THE X EFFECT

During the 1968 election campaign, Nixon paid for TV ads showing students with long hair and denims attacking him because he knew that this would win him votes. The students in question were not as lazy, unwashed, and promiscuous as the blue-collar voters feared. People exaggerated to feed their fear. I think the point of this was to shorten processing time. People intended to reach a certain conclusion but the facts were in the way. To get to grips with a whole culture threatened to be very effortful. So being given ringing examples of failings of the new culture (or, of the old culture) got you to a conclusion quickly and was the convenience food of the intellect. 1970 is an unstable moment, and polarisation in the cultural world will grow rapidly during the Seventies: if you showed any art, there was a strong likelihood that parts of the audience would react not passively but with vocal protests against the kind of social interaction and behaviour the art is showing. The negative reactions of the time may outweigh the vision and recording of ideals.

D.J. Enright edited the *Oxford Book of Contemporary Verse 1945–80*, in 1980. My calculation is that the average age of Enright's contributors in 1980 was 60. One has to ask, contemporary to *what*. He could certainly please patrons by ignoring almost all the poets who had made a debut in the Sixties and Seventies; Thatcher and Reagan were trying to roll back all the liberal social changes and wage increases which had happened since the end of the 1950s. Another way of looking at this is to observe that Enright found no mainstream poets from those years. That is – the mainstream collapsed, just as the Underground said. Were the Seventies the root of the crisis in poetry where collective memory was damaged and lost integrity? Consider Nixon – he made his career out of red-baiting, in the Fifties – which was a decade of classic depersonalisation and silencing of cultural radicals. There was no moment before depersonalisation.

## Mutual hatred

Geoffrey Grigson (1905–85) published an essay in 1980 called "How many sprigs of bay, in fifty years?". My recollection is that it was in the *TLS* – the book version does not credit the sources. He is taking the long view, from the late Thirties up to 1980, and says that in that time only his personal friends are of any literary value. "Since […] the leading poets (now dead) of my own Thirties generation, there have been no major poets, no 'good' poets at all, and perhaps only six middling poets worth attending to[.] And the bad poets? […] I count up to forty or fifty poets, now published, discussed, and praised, […] whose work requires to be called inept." He leaves out an uncounted number of the bad and unconsidered. The erosion of the centre makes life difficult for the managers of culture.

Hundreds of other people are trying to take their decisions for them. In this period of factionalism, there is an element of mutual provocation. One group says, *They dislike my poetry because they are a kind of person whose attitudes I dislike and this shows that the poem is working.* Of course, critics like Edward Lucie-Smith, Peter Porter, or George MacBeth didn't twitch along with the polarisation reflex, and didn't lose sensibility to new cultural creations. Art is only there for someone who seeks art.

No small part of the recorded prose about the period is nothing more than high-pitched distortion, aimed to satisfy this craving for what you dread. The *X effect* of mutual distortion, where culture is scattered on an X pattern and people on opposite tines of the X cannot hear each other (*and* refuse to listen), is one of the most important of modern symptoms, given that breaking up into autonomous groups is the main feature of the modern cultural market. On the X, there is much *crossing out* and *cross purposes*. It is benign to pay attention to different views of the same evidence. I am trying to do this, but for a lot of this poetry it is difficult to establish what the response was, if any. There is a doctrine that nobody in the mainstream has read any small press poetry since 1972 and nobody in the alternative sector has read any mainstream poetry since 1972. Accepting that this X effect is true, how have people formed opinions of the realm where they do not tread? Commentators on the time seem to have mastered a line of writing off entire realms of poetry without naming even one actual poet. The write-offs do not use recognisable descriptive terms, so that working out which poets they refer to is not easy, and comparing them with textual evidence is only guesswork. Poetry which never got reviewed never got negative reviews. On the other side, explanation tends to leave out evidence altogether in favour of Theory which has no obvious connection to British poems except to supply a "nimbus of sovereignty".

Reaching 24 at some point in 1980, I had missed the poetry of the Seventies. Responsibility for this lies mainly with the *TLS* and Grigson, as their poetry guru. I believed the *TLS* and they didn't have a warning at the head of every page saying that "we are thirty years out of date when it comes to poetry". Grigson not only published three books about poetry (modern poetry – sort of) in the period but also published magisterial texts in the TLS explaining why young poets were no good, along with long reader's letters in which he loftily demolished everyone who disagreed with him. If you saw Grigson (who had after all been associated with vital new poetry once, in the 1930s) as the sage who had defined the new age and its follies, it followed that you wouldn't read new poetry at all. So it was that in 1980 I was thirty years behind. My contemporaries generously pointed this out to me once they found out who I was. My impression is that Grigson was allergic to talent. He voted for Auden as Best New Poet for 40 years running – he felt he owned a stake in Auden. His attitude, extreme as it sounds, noticeably resembles that of Larkin, in *All What Jazz*, William Cookson's editorials in *Agenda*, and Davie, in *Under Briggflatts*. It is a whole cultural style. It was both paranoid and fraught with institutional power. Put simply, my task is to pile up all the evidence which proves Grigson wrong.

## Saturation, queasy feelings, boredom

There were three big cultural waves of the Seventies: the advanced leftism of Sixty-Eight, the punk movement, and the New Right. Each of them had in common a feeling of disgust and saturation, their "package" included rejection of a component of the existing cultural offer. Clearly a big part of the atmosphere was cultural saturation and fatigue.

Cultural innovations started in disgust. A regime of satiation has an especially crushing effect on poetry, because a poem only happens if you co-operate with it. This is so unlike a film or a concert, which throws buckets of data over anyone present. You read ten bad books of poetry and miss how good the eleventh is because you were too fed up and dulled to read it. One response to saturation might be to develop a new product – a new stimulus offering a new sensation. But, in a regime of over-production, most books of poetry lack a retail justification. And the "cultural vocabulary" includes rather violent consumer experiences of frustration, contempt, boredom, dissimilation and walking out.

I had thought to explain why the young and unknown poets moved out into the Alternative sphere, but really it is an effect of miasma, and miasma was convulsive, irrational, and irrecoverable. You might as well ask spilt brandy why it evaporates. There is an exhibit, a book named *Poetry Dimension 2*, curated to explain what conventional poetry was in 1974 and why young poets feared being contaminated by it. It is grey sludge and the invitation to join the merry throng had the implication that you too would come to write grey sludge. Was there plenty of the grey stuff? Yes, and if you look out over the North Sea you can see vast banks of it waiting to find young academic poets to realise itself through. No point, either, looking for what unifies the Underground; the loss of barriers brought a thousand possibilities within reach, and the factor of unity was no more than the giant negative reaction against tedium, conformism, greyness, empiricism, etc.

Cultural critics who showed an energetic version of polarisation developed much more cultural energy. Cultural dynamism may come from a particular kind of person who thrives on high conflict levels and who manipulates situations to make conflicts worse. One way of doing this is to degrade things precious to the other side. Reviewing can become a hostage situation, a matter of capturing someone else's poem and torturing it, publicly. Not only do the images make you ill but you pay people to bring you more extreme images which will make you more ill. If any artist conforms to their audience, then the cracking of an audience into mutually ignoring fractions forces art to evolve – 10, 100, 1,000 times faster.

The 1970s saw artists in Britain racing to catch up with the audience.

## FALIKENSYMBOL? PHALLOCRITIQUE?

In the Seventies, most new poets were men (and most good new poets), and a shift in that balance had to wait for the Eighties. Frances Horovitz arrived as a genuine lyric poet. The combination of generic imagery and minimalism could bring an impasse about, but the discarding of factual and analytical structure allowed her to write something ethereally light, lifted by acuity to timeless energies and patterns. The Seventies were the era of derepression, of the X-film: raw fantasies are on screen; and women have disappeared from the cinema audience. Plausibly, the '70s with their loss of inhibitions and moral standards were less friendly to women artists than eras of more restraint. Feminism was partly a reaction to a new wave of the aestheticisation of violence and escalation of films to sexual fantasies, part of the contradictions of derepression. The gross civilisational process is normally to the benefit of the weak – meaning the physically weak but also those less willing to engage in conflict. To remove the inhibitions menaces the return of unassuaged feelings of aggression. Literature was experimenting, in our period, with the thousand-year cultural project of inhibition. For women, lowering the barriers required a safe space, one separated from the space owned by men and where the listeners are part of the safety. To get the story of derepression, we have to look at defensible space and at an audience small enough to have strong group feeling. This new group legislates to charter new territory – where defences can be dropped. Poetry logically breaks up into tiny but interconnected spaces, with their own histories. Someone who was a vocal feminist in 1975 had to put up with pity, ridicule, and abuse. It was quite common for people to treat feminists as crazy, so that their ideas had no equivalent in the real world and didn't need to be discussed. The pathfinders had to go through ritual humiliation and in the end they changed society. Most probably, men who felt threatened by a shift of social power produced all kinds of verbal counter-measures, and some of their cultural production was made up of these. My impression is the anti-feminism was said but didn't get recorded. I can't write the history because the documents aren't there. The key thing is change over time and this is where you need objective, dated, evidence. I accept failure – maybe you can't trap the floating and incomplete images, which pervade our cultural life and disappear.

Going through digitised newspaper files, I did find a moment when antifeminist protest actually made it into print. For a while (roughly 1979–81), Jeff Nuttall was working for *The Guardian*, as a sort of house hippy or counter-cultural sound-off. In the online archive, he says briefly: "Old fashioned bluestocking prudery crawls back thinly rationalised as feminism. Pornography spreads like soft margarine." (January 1980, opinion piece). To be fair, that opinion piece is overall a disaster-movie "decline of western culture" thing which attacks almost everybody.

What was Nuttall defending? His poetry is repetitive, overexcited, crassly physiological. It is about sexual arousal. The word *phallocratic* (which has gone out of usage but was big in the '70s) gets right to the heart of the matter. Someone like Nuttall who thinks that the whole process of aestheticisation corrupts what the Id wants and says is going to come out with something phallocentric – justifying the term. Traditional art aestheticises human conduct by winding it around with restraints, making the pursuit of appetite social and integrated with other people's wishes. A belief that everything repressed should be the subject of avant-garde art was bound to arouse doubt and disgust, among other things. If you cast off all restraints, you are going to remind people of a pig. You can't solve the problems of art by declaring that the conscious mind is wrong the entire time. I think he wanted to be Dylan Thomas (drunken, anarchistic, highly sexed). *I'm so attractive when I shed all my inhibitions*, I don't think.

1975 shows an anthology of *Contemporary Women Poets,* edited by Trevor Kneale. This may have been the first of its kind since one in the 1940s. It does not mention the feminist word, and may be a sign that feminist poetry has not yet got going – it is in development, you have to leave the old society before you can live and speak in the new one. The contents (41 poets) are not strong. Valerie Sinason's issue Three of *Gallery,* her 1975 collection of women's poetry, refers to Kneale, discards 35 of his poets, picks up the good ones, shows a new world. The floodgates have opened. Her editorial note explains the weakness of women's poetry in terms of fear of success, exposing why it was so bad before 1975 (and abandoning the possibility of denying this). *Gallery 3* is a huge advance on Kneale, an unconventional set drawing on folklore and dream, rich in imagery and often scary. In this showing, Harriet Rose, Sue Jackson, Nicki Jackowska, and Penelope Shuttle sound quite similar. There is a link to naïve art in this wide-eyed style with its simple syntax and simple nouns, its lack of classification or abstraction, sounding as if the speaker has never seen the sight before. The subtext is that what is social is alienated; and derepression is the key. Sinason praises "(a)nything that encourages women to explore their angers, their inner core, their creative selves[.]" The notice on how to submit to *Gallery* says "emotionally complex, no landscapes." Dates of publication can be misleading, so let me specify that developments prior to 1980 are found also in these books: *Alto* and *Body of Work* (Maggie O'Sullivan), *Dry Air* (Denise Riley), *The Wicked Queen* (Judith Kazantzis), *The House That Manda Built* (Nicki Jackowska), *Mwyara* (Menna Elfyn), *The Orchard Upstairs* (Penelope Shuttle), and the anthology *Purple and Green.* Sinason says "truly strong sexual female poems are minute against the thousands of women writers sitting on uncompleted piles of 'almost a man' poems". The 'almost a man' category implies that she can decide which women are really women, taking that jurisdiction away from other women. This was not the only effective feminist poetry – Denise Riley and Judith Kazantzis were writing in a much more adult way, able to connect with civil society and public policy. We read on the next page that Kazantzis is "part of a women's writing collective", something which proposes that empathy and interaction might be more valuable than straight self-release.

# Speaking Volumes

*Reading list for the 1970s:*

1970
W.S. Graham, *Malcolm Mooney's Land;* Frances Horovitz, *The High Tower;* Ted Hughes, *Crow;* Emyr Humphreys, *Ancestor Worship;* Will Parfitt, *Midnight on the Diamond Air;* Peter Porter, *The Last of England;* Tom Raworth, *Lion Lion;* John Riley, *What Reason Was; Penguin Modern Poets 16* (with Beeching, Guest, Mead).

1971
George Mackay Brown, *Fishermen with Ploughs;* Paul Evans, *February;* Peter Finch, *The End of the Vision;* Roy Fisher, *Matrix, The Cut Pages;* Geoffrey Hill, *Mercian Hymns;* Norman MacCaig, *Selected Poems;* Barry MacSweeney, *Our Mutual Scarlet Boulevard;* Roland Mathias, *Absalom In the Tree;* J.H. Prynne, *Brass;* Tom Raworth, *Moving.*

1972
Peter Finch, *Whitesung, Blats;* Paul Gogarty, *Snap Box;* John Hall, *Days;* George MacBeth, *Lusus;* Edwin Morgan, *Instamatic Poems;* Peter Porter, *Preaching to the Converted;* Peter Redgrove, *Dr Faust's Sea-spiral Spirit;* Alan Riddell, *Eclipse;* Sacheverell Sitwell, *Tropicalia;* Ken Smith*, Work, Distances. Poems.*

1973
Gerard Casey, *South Wales Echo;* David Chaloner, *Chocolate Sauce;* Peter Finch*, Antarktika;* Edwin Morgan, *From Glasgow to Saturn, The Whittrick;* Tom Raworth, *Act;* Peter Redgrove and Penelope Shuttle, *The Hermaphrodite Album;* Alan Ross, *The Taj Express. Poems 1967–73;* Adrian Stokes, *Selected Poems (in a* Penguin Modern Poets*);* Anthony Thwaite, *Inscriptions;* J.P. Ward, *From alphabet to logos;* David Wevill, *Where the Arrow Falls.*

1974
Allen Fisher, *Place* (four volumes, published 1974–81); Flora Garry, *Bennygoak and Other Poems;* Jeremy Hooker, *Soliloquies of a Chalk Giant;* David Jones, *The Sleeping Lord and other Fragments;* J.H. Prynne, *Wound Response;* Tom Raworth, *Ace;* Anthony Thwaite, *New Confessions.*

1975

Anthony Barnett, *Blood Flow*; Asa Benveniste, *Grip Edge Lay Edge*; Andrew Crozier, *Pleats*; Allen Fisher, *long shout to kernewek*; Ulli Freer, *Rooms (1975–82; never collected in volume form)*; John James, *Striking the Pavilion of Zero;* Glyn Jones, *Selected Poems*; George MacBeth, *In the Hours Waiting for the Blood to Come*; Peter Porter, *Living in a Calm Country*; F.T. Prince, *Drypoints of the Hasidim*; Peter Redgrove, *Sons of my Skin (selected poems 1954–74)*; Alan Ross, *Open Sea*; Iain Sinclair, *Lud Heat*; Iain Crichton Smith, *From the Notebooks of Robinson Crusoe.*

1976

George Mackay Brown, *Winterfold*; Brian Catling, *Pleiades in Nine*; Allen Fisher, *Paxton's Beacon*; Alastair Fowler, *Catacomb Suburb;* Harry Guest, *A House Against the Night*; Mahmood Jamal (poems in a shared volume called *Coins for Charon*); Peter Levi, *Collected Poems 1955–75*; Jeremy Reed, *The Isthmus of Samuel Greenberg*;
Colin Simms, *No North-Western Passage*; Gael Turnbull, *Residues.*

1977

Anthony Barnett, *Fear and Misadventure / Mud Settles*; David Chaloner, *Today Backwards*; W.S. Graham, *Implements in Their Places*; David Harsent, *Dreams of the Dead;* Ted Hughes, *Gaudete*; Judith Kazantzis, *minefield*; Sorley MacLean, *Spring-tide and Neap-tide* (Selected Poems); Edwin Morgan, *The New Divan*; Eric Mottram, *Tunis*; J.H. Prynne, *News of Warring Clans*; Peter Redgrove, *From Every Chink of the Ark*; Denise Riley, *Marxism for Infants*; John Seed, *Spaces In*; Martin Thom, *The Bloodshed the Shaking House*; Anthony Thwaite, *Portion for Foxes*; Geoffrey Ward, *Tales from the Snowline.*

1978

Peter Abbs, *For Man and Islands*; John Ash, *Casino*; Paul Brown, *Meetings and Pursuits*; Andrew Crozier, *High Zero*; Roy Fisher, *The Thing About Joe Sullivan*; Geoffrey Hill, *Tenebrae*; Ted Hughes, *Cave Birds*; Alexander Hutchison, *Deep Tap Tree*; Philip Jenkins, *On the Beach with Eugène Boudin*; R.F. Langley, *Hem*; Tony Lopez, *The English Disease*; *Change*; Barry MacSweeney, *Black Torch, (part 1)*, *Odes*; Brian Marley, *Springtime in the Rockies*; Peter Porter, *The Cost of Seriousness*; Jeffrey Wainwright, *Heart's Desire*; Nigel Wheale, *Answerable Love.*

1979
James Berry, *Fractured Circles*; D.M. Black, *Gravitations*; Paul Evans, *The Manual for the Perfect Organization of Tourneys*; Paul Gogarty, *The Accident Adventure*; W.S. Graham, *Collected Poems 1942–77*; Ted Hughes, *Remains of Elmet, Moortown*; Roland Mathias, *Snipe's Castle*; J.H. Prynne, *Down Where Changed*; Peter Redgrove, *The Weddings at Nether Powers*; Jeremy Reed, *Saints and Psychotics*; Iain Sinclair, *Suicide Bridge*; George Szirtes, *The Slant Door*.

**Anthologies:**
Edward Lucie-Smith, ed., *British Poetry Since 1945* (1970)
Peter Finch, ed. *Typewriter Poems* (1972)
*Seven Women* (1976)
Meic Stephens and Peter Finch, eds., *Green Horse, an Anthology of Young Poets of Wales* (1978).

Much Seventies poetry was published after the decade closed, so for example Iain Sinclair, *Red Eye*; Jeremy Reed, *Black Russian Out-takes at the Airmen's Club*; (parts of) John Hartley Williams, *The Ship*.

The core of the Seventies is the creative work collected in these 120 titles. There is little point having the arguments without reading the evidence first.

## CEREMONIAL DEVICES: BOOKS OF 1976

Porter: "In the world of poetry publishing, the Little Presses are now overtaking the Big Houses. The range of poetry and production standards are very wide but the emphasis is on imported Modernism and beautiful typography and lay-out. The first wave which included the achievements of Fulcrum Press and Cape Goliard has now subsided, regrettably, after economic retrenchment. The second wave is devoted more to home-grown poets." (*Observer*, February 1973)

One consequence was that, in 1975, someone based in Cleethorpes named S.T. Gardiner began compiling a list of all the poetry books being published. He did this by writing to about 900 publishers to ask for a list of their new poetry publications. The outcome was about 796 titles. Gardiner says that the figure for 1975–6 was 770 titles.

These were by some 532 individuals, of whom 18% were female. This gap of 64 points (18:82) is striking. There are probably 64 different explanations. The count for 1976–7 is 906 titles. The figures I have make it possible that 3,000 individuals published a book or pamphlet of poetry in the decade – but extrapolation is always a stretch. The corresponding decade figure for titles is 6,000, accuracy limited of course by the manifest limits of the data.

In the 1977 yearbook, Gardiner gives sales figures – roughly three-quarters of sales were by post. The shops just weren't keeping up. While this points to a persistent, well-informed, and demanding market, it also points to a break-up into different fractions of taste. Social contact constrains language: without it, you develop far and fast – and then most of the audience can't understand you. Over a long period, I have been searching magazine files for reviews of poetry as it came out. The problem was that the hip people in the Seventies were preoccupied with American poetry of the Fifties, and wanted to slot the development of English poetry into a frozen landscape tied down by those marginal/authoritative figures. Analysis of the new British poetry in its own terms was rare. More broadly, the organs of reception were just overloaded by the demands of assimilating the new poetry. This certainly limited how far poets or readers could keep up with the advances of technique. It is an open question how far several hundred poets in the Underground understood what was happening around them, or if each one had a partial and fragmentary and even creative vision of it all. That is, if you could capture the view of 100 poets about 1975, you would be collecting 100 different pictures. Everyone *thinks* they're modern. The conclusion was that the initial reception record was missing and I had to start from the texts.

Gardiner's figures can't be assailed, since he lists all the titles. In volume 1, the publishers were given a specific date range, but if you look closely it emerges that they thought "this is free publicity" and didn't stick to the date limits. Therefore volume 2 has fewer titles than volume 1 (and at least one title is in both volumes). His dates run from June to June so don't map onto the more legal year of copyrighting. I looked for missing titles, but couldn't complete because of the runover between two calendar years. The yearbook includes a list of magazines, but this is clearly incomplete. Gardiner says that roughly half of the sales were of magazines. So, although Raban says that the modern poem is a monologue, readers may have preferred a turmoil of voices.

SURVEY OF BOOKS FOR 1975–76

These are titles from Gardiner's survey which was closed in June 1976. Sacheverell Sitwell, a survivor of the first moment of modernism in Britain (the *Wheels* anthologies, around 1917), issued two new pamphlets, self-published. A retrieval from a just later phase of literary memory, Edgell Rickword's *Collected Poems* – Rickword was probably at his peak in the 1920s; Carcanet connected with the old Marxism of Rickword but not with the New Left. Ewart Milne, a '30s Marxist poet, put out a pamphlet, *Drift of Pinions*, and a book (*From the Joke Shop*), and a pamphlet (*An Ill-governed Coast*) came out from Roy Fuller, another Thirties Marxist who had achieved great things but whose energies had sunk to a low level by this time. An odd object, a "verse scenario" of 16 pages with musical score, by D.S. Savage, a pacifist and New Romantic poet of the 1940s. Denis Goacher, who had been almost the only young modernist of the 1950s, and a right-wing Poundian, put out a pamphlet – I haven't seen it. Eric Ratcliffe, editor of *Ore* for many decades and a forgotten loyalist of the 1940s New Romantic style, put out *Commius*; Commius was a Gaulish king of the Atrebates who fled to Britain under the pressure of Roman invasion in the later 1$^{st}$ century BC, so presumably this is another piece of romantic history. Two books gathered Pop and live poetry from the Sixties, *The Best of Henri* (by Adrian Henri) and *The Apeman Cometh* by Adrian Mitchell. Aloes Books put out pamphlets by Colin Simms (*Flat Earth*) and Paul Matthews (*Blank Walls*). Anvil put out a long book by Harry Guest (*A House Against the Night*) and Peter Levi's *Collected Poems 1955–75*. Guest also released a pamphlet, *Mountain Journal* – I haven't seen this. From Jeremy Hilton, *Metronome*. From David H W Grubb, an unclassifiable poet, the pamphlet *Falconer*, and the book *Last Days of the Eagle*. From Mark Williams, a poet from the Cabaret 246 performance writing class at Cardiff, fondly remembered by the other members, three publications: *Only the Spaces, Blame the Music*, and *Sophisticated Raspberry*. Poetry flaring in performance tends to disappear when the moment has gone. *Only the Spaces* was published by two different publishers, according to this list. A dual volume by the anarchist authors, Bernard Kelly and Ulli McCarthy, title *Sonnet Brushes*, another pamphlet by McCarthy, *Errire*. A book of Charles Tomlinson's graphic work, which I believe includes poems as well. A pamphlet, *The Rex Quondam File*, by Steve Sneyd, of Huddersfield, one of the mainstays of the small press world. George Barker is listed as bringing out two books,

*Dialogues etc.* and *In Memory of David Archer*. The David Archer book came out in 1973 so someone at Faber seems to have been confused about dates. Penelope Shuttle published *Webs of Fire*. George MacBeth published *In the Hours Waiting for the Blood to Come*, another explosion of inventiveness and superficiality. Glyn Jones, one of the greatest poets to emerge from the 1940s, issued his *Selected Poems*. Andrew Crozier issued *Pleats*, and Michael Haslam his pamphlet *The Fair Set in the Green*, not yet fabulous, and the much longer *Various Ragged Fringes*, while the same publisher issued a pamphlet by Peter Philpott, *The Bishop's Stortford Variations*.

Standing Waves came out from Geoffrey Ward, a fan of the New York School who published a limited amount of work. *Grosseteste Review*, the headquarters of the Cambridge School (i.e. the Ferry/Grosseteste school), published pamphlets by Anthony Barnett, Roy Fisher, and Gael Turnbull (*Residues*). Barnett also released his major work *Blood Flow*. London Magazine Editions put out two volumes by the poet Brian Jones (one a reissue). Jones' style was too plain, probably, to make a revival possible, but he was close to doing something good. They also did *The Taj Express* (poems 1967–73), by Alan Ross, with travel poems from eight countries, surely a good thing. The dust jacket of my copy advertises Ross's *London Magazine*: Art Architecture Films Theatre Music Poetry Stories Criticism Memoirs Posters Jazz Books, hurrah. Iain Crichton Smith released *The Permanent Island*. John James' classic *Striking the Pavilion of Zero* came out. Eric Mottram's *Local Movement* came out (for the second time), also his *1922 Earth Raids*, from the same source as Allen Fisher's *Long Shout to Kernewek*. Martin Thom issued *Ceremonial Devices*, his first pamphlet. An anthology of three Glasgow poets came out including Tom Leonard, someone who formally belongs with the Underground, even if the quality of his critique never reached the starting line (he also put out a pamphlet). Antony Lopez put out *Snapshots*, Lee Harwood *HMS Little Fox*. Cory Harding, publisher of X Press, put out two pamphlets, which I haven't seen. *Omens*, in Leicester, put out *Cordelia and Other Poems* by Veronica Forrest-Thomson, something of a cult figure, who also released a book, *On the Periphery*. Peter Porter released *Living in a Calm Country*. J.H. Prynne published *High Pink on Chrome*, a exploration of his new and, for many people, radically alienating or disorienting style. The underground scene-maker Jeff Nuttall put out *Sun Barbs*. Tom Raworth issued *Bolivia: Another end of Ace*, a pendant to his staccato long poem *Ace*. Paul Evans put out a pamphlet, *Prokofiev's Concerto*. Back from the USA, Ken Smith released a pamphlet, *Wasichi*, in the Red Indian style. *Dense Lens* was a collaborative volume containing poems by Brian Marley and Asa Benveniste, owner of Trigram, who also put out a pamphlet on his own, *Edge*. There are a few titles in dialect scattered through the list. Two volumes exhibit what seem to be poems in Shetland dialect, presumably the most marginal in the whole Anglo-Scots continuum, two being probably more than they managed in the average year (a third book is Shetland poets but possibly writing in English). Two pamphlets by Jeremy Reed came out. Poems by Mahmood Jamal were in a volume shared by 4 poets, perhaps his debut. He has written both in Urdu and in English. The great Orkney poet, George Mackay Brown, published his book *Winterfold*. The Scots poet, Tom Scott, issued *Brand the Builder*, which is a recollection of his early life (Ibsen used the same title). This isn't so good but it does contain one good poem. Alastair Fowler's *Catacomb Suburb*, one of this scholar's two collections of poetry, was a couple of generations ahead of Scott.

The anthologies section does not include any significant set of contemporary poets – in my estimation. It is strong in regional selections, quite often linked to local writers' groups or classes. Anthologies of *Modern Scottish Gaelic Poetry* and of *Poetry of North-east Scotland* certainly stick in my memory as significant books, but dealt essentially with older poets. We don't seem to have any publications which you could recognise as Beat poetry, this was perhaps a youth movement which dried up as youth passed on – in contrast, the Pop thing was still happening in 1975. James Berry's *Bluefoot Traveller*, an anthology of West Indian British verse, was a sign of future developments – there wasn't so much to gather but Berry's dedication was a great asset. No titles in Welsh are included (except a couple of posters, for some reason), but that isn't the main thrust of the book, and anyway nothing is perfect.

## Origins of a Split World

Around 75% of the titles in the 1977 *Yearbook* (which runs up to June 1976, recall) are from small publishers, known as the "small presses", although they didn't use presses.

Meanwhile, the editorial policy of the national magazines, the ones that reached the High Street, was never to review small press poetry. This was an economic decision rather than an act of oppression, but it did create a cultural deficit which grew from year to year. Out of 770 titles coming out in 1976 (plus 88 anthologies), Peter Porter reviewed about 15 in *The Observer*. Brilliant reviews, but how frustrated did everyone else feel? The little magazines did run some key reviews, but only sputteringly and sporadically. There was some counter-pressure, for example Jeff Nuttall in his stint as poetry reviewer for *The Guardian* (1979–81) looking only at small press poetry, and the Mottram-era *Poetry Review*, but generally it was impossible for bookshop managers or librarians to find out what the course of events was.

The awareness of the market was going down even if the new poetry was more likely to arouse enthusiasm and commitment than the old, educated poetry. The beleaguered quality was so much at the forefront for many people that it drowned out the identity of poetry as a form of art which dealt with evanescent feelings and styles and which was there to be enjoyed. If the siege is raised, you can get back to normal life and to moving on to new styles whenever necessary.

The flood of compositions means primarily a deluge of enthusiasm among poets who believed in themselves and the audience, secondarily a shared lack of belief in what critics said. The reception history is of most of the valuable poetry flying into oblivion through a huge market gap.

Like other gatekeepers, a bookshop manager only had so much display space (and could only shift so many books). A constraint which applies is the rigidity of retail income: if you look at the list of poets in Mottram's definition of the British Poetry Revival, most of them did make it into the High Street and did get taken on in anthologies and in the selective memory of critics. Some of the poets who were accepted, and widely sold, were difficult and extreme, thus Hughes, Redgrove, Middleton. The limit was that not every radical poet made it into the market place. The market wasn't wholly rigid, it expanded, but it wasn't going to expand enough to take on 100 radical poets. So, perhaps the lack of acceptance wasn't due to malevolence. Some people cherished organs of malevolence, but the key thing was non-awareness. Critics weren't being paid to read all the new stuff.

How would a commercial approach deal with an over-supply of similar products? Differentiation. Poets must dissimilate from each other to reach an identifiable voice. Where the market is satiated, it is rational to develop product lines of poetry that exit into the unknown, the repressed, and the unbearable. This is where the Alternative came from. It is credible that poets differentiated far and fast because they understood the laws of the market place. This advancing line also involves the development of the audience, desires becoming more acute and sophisticated. It is credible that parts of the market evolved away from each other. It's not clear why the business shouldn't satisfy all of them.

# *Sounds surround the icy waters underground*: Psychedelic Coding

## IT'S COSMIC, MAN

To get the time, you have to practice using the phrase *it's cosmic, man* until you can use it at exactly the right moments.

Why cosmic? The source is presumably an acid trip in which the tripper is hypersensitive to patterns, links things remote and close by, sees large-scale patterns and progressively sees past the impedimenta of daily life so that everything which hid the cosmic patterns from view disappears. In the end, the largest and most comprehensive patterns are the ones which are most prominent, and so the voyager is closest to them, and rightly observes *It's cosmic man*. The phrase is of course suited to the experience of reading one of the new cross-disciplinary maestros, the Western gurus, who juxtaposed historically incommensurate fields of knowledge, using the new systematics and the new cheap data, to produce a new insight into truly deep patterns; so that it was right to notice *it's cosmic man*. Also, the photographs which began coming back from journeys into space, as released to the media by NASA, showed the earth as a round object floating in a space whose extent is palpably far greater than an earth diameter, a reach justly called the cosmos and referred to as cosmic. As Sheila Whiteley points out, the use of two-chord structures in music removed the distinction between moving forward and moving back, an analogue to the loss of up and down in outer space.

It is logical to deal with the Seventies via a poet whom at least one reviewer totally failed to understand at the time, and who abandoned poetry as the decade was ending. This is Brian Marley, who wrote:

With steam striking his jug-handle ears, our
new luggage, smell of old newspapers in
the hall – surely something vivid must happen
without a slump in torpedoing the twentieth century
'Courage, Morris, courage…' I neither neglect
to brush my teeth nor prune a handful of stars in
the early evening – as such, I know one true
particle in the mystery of bone-setting old
ceramics; the motionless dark, occultist
theorem, crumbs inevitably remaining

and I am (in my soupy way) blocking the nerves
from their coffee-veined stimulus – droning cellos!
    The known-to-be-positive by *reason*, adjusting
a small knob – will frenzied faces appear on
our scanner? Duplicity, when peering up the
gun barrel, fingering the trigger: *memories
are made of this!*
                    (from 'Bargain Basement Sonnets #5',
                        from *Springtime in the Rockies*, 1978)

Although forgotten by successive generations of poets in fierce
competition with each other, this is splendid poetry. How is it possible for
someone to achieve such lightness and brilliance in such a sustained way?
When the style is more important than the subject, we have to qualify
the style as far as possible – including tracing its external associations.
All the new style poets of that vanished decade have in common the
rejection of traditional genres, with their firm rules for the ordering and
design of parts, which neither readers nor poets could easily get wrong.
It is hard to summarise or paraphrase Marley's poem – isn't it valid to
see this as virtuosity, and to see this capacity to hyper-associate, and to
take over experience from the fatal cycles of memory and conventional
behaviour sequences, as counter-cultural heroism? The aestheticisation of
everyday life is represented by – the aestheticisation of the poem. Not by
chance do 'reason' and 'memory' appear in the poem – it is telling us that
consciousness has access to *other* processes. The poem is dominated by
style – we can see this as like the lingering over ornament, at the expense
of 'purposive' and busy musical structures, which features in the songs of
that time. All of their poems can be seen as interstitial to 1950s poems –
they burst out into the space between the lines. They are unpredictable,
unaccountable, non-functional – and, from the point of view of a critic
like Allott, unnecessary. Ornamentation and hyper-association are closely
linked – the ornament breaks down the functional patterns to create
an 'aesthetic', uncoded, space, which is filled with a purely subjective
message, about the poet's state of mind – the hyper-association *is* the
message: I'm loose, I've got time, and I'm having a good time.

    If we define this kind of poem as an improvised variation on
moments within the traditional poem of the 1950s, with its rational
account of highly conventional and involuntary behaviour sequences
– we connect the new poetry to a new lifestyle of affluence, leisure

and exploration – and simultaneously designate an 'out group' of poets who couldn't manage the incredible virtuosity needed to invent new structures that had an inner logic, and to get through poems without 'touching the ground', and relapsing into explaining and instructing.

The new society was one of status competition, and radicalising leisure actually made things more competitive. Any loss of nerve would make the poem relapse into the familiar Fifties drabness, and while the programmes of readers and editors involved evading or excluding this kind of poem, much of the ideological promotion around the texts has been an attempt to disguise the conservatism which makes the poet acceptable to the mainstream. There is a secondary question about the *reader* being baffled by poetry which doesn't pause for explanation. No-one likes being in the middle of a party where they don't know anyone and can't understand a word that is being said. But I feel that the youth culture of the Sixties and Seventies has spread, as youth got older, to become simply mass culture. The generation born in the 1920s which indicted and fought off the new poetry is marginal now; the preoccupations which blinded them seem eccentric to us.

I wonder if we can find a way of modelling this intractable material by borrowing the rock critic Sheila Whiteley's idea of psychedelic coding, in her book *The Space Between the Notes*. The specific 'ideal-typical' bands she names are Cream, the Jimi Hendrix Experience, The Beatles, and Pink Floyd (although hundreds of other acts recorded psychedelic material). In a complex exposition of a musical language, she points to features which had for the target audience a social meaning – referring to the counter-cultural lifestyle, to recognised 'affective identities, attitudes and behavioural patterns'. The musical conventions involved originated, she says, with the Charlatans' residency at the Red Dog Saloon in Virginia City, Nevada, in the summer of 1965. Dan Hicks, their drummer, explained that the people who ran the Red Dog Saloon were strong hippies. When they ran into certain Charlatans on the street, in North Beach, they first asked, "Are you the Byrds?". Then they hired The Charlatans without pausing to hear their music, based on how they were dressed. The Charlatans went to Virginia City to audition and the people running the audition gave them LSD before they began to play. This is how music came about which expressed a state of mind of certain young people in 1965. Because youth culture was international and fashion-conscious, the style-package spread rapidly to the 'underground' in San Francisco, Los Angeles, London, and other places. The music refers to hallucinogenic experience by means which 'include the manipulation of timbres (blurred, bright, overlapping), upward movement (and its comparison with psychedelic flight), harmonies (lurching, oscillating), rhythms (regular, irregular), relationships (foreground, background) and collages which provide a point of comparison with more conventionalised, i.e. *normal* treatment.' She talks about virtuosity – the wild exceeding of the norms of blues-rock musical structures, while essentially obeying those norms. The elaborate variations on musical form are spontaneous: they vary all the time, and are decorations of the basic form. She identifies 'tripping' as the lingering fascination for a texture, or a sound, experienced while tripping. Typically, the style uses dislocation of time – two-chord tunes where the listener cannot recognise whether the chord shift is going forward or backward; and blurring of notes which partly contradicts the 'progress message' that one note has finished and another one is now due. 'Don't know if I'm coming up or down.' She says of Hendrix's recording of 'Purple Haze': 'Whilst this is basically a pentatonic blues riff, the extremes of distortion blur the actual pitching of the notes and the discordant partials make it practically impossible to hear the pitch … the electronic distortion, the fuzz … and the resultant discordant partials. For the listener, the sheer volume of noise works towards the drowning of personal consciousness. The simultaneous underlying pulsating rhythm and the heightened sensation of raw power rip through the distorted amplification of the guitar sound with its sinuous *tripping* around the basic notes.' Again, of 'Love or Confusion', 'The use of distortion and fuzz creates an unknown element which can suggest uncertainty. This also comes through in the way in which Hendrix tuned his guitar. The top string was often tuned to D or Eb and the excessive bending and use of the wah-wah pedal served to obscure the actual notes played.' The belief in new possibilities for social institutions was expressed musically: "Stylistic complexity, the elements of surprise, contradiction and uncertainty suggested alternative meanings which supported the hippies' emphasis on timeless mysticism."

I wonder if we can draw lines of analogy between the songs and the poetry. The timeless effect of two chords can, very weakly, be connected to indeterminacy in syntax – lines floating without tense, etc. Although paradox was something recommended (i.e. posited for all truly significant poems) by Cleanth Brooks, in a classic of the new criticism, the use of fundamental tensions and oscillations by 'underground' poets clearly goes beyond paradox, and can be equated with the uncertainties of pitch, rhythm, etc., which Whiteley describes for the classic bands.

We need to draw our attention away from psychoactive drugs. Extensive availability of biographical data has made it quite clear that a lot of 'psychedelic' musicians never took any of the drugs. The innovations of the period 1967–70 are logical extensions of what was happening in 1964–7, and one can easily find hundreds of recordings which are 'proto-psychedelic' at dates which unconditionally didn't see any use of lysergic acid in the places concerned. It is equally valid to see the new sounds as the product of new electronic devices – the maturing of electronic instruments and studio techniques. Whiteley quotes two sociologists to the effect that 'But this culture has already been defined in this way partially because of the existence in it of this particular kind of music. The system is perfectly structured internally... but has no necessary *purchase* on it from without.' People who take hallucinogens see the figures and narratives in the Otherworld which their culture has taught them to expect, and indeed one of the purposes of teaching children myths is to ensure this. 'Acid rock' pleased millions of people who had never taken any drugs at all. I have no evidence that any of the poets used any chemical assistance to their purely neurological resources. The issue of drugs is a big distraction.

The most important aspect for us is the coding which relates specific linguistic traits to a view of how life should be led – liberal, exploratory, hedonistic, not preoccupied by status and possessions. This wished-for new life was political – because it inevitably led to clashes with the captains of 'bourgeois guardianship'. It was also apolitical – because it was essentially about the dominance of leisure, and pleasure, over work and duty. It lost many of its qualities when the living people who made the coding moved on to new personal interests and rules. At the time, it 'pointed' to this group (of 'concrete living people who can be loved', as we say) – and was therefore as indefinitely complex as the behaviour of those people.

Because the people were three-dimensional, the 'counter-cultural' concept is too. Precise, contract-like, definition of the meaning is inappropriate. The question of what it means now (when the people are 40 years older and quite different) interests me a great deal.

Whiteley speaks of *affective identity*. Certain features of music became signs of belonging – music was not merely a pastime but the seizure of a group identity. I suggest that, similarly, there were poetic traits which readers at that time created and recognised as signs of the counter-culture. One of these is contradiction – the confrontation of two cognitive frames which don't really belong together. Along with this, is the move of flowing two levels of knowledge into each other, so that the reader is destabilised (confused?), and responds (in theory) by a reorganisation of their existing knowledge. Reversion to the origin of social forms is held to invite the question why do we do things this way – and conjecture about how things could be different. Montage suggests a rapid shift of psychological horizons – preparation for revolutionary change. It challenges the predictable structures of consciousness. The key to the style is found in the anti-functional quality of virtuosity. These poems are not simply methodical philosophical enquiries. Art as something logical, a form of work, a piece of evidence, a test of character, is being discarded – hollowed out to leave space for the rhythms of pleasure. The shifts and leaps of the poets need to be compared with the rock guitar solo to be properly understood – they are outbursts of spontaneous virtuosic display. The flouting of preset procedures is a form of hedonism – the play principle.

Defining this new style points to an elite of poets who could go far enough in abandoning traditional concepts of logical coherence: Prynne, John James, Barry MacSweeney, Tom Raworth, Allen Fisher, Martin Thom, Brian Marley, Iain Sinclair, Eric Mottram. At a certain distance, we could add Ted Hughes and George MacBeth. Of course, there were any number of people hanging around with the underground and writing poetry which was too feeble, prudent, or inconsequential to make its mark as part of the New Thing. The reference to something external, making art a proxy contest about social ideals, can make the art collapse when the referent migrates, but also makes it plausible that the conservative hostility of critics like Davie, Grigson, Hamilton, or Enright was due to misplaced authoritarian politics rather than to serious artistic judgment. So many products from that era look ridiculous now the libertarian Utopia has been dissolved by its creditors, but work like Marley's, which has a richness of internal organization, is a permanent now, undamaged by time. Eric Mottram wrote:

> a helmet set on a head
> for the horns reach from brain folds
> to planets above towers
> beyond a lens
> moon light in his antlers

curl and spiral of universe
curve out of the brain
skill of mountains      receptors to wind curve
from space to caves in the heart
a coil of horn around a nerve

which tunes the herb
    (from *A Book of Herne*, 1981)

The imagery comes from Ferenc Juhász, and no doubt Eric would connect the physiological equations to Charles Olson, but for me this fits perfectly as a piece of psychedelic cosmic poetry. Besides, the part about linking caves to space is too much like Syd Barrett's lyric about 'the stars [that] surround the icy waters underground'. I can't read 'moon light in his antlers' without hearing 'blue moonlight in your hair', from an old Cream song. The animal imagery comes from a shamanistic context, although mediated by Juhász, and this echoes Martin Thom – we can see this as the poetic equivalent of the counter-cultural interest in Asian religions. (Eric's *Peace Projects* also draws on the great poem, 'The Pearl', from 3rd century Syria.) I don't like Eric's poetry, but at the same time almost everything I like in the cosmos appears in it somewhere. I counted eight radical cuts/discontinuities in the first 40 lines of 'Peace Project 5'. I see this merging of different conceptual/cognitive frameworks as intrinsically psychedelic – although Whiteley does not actually explore the use of montage, incongruity, recontextualisation, and merging in 'alternative' art. An example would be the cover design by Hipgnosis for the Pink Floyd's second album, *Saucerful of Secrets*: an uncalculable space unifies images, partly overprinted, of a real photo of outer space, what may be the fluid slide of a light show, a painted illustration of the planets, a row of green glass bottles (or alembics?), a photo of the band by a lake and against the sky, the Zodiac, a coloured print of a man in green (a magician?) in a forest, etc. This collage style, with its disorientation and overload, was coded as 'counter-cultural' at the time, and you certainly wouldn't have found it on record sleeves for jazz bands, family entertainers, or 'pop' groups. (Whiteley does talk of 'blurred/overlapping timbres'. The sound collages of a track like 'A Day in the Life' are a musical analogy.) Eric's manically branching associations parallel the hyper-associative state of a trip – and the stunningly rich sheafing of variations in musical improvisation. His edits are bewildering – much unlike the perfect smoothness which Martin Thom achieves. What I think is significant about the way Mottram writes is its aestheticisation of knowledge structures. The really big revolution in poetry was the loss of anxiety about intelligence – the recognition that the boundless landscape of human knowledge was material for its own landscape of poetry. The counter-culture called a mighty subjectivity to life – vigorous enough to burn away the problems of the monotony of so much of human knowledge, the exasperations of accuracy, the company of dusty and sanctimonious pedants. His poems are designed like bibliographies – but his bibliographies are incredibly exciting and pushed a whole generation of underground poets into poetry.

J.H. Prynne wrote:

> A dream in sepia and eau-de-nil ascends
> from the ground as a great wish for calm. And
> the wish is green in season, hazy like meadow-sweet,
> downy & soft waving among the reeds, the
> cabinet of Mr Heath. Precious vacancy piles in
> this studious form, the stupid slow down & become
> wise with inertia, and instantly the prospect of
> money is solemnised to the great landscape.
> It actually glows like a stream of evening sun,
> value become coinage fixed in the grass crown.
> The moral drive isn't
>              quick enough, the greasy rope-trick
> has made payment an edge of rhetoric;
>                   the conviction of merely being
>          right, that has
> marched into the patter of balance.
>         (from 'A New Tax on the Counter-Earth', from *Brass*, 1971)

While this passage is clearly rational (and even waspish), we do seem to find psychedelic traits in it: the blurred, shimmering, quality, the pastoral feel, the aspirations to shed material values, the prominence of disembodied colours, the dream state so often invoked, the use of hazy textures (the delicate seed-heads of the plant meadow-sweet), the virtuosity, the sudden leaps of cognitive level. Perhaps not only musicians were sitting in meadows thinking anti-capitalist thoughts? how far *is* it from 'lime and limpid green' (in a Syd Barrett lyric, 'Astronomy Domine') to 'sepia and eau-de-nil'? is the "counter-earth" (described by the poet as nature and where we go in dream) where the "counter culture" was thriving?

The poem starts with "the wish for calm" but is probably not underlining that wish, but instead hoping for alert and experimental action to take society through a crisis. Its main theme is, however, evoking a dream state – illustrated by seven 'dreams' in its course. The counter-culture is thus the subject of the poem, rather than the poet signing up to the counter-culture. A quote from Dr Freud sets out how dreams work to prevent someone from waking up, under the pressure of ideas – this is the link between dreaming and the wish for calm. Presumably a feature of any counter-cultural imaginings was that they did not include a statement of cost, or name a source of funding, or say what would be an acceptable interest rate on loans – and this is why money appears so often in Prynne's poem. Several lines report the views of Lord Cromer, presumably the one who had been Governor of the Bank of England up until 1966 – bank managers are figures likely to appear in dreams, as the voice of anxiety. The "cabinet of Mr Heath" appear as one of the figures who wish for calm, and one of the dreams may be theirs – in context, no doubt Heath's core project of reviving industry and exports by directed investment, which the City of London treated as fantasy.

The method of quotation neatly excludes exhibition of the effects of loss of boundaries on the duration of poems. While we can only point to exhibits here, it is clear that the 1970s saw an explosion in the number of long poems, and that this wish for new volumes was related to 'space rock' and the infinite reaches of subjective experience opened up by the counter-cultural emigration. Allen Fisher's 1970s work presumably does overload, destroy, and transcend inherited structures of the poem, and the poet/self audible within it, just as Pink Floyd destroyed the 'song' and 'the pop star' by plunging into half-hour improvisations as the audience sank into the objectless swirl of the light show.

Many of my readers will already be familiar with recordings by The Beatles, Cream, the Jimi Hendrix Experience, etc., and so can draw on memories of the music of 1968–73 to form a concept of the poetry. The 'era feeling' obviously changed around 1974, by when most of the bands had either vanished or mutated unrecognizably. So, how successful is this comparison as a way of describing the new feel in poetry? I think there are considerable problems with it. The verbal art is not music – Prynne's poem may have as a start point hyper-association and a rebel attitude towards the social order, but it is not subjective or free of logic as the music would be. The music comes into existence because it refers back to itself and the poetry has to contain everything outside itself in order to exist. The hyper-association is arguably a realistic view of how interconnected things are, the subject entangled with material objects, which everyday perception blocks out in order to achieve short-term goals. I feel that the poetry had got going later, and went on for longer, but we are left with the questions of what happened after 1977 – and what the poets of the underground era have been doing over the last 40 years.

The psychedelic feel is as timeless as any other style of art. It offered a feeling of being outside time. However, there is another dimension in which it was tied to a specific group of people. The coding referred to being part of that group. Whiteley talks about "the space between the notes", and the space corresponding to this in poetry is the domain of the implicit. Porter's reviews in the Seventies keep on saying that information is missing from the books. The domain of the implicit was out of control; my guess is that the unstated meaning permeating Seventies poetry was to do with radical social change, and that this was literally a state of being out of control. The feel was soaked into the musical patterns of a class of recordings. It referred outwards to people who were young in 1968. They objectively were young, leisured, incredibly optimistic about a future of unlimited economic growth, liberal, generous, fascinated other people, without ties, sexually active. All of this was fragile. The same people did not have those qualities, or only some of them, in 1980. At the outset, a large fraction of the poetry audience could not get into the new poetry because it was not sociologically congruous with them. They felt awkward inside it – it went through them as if they were ghosts. But, one or two decades later, the new poetry was "coded" to a life-style which its proponents were no longer leading. We have already heard Michael Gibbs describe the loss of optimism about the future. It had certainly been an asset of a kind of poetry, and it certainly disappeared. It shifted from being the Future into being the ghost of a landscape. This leaves us the question of when the wave broke. A variety of sources indicate a wave of pessimism sweeping through in about 1974 – the children of 1968 stopped living outside the official economy and scrabbled to find jobs, rental contracts, and career paths. Like most great highs, the surge of the underground and the radicalism of 1968 left a terrific hangover – the biggest down of all time.

# Short Poems of the 1970s

Ads and magazines have to be attractive. Poetry from within the London media world had qualities of hedonism, attractiveness, and flow which the staple academic poetry lacked. Poems in magazines like the *Listener* and the *Times Literary Supplement* reached a large audience otherwise hardly attainable. Some of the most enjoyable poetry of the decade was in volumes by Peter Porter, Alan Ross, and George MacBeth, who wrote very social poetry along with working for the *Observer* as poetry reviewer, at various magazines as a sports journalist, and as a poetry editor for the BBC (respectively). There was an audience whose tastes were not those of academic reviewers. Critics who expressed this taste included Porter, Lucie-Smith, Martin Booth, and Jonathan Raban.

### The monologue

Jonathan Raban's *The Society of the Poem* is a complete account of the surface of the poetry world as it was in 1971, an astonishingly vivid capture of what people were saying and what it felt like to be in the room with them. He plumps for the monologue as the guiding force of the time:

> The dramatic monologue is *the* modern verse form; as a style it enables the world to report back to, and inform, the poem. [...] the constant tension between the swaggering energy of his own voice and the containing shape of the poem makes for a continuing dialogue between the profuse, muddled pluralism of experience and the ordered, rhythmic design of art. But monologue as a form cannot bear too much instability [...] For Pound, as for Browning, the monologue is rooted in a basic confidence – in society [...] and its shared consensus of values, in social language and its expressive deviations, and in an essentially nineteenth-century, novelistic notion of character. In our own times, so much has changed that we have been left with the mere technical husk of the dramatic monologue[.] (p.115)

Porter writes –

And victims sitting in the tireless hall
Before the second paper of the afternoon
Are answering shadows. Who'd start
The heron of the Eighteenth Dynasty
From painted reeds; who'd say Paul
To a persecutor from a quarterly?
The blind man is called in as
Adviser and the tone-deaf President
Buys Wagner's bed – our only protection
Sacred objects with a patina
Of fear. And that there are too many
Of us will never refer to one.
     (from 'There Are Too Many of Us'
      in *The Last of England*, 1970)

This is a brief example of a kind of poetry which is centrally a monologue, you are always hearing the poet's voice and he is constantly describing individuals through their speech, possessions, and habits. The poem seems to be about evanescence and the provisional nature of artistic patterns. "Who would have guessed/ That final seriousness is temporal?" The title is a quote from Yeats, at a club of poets, saying "we are too many" – the passing of a generation will make most poets simply vanish. This "will never refer to one", i.e. 'it doesn't mean me'– everyone thinks they are the exception and this self-awareness will be proven wrong after an interval. He is a social poet. The lines about the Egyptian painting seem to say simultaneously that art is an eternal moment and that it is just a shadow. Paul persecuted Christians before a conversion – which left him (temporarily) blind. Sniggering critics are just a *shadow* of a real persecutor. The "sacred objects" are classical works of art from the past, whose afterglow fitfully invests living artists. I find Porter's poems simply terrific. It is just unbelievable how he can be dealing with existential problems, long-term conditions, and yet have that quicksilver speed of movement. He has "swallowed" Auden, totally absorbed him, but it had been a geological era since Auden had written anything as good as *The Last of England*. Porter published four books during the Seventies.

    The giveaway is Porter's brilliant volume of translations, *After Martial*. Martial had written satires with lavish social detail depicting characters of the urban society he lived in. He was doing this in the 1st century AD. The similarities with chic Seventies poetry are all too obvious, and if a model had been around for two thousand years even a slick operator couldn't define it as original. Over-familiarity sensitised people to the weakness of this version of the poem, and that led to irritation at some features of it. More profoundly, the design of a poem that produced an individual voice was not going to answer the significant questions raised during a political crisis, where interaction between competing groups was the central event. The idea of character rejected the idea of crisis; almost, it relied on stable social roles and Raban's "basic confidence".

Raban links the belief in a speaking voice with the setting of the public reading. However, poems also lived in the setting of magazines. These were the most visible poems but maybe not the best. The news industry has a homogeneous product, it is the same every day and the same shape on every page. They may have an inlet poem, to fill a space otherwise unused and unsold, but the poem must fit in. A crew of poets, indeed, was able to write bright and undisturbing poems that an editor could rely on. These were knowing poems. Satire has a conservative geometry, it assumes that social values are right because they are the means on which it relies for the bulk of its information, and it reinforces those values by exploiting eccentricity for laughs. The deal by which such poems reached great concision was to accept prevailing social prejudices as accurate, and to ride on them. This matched the typical publication site, in a magazine surrounded by prose which embodied the prevailing values of the day, the news and the customs. This asked the poem to be concise and yet also to fit in, to go along with the assumptions of someone reading the news. To undertake anything critical, you had to get out from under the overburden of that matrix and build a context as well as moments of poetry. Many people felt that a poem fitted into the entertainment and news industry so well because it was unoriginal and made no difference. It was there to prove that the poet was witty and sophisticated rather than to achieve anything on the artistic front. Because so many people were writing it, readers were used to carrying out a predictable reaction pattern when facing it, and this had led to a curve of diminishing returns which had been sloping down since sometime in the Roman Empire. So, this was a path for a successful mainstream poem of the 1970s.

The quality magazines did publish poetry, but it didn't *sell* magazines. It was an afterthought, and this is partly why the poets they favoured didn't produce much that you can read today. Poetry in the media was out of time, historically; it was a lake which was slowly draining, year by year, as editors did the costings. Just as a certain restaurant in Greek Street could cease to be fashionable and be empty every night, so poetry as a form of cultural pleasure had ceased to be necessary for those people. An obvious effect of the pressure on space is 'thrills and frills', the superficial effects by which you take a poem model which a thousand other people are generally using and give it a slight twist – a commodity effect. This genre of poem goes on working because it resembles conversation so much. If you wholly reject it you are rejecting conversation also – cultured discussion, empathy, being social, amusing people and telling them about your feelings. All that.

However, this route was open to the most politicised people at the time. And empathy was seen as something bourgeois and reactionary. It was only permitted to empathise with people of the right political fraction. Conversation fires a flare illuminating social actions more vividly than nature. If you went there, it would be less vivid than the conversational account. There is an element of shared fantasy. This style wasn't going to disappear but it could become non-prestigious. The narcissistic approach relies heavily on the reader liking the poet. Poets may not be so likeable as they think. Many of these poems also relied on circulating privilege as an aura. So the feeling of "being at Oxford", being metropolitan, etc. was the hospitality area of the literary realm. This also may not work for every reader.

I don't see a raft of urbane poets around Porter, gregarious as he was. There was just more money in other kinds of journalism. The admired London poem was witty but not academic – a touch of urbanity, of *savoir-faire*, separates it from the earnestness of Existentialist academic poets. It is native to the media world, to certain bars and certain manners of being brilliant. It is the high wheedling of a couple of square miles in London, without much link to anywhere else. This was an elite group, but a productive one in terms of retail success. It produced the magazines, the television, the advertisements, which everyone else was eager to soak up. Its members were unceasingly competitive – this kept outsiders down. The put-downs were also very funny. They were a kind of revenge on the stupid. But being competitive and sarcastic did not mean being socially critical. That was associated with being provincial and Puritanical, and under European influence.

Was this kind of poetry wholly bad? No, the reaction against it by the generation of '68 was dramatic and energetic and not a scholarly analysis which isolated good patches hidden behind torrents of slush. Juvenal and Martial were good poets – although obviously cynical ones. They wrote in a period where democracy was disconnected from the governmental process. Porter was a great poet. It's just that there is a wider poetry world. Porter is not a credulous citizen, he is not a supporter of the ruling class, politicians, businessmen, or media men. He is not preaching the bourgeois lifestyle with the piety of belief in commodities. But people didn't expend years of study before fleeing the mainstream. It was the decision of a moment. The collapse of the prices-wages policy implied the collapse of the know-all poem. The post-war settlement disintegrates, and at that moment the conventions of poetry stop looking like a kind of rhythm and start looking like deceptions.

The Underground was reacting against this model of poetry and the first consequence was that you could have a different reaction pattern. The second consequence, probably, was that the editors of bourgeois magazines like the *Listener* and the *TLS* wouldn't publish you. Questions. Is this the collapse of shared norms in real society or of legacy conventions in an artificial but self-consistent genre of art? And was it that the quality magazines dropped poetry because mainstream poetry was so stultified, or did a generation of new poets reject the mainstream because the sales tills had already rung its death-knell? There is no obvious answer, but if you can get how the exhaustion of a form matches up with the way a large number of people are moving, the colour of the time will become visible. Evidently the mainstream was in crisis and this explains why a generation of young poets abandoned it. That doesn't explain why the mainstream failed to co-opt the new vigorous and expanding thing. If you get that, you know why they had a crisis.

People move to the margins, and this is a geological moment, a way of locating the boundary between different factions. The split must have to do with thinking about sociology. Can you be a social poet, a poet writing about experiences in society, about manners, and never think about sociology? Once sociology sashays in, approaching human processes through a single special individual seems ridiculous. It reaches wrong answers all the time. So you want to portray a group. Not one feeling which everyone shares, but interactions which include conflicts. And you want to do this inside the poem. But when you do that you take the wheels off the existing clever monologue poem, as practiced by

Porter (and previously by Auden). You break its paces and so when it comes to marketing your poem will be failed by editors who specifically want clever narcissistic monologues. In fact, you have just opened an entire career of being rejected by mainstream editors.

An advertisement is structurally about a link between commodity choice and personality. It twines the two together. You define yourself in the act of consumption. So writing poems which did that used logic which everybody understood but which simultaneously meant you were trapped inside the world of commodification. The conclusions of the poem were already there before you started to write it. Can you write poetry which rejects the social structure and expresses a wish to start again? what is the content of such poetry, what sights is it showing? This is much the same question as, if you are portraying what is familiar to everyone can you also be interesting?

Raban goes on to identify a weakness of the monologue and of the self-reproducing self: after quoting Ed Dorn (on a talking horse) he says, "The style of monologue has become supportable only when it is accompanied by this sort of dicing with language; a nervous, ironic game played out on the edge of the poem, which opens everything that is said to an overwhelming lexical question." The "premises condemned" notice, that there is a product which a current of culture is embedded in, and that as a product line it is used up and close to its exit, is a display object. At one level, it is an utterance compulsory for the hip market maker, an assertion of being up to date. Everyone knows that when a poetic convention wears out, people go on using it for ten to twenty years without realising it. If you sound like you know that, you come over as the guy who knows. At another, it reflects a consumer society: any leisure consumption pattern is temporary, the public and the profitability move on. At another level, it is the effect of exposure: having read even two books based on the same assumptions, you get to realise what the assumptions are. Raban sees Dorn as the way out of this exhaustion, and this is actually a prediction of the necessity for Prynne as the voice of the era: Raban never mentions Prynne, but the later manner of *Brass* and *Warring Clans* is a direct development out of *North Atlantic Turbine*. Dorn was Prynne's best friend.

Raban goes on to say that "The talking heads of contemporary verse may well, I suspect, turn out to look like so many insubstantial spooks; summoned by a society which needed them for its own therapeutic reasons[.]" He has got to the idea of the speaking voice as a kind of self-deception, simply by reading a large amount of poetry. The "ghost" phrase is much favored by neurologists, these days, convinced that the inner voice is a phantom, something with a problematic relationship to what the brain is actually processing. The idea that the story is something the human mind needs rather than how society verifiably works is not yet there, for Raban, in 1971. Not explicitly. Of course, for the radicals of 1971 the media were precisely a phantom discourse within which everything significant happening, for example to income groups D and E, for example in Sunderland or Birmingham, was silenced. The belief that there is another flow of knowledge and that you can break through into it was constitutive for the Left of the time. What media people produced seemed like the chattering of parrots.

A small step further on is the chain "consciousness is a flow of deception. Consciousness is how my self is audible. It is what I can hear. I can't stop it and replace it with anything else. The rest of the universe is cold and silent and consciousness is all there is". Raban is keen on the idea of the voice of a poet as humanising the universe, even if the universe is not human and that coherence is ultimately based on omission and false recognitions. We have also to ask what kind of poetry you write if you agree that consciousness is a deception stream and try to produce language by other methods than recording self-awareness. This is discrete from someone who simply thinks "the media are full of illusions but what I think and feel is perfectly true".

We could define a moment where the poet becomes aware of the unreliability of consciousness and, instantly following, a moment where the poet solves this problem and produces a way of writing which satisfies epistemology. The second moment simply does not exist. It is a sort of 64-dollar status symbol which nobody owns. It seems abidingly true that *the universe is not human* and that *human awareness is the only kind we have.* You have poets who disable criticism by bringing on fascinating distractions, but not poets who have faced epistemology and won. The poetry flows past this.

Brilliant conversation enhances memories. We have to look at the poem which is an artefact, a precious thing in itself, rather than a record of experience. It adds value, enhances by various orders of magnitude. It is convincing but not realistic. It does not simply match actual recoverable social events. If you ask about the mismatch, you have punctured the poem. So, when conventions fail we have to ask several times why. The monologue puts one voice at the centre of the universe and the problem which radical poets had with legacy poetry, generically, was this egocentricity. It matched too accurately with the individualism basic to capitalism and the ownership of natural resources by individuals. It is only fair to add that conventional poetry was less reliant on arbitrary personal attitudes because it embodied the attitudes of a whole party or clique – because it obeyed conventions. Did these conventions embody wisdom or falsehood? If you combine the falsehood implied in heightening effects with the narrow focus on one individual self, you get a product which is not only narcissistic but also designed to falsify tone values in order to make one person seem more glamorous. This was very provocative for anyone who didn't simply identify with it.

# Post-western?

We will start with a riddle. I found extensive use of imagery from Ancient Egypt in poems by Iain Sinclair, Lee Harwood, Allen Fisher, Philip Jenkins, Eric Mottram, Martin Thom, and Jeremy Reed. Why all these Egyptians? This could be debated. In their origins, myths are linked to the working of the society which invents them, connected to teaching values to children, to rituals and celebrations of the village or the family, to the rules, to the political order. They are *operational*. Taking myths from a society which you were never part of is wholly unlike this. Egyptian forms are *non operational*, we have forgotten their sociology and they are loosed from effort or effectiveness. The use of such myths is central to Seventies poetry. It prefers to be fact-free and pattern-rich. In *Lud Heat*, the Egyptian motifs in Hawksmoor churches in the East End are used as the anchor points of a weird geometrical transform:

> St Anne, in plan, is seen to be closely related to the horned scorpion gate form, described by G.R. Levy; *The Tombs of the Giants,* Sardinia. And this goes back, once more, to Egypt… not by direct route, carried by migration – the plodding cultural-transfer theory – but by sap connection… archetypal expression of common needs. It is the essential shape of a peculiar kind of fear. Hathor, the Moon goddess, whose horns hold up the moon disk… contains Osiris, by assimilation. Our rapid spirits trace out a moving cage of paths and tracks around the pyramid… are bees, pieces of the sun. (…) The church is a mummified bee surrounded by water.

turning parts of London into a re-enactment of the Nile as the highway of the dead and the Isle of Dogs into the lair of Anubis. If you look at H.J. Massingham's original diagram of how megaliths evolved from Egyptian rock tombs, reproduced by Elliot Smith, you see the same Sardinian design: the Tombs of the Giants. The idea of diffusion, 5,000 years ago, around the Mediterranean's coast and then up the Atlantic littoral, to Neolithic Britain, was proposed by Elliot Smith and accepted by Massingham. This would give us a reason for re-enacting Egyptian ceremonies. But did Sinclair believe in it? Mottram didn't believe in it. Gertrude Levy didn't believe in it. Even I don't believe in it. Sinclair says "not by direct route". His use of the power of buildings to draw down recurring events connects with Renaissance occultism (as described by Frances Yates) and with sacred geometry (imagined by John Michell as the force shaping the originally blank land) but only as a charade, a plot supposition in a horror film. Allen looked, in *Paxton's Beacon*, at the Egyptian fantasies of the Crystal Palace and recorded what he saw – a delirious recreation of a far-away realm. Eric Mottram said in his 1973 book *Local Movement*:

> after coffee in the Heliopolis Hotel 1955
> under dome and propeller out to Giza
> crawling night into the Great Pyramid
> down the stone tube to a centre
>
> thunder of beaten sarcophagus weight of stone measures
> in that night a terror of ignorance I should have quieted
> meditated on measure but framed by knowledge I lived blind
> old untouched by *harmonia mundi* and magic techne
>     ('Homage to Denis Saurat')

Jeremy Reed wrote:

> The January sun mulled. A poker-point
> of cinnamon. Words are the offertory,
> the rites to establish a counterpart
> I work inside a simulacrum. Gold eye
> to the lens reanimating Kher Heb
> the twelfth rite, Opening the Mouth: office
> of the poem. So too with passing geese
> you are form between a rice-paper's double fold:
>
> motion invested with cabala. Red A
> in Chepera's vision. I can never
> arrive without a diaphragm of gold
> the occult alphabet in mineral
> veining the poem from shoulder to wrist.
>     (from 'Stratton Elegy')

The sociology does not matter and several societies are being used to add to the pattern library. In this new world, the point is the intellectual elegance of each proposition and the calm with which the poem allows its developable surface to develop.

The forms are empty after their long journey. The poem is a mask for something which may be closer than Egypt or the Hopi and their kachinas. The wish to get out of the so-called "Western box" expressed itself as a change in the grammar of art, the unit structures from which poetry was constructed. The new poetry could therefore propose a "grammar without a society", or a language without a grammar, something asymmetrical and without counterpart or standards. If someone proposes to you "I am going to throw away the shared assumptions of our society and write a new literature which is completely alien and without legacy", you are likely to ask them "who exactly is going to read this literature?"

## CULTURAL CRITIQUE AS HOME

Clearly any hippy was saying, on day one, I am no longer part of the West. This connects back to the earliest stratum of our data-set: in the 1920s, David Jones was part of a discussion group, Catholic in orientation, which was primarily reacting to Spengler's *Decline of the West*. Spengler had created the intellectual game of regarding the West as merely a culture, to be studied by "culture morphology", even if all his specific assertions were wrong because of his scant knowledge of anywhere else. Theodor Adorno had started his career in the wake of Spengler: even though he disagreed with Spengler's non-factual, if mythologically suggestive, doctrines about Faustian culture, Magian man, and so forth, he could devote himself to cultural criticism because Spengler had just made it central. Jones had spent his poetic career defining the life of a culture which he thought had already come to an end: the young of the 1920s no longer believed in it.

Farrenkopf's book about Spengler describes some of the things Oswald saw as elements of culture, distinctive (and symptomatic) of the "Faustian" Western culture:

> Soaring Gothic cathedrals, symphonic music, perspective oil painting, double-entry bookkeeping, differential calculus, cannon, machine technology, [...]
> (Farrenkopf, *Prophet of Decline*, p.34)

These offer meaning-bearing elements which can be deployed in poems – on condition of being viewed critically and as starlike gleams which show great historical depths. These components are agitated and self-willed enough to forge their way through poems, and cultural criticism can use them as symptoms mimicking the movement of the illness. Spengler may be like a neurosis, a swarm of symptoms with no valid external cause.

I am still wondering why poets of my generation went the way they did. Sometimes it looks as if a path was the exit from capitalism; raising all the rules involved in the local arrangements of the West since the 16th century or so to the conscious level, and slipping out of them. The suspect area involved not only the design of corporations, the breakdown of community, the obsession with objects, but also competition between people, the sense of power and superiority. These rules could be identified quite accurately and the critique dissolved the structures of daily life. The long act of reproducing the old society in young individuals could be turned on its side to allow an exit into another world. This was an educational project, a course with no definite ending. The poems are not records of experience but an exit – objects leaving the ego. They began with a blank. Outside capitalism was a non-place, a suspension. Non-capitalist societies were readily to hand, although as theories or travellers' tales. The range of objects or customs which we saw Spengler fussing about propel poetry, they move out and in and give us instability. In the 1970s, there were few counter-cultural poets who would admit that "I can't think outside the Western box". What happens to the merely-western reader in the middle of a poem which has suppressed western structures of meaning and symbolism? Couldn't this be like a surfer coming off his surf board?

There are obvious differences between the new poetry and psychedelic music, or underground music, or whatever you call it. To visualise the connections between the Counter-Culture and poetry, we have to accept that the music was a free realisation of a fraction of the possibilities latent within the Counter-Culture. Poetry realised another fraction of them. Also, the Counter-Cultural ideal involved liberation and so divergence: a hundred poets were not going to re-converge on a new convention, or if they did that was a proof of failure. The magazine *2nd Aeon* may have defined the new ideal, while it lasted, but it is also plausible that most of the poets had only a vague idea of what they were aiming for, and that the ideals came from a new life-style rather than from model poems.

How do we get from psychedelia to poetry? In *Flying Saucer Vision* (1967), saucer-seer John Michell expounds Jung on the meaning of the flying saucer cult as a sign of a historical shift of axes as mankind enters the age of Aquarius. He goes on to say, "The arbitrary framework which limits our way of thinking, our western liberal-humanist system, based on the Hebrew-Christian tradition and seemingly confirmed by the superior technology which enabled us to exploit and patronise the natives of our colonies, has evolved to its limits and is now approaching a state of decadence." (p.20) It is reasonable to say that everyone under 30 in 1970 would connect to those words. That is not to say that more than a few people even believed that they had knowledge of anything else than the western thing. It may come as a surprise to people today that hippies (flying saucer spotters or not) thought that they could stop being westerners just by an act of will. Further, you can't directly record or versify this breach realm, this post-exit condition. Another way into this dropping out is to recall Gavin Maxwell's *Ring of Bright Water*. This was a book inevitably read by children in the Sixties. The book did describe life with pet otters, but the main appeal was the wilderness aspect: the protagonist lived somewhere (fictional name Camusfearna), on the coast near the isle of Skye, where there was no road, not much of a harbour, no television or radio reception, and the nearest telephone was six miles away. In the absence of shops, supplies had to be carried from where the road ended. Fuel was driftwood from the sea-shore. I want to imagine, just as an experiment, that the impulse to drop out came from *Ring of Bright Water* rather than from legends of life in Haight-Ashbury, and that the rejection of legacy poetic means corresponds to the lack of infrastructure inherent in this wilderness life.

Dropping out meant the erasure of the existing literary conversation, where you would write poems about your garden or Emily Brontë or the sullenness of A-level pupils or whatever. The legacy poetry was like having a telephone 100 yards away. It was very hard to define it as an insult or abuse. But the Camusfearna fantasy involves the nearest phone being six miles away. This casts the legacy poetry as circular twittering which interferes with awareness. A whole mass of literary rules was scrapped in line with this journey away from the infrastructure. Empiricism was thrown out because it was the central dogma of an older generation. The things to be scrapped also included law, property rights, commercial behaviour patterns, institutionalised knowledge. This jettison affected the way poems were constructed. In fact, the project could include scrapping all knowledge which the older generation had. After all, the point of fleeing to the coast of Inverness-shire was to get away from other people.

The clear-out left an empty space, and part of the new poetry is the act of re-populating the data space. The appeal of gurus was that they filled up the hole quickly.

Spengler said that civilisations differ in their conception of space. Inscribing those conceptions in the fabric of visual works means that a few square centimetres of textile embody entire civilisations. Ominously – this means that a poem can quote a small stretch of cultural fabric to put a whole civilisation on stage. Alterations to those small and yet productive patterns can express views on them – showing flaws perhaps, expressing distance, in fact the whole programme of what we call critique. It is supremely economical – there is no other way of getting entire civilisations into view without hundreds of pages of exposition which fundamentally do not work in a poem. Yet it is artificial – the small object you hold in your hand may be precious and fascinating but it can hardly contain the complexity of human affairs. This is an investment for poetry in the double sense of depositing value and reducing your ability to buy anything else.

This chapter was originally entitled *Are you serious?*, because the idea that you could become post-Western just by an act of will was so ridiculous. A test case might be Cubism. This used different conventions for depicting space from painters of the 19th century. It could be claimed for these older painters that they continued conventions used by classical Greek and Roman painters. If you accept Spengler's claim that conventions for representing space (in pictures or intellectually) are what differentiate one civilisation from another, then a Cubist painter has exited from the *Abendland* and is post-western. A painting is a clash with civilisation. Montage of images showing different sets of spatial rules throws us out of site into a fore-time where everything is arbitrary. There is more than one geometry. Early in the 19th century Riemann invented a world of alternatives to the Greek/Western, Euclidean, standard geometry, without ceasing to be a European.

## Fringe Science

Following the First World War, where various European societies had almost succeeded in destroying each other and themselves, the 1920s saw a unique collapse of belief in the wisdom of society. This was a moment when cultural critique reached a great flowering, recording a generational revolt. The 1970s were also dominated by cultural critique and so the cultural practices of the 1920s came back to centre ground. Although Spengler was not trying to get away from being Western, he did pull the camera back far enough to see the West as an exhibit, one cultural complex among a number in neighbouring regions.

Until this de-Westernised knowledge is inside a mind, it isn't there. Several classes of possible pioneers present themselves. First, the colonised. Someone who possesses more than one culture, by virtue of being one of the dominated in an unequal society where democracy is not the means of choosing a government, clearly has access to non-western values but at the same time understands Western values and can judge them. Secondly, the gurus. The West produced figures who, very soon after the change of awareness, could lay claim to speaking from the future. Marshall McLuhan and R.D. Laing spring to mind straight away. Many others produced paperbacks. Third, social anthropologists. Poets who had studied social anthropology are a special group. Their idea of the West was less simple than that of some other poets. This might include sociology using social anthropological techniques – like the Nuffield-funded study of Banbury in the 1950s. Fourth, a line of anti-rational thinkers, within the boundaries of the old East Mediterranean civilisation (and its offshoots), offering knowledge of magic and believing in trances and visions. These can be appropriated as legacy gurus, anticipators of the Counter Culture. And fifth, of course, gleaming new poets, products of the Spirit of '68 as well as of the Psychedelic Summer of 1967.

Several of the poems examined had an interest in the fourth group, and its unvalidated knowledge. Outside the validated realms of science and of official Christian theology, there is a large area of surviving works from pre-modern times which record a different kind of knowledge. Knowledge, to be sure, may be the wrong word. One line of interest in this class of texts (unlikely to be found in university libraries) came from Aby Warburg. He acquired some astonishing knowledge which was of use to clarify the programmes used by certain Renaissance artists. His library came to England, where he founded the Warburg Institute, in which for many years scholars with remarkable knowledge of the suppressed and forgotten pursued Warburg's themes. Frances Yates is the best known of these scholars. Another line was C.G. Jung, a late follower of Symbolism who continued their interest in occult knowledge and specialised symbols. Another line was interest in Blake, for example Kathleen Raine set out to read everything which Blake had read. She had some associates in 1950s Cambridge who carried out similar research into poets like Shelley and Yeats. The hippy movement moved Blake to the centre of English literature and so found his sources to be of the first interest. Of course, this fringe science had continued after Blake's death, and the hippies themselves produced an outpouring of it which reached hitherto unknown dimensions.

RESOURCES

Scholars are competitive and paranoid about being new. Recovering the intellectual milieu of 1970 or 1975 is going to take something more than just reading what big-shot academics are pumping out today. The ideal way of reading this poetry is to know about all the intellectual background from which data structures flow into it. The books which students normally read in 2017 were not around in 1975 and so their knowledge units were not the fuel cells which animated the poetry we have in mind.

A minimal statement about books circulating at the time may be helpful. It goes without saying that this was a competitive area and poets were eager to find sources which no-one else had heard of. Perhaps it is simpler to spend a dedicated month in which you only read books available in 1975 and only watch films or TV from the Seventies. It was an era of saturated media productivity and the evidence is available in vast quantities. Some books:

Ezra Pound, *The Cantos*.
Charles Olson, *The Maximus Poems*.
William Blake, *Poems*. Everyone read this. Raine's books on Blake were also influential.
Donald M. Allen, *The New American Poetry*. Widely available source for the American poets of the 1950s.
Frances Yates. *Giordano Bruno and the Hermetic Tradition*. The Warburg tradition. Of course, Yates was discussing a whole flock of fringe writers.
H.J. Massingham, *Downland Man*. A source of mythological thinking about the ancient past, the landscape, artificial hills, pre-industrial harmony, etc.

John Michell, *The View over Atlantis.* This was a central statement of hippy thinking and made the connection between ley lines and flying saucers. Related works are Paul Screeton, *Quicksilver Heritage,* and Guy Underwood, *The Pattern of the Past.*

Paul Devereux and Nigel Pennick, *Lines in the Landscape.* Continues the interest in ley lines and offers a way of reading symbolism in the landscape.

E.P. Thompson, *The Making of the English Working Class.* Stalin's academicians invented a history of the area of the Soviet Union which built up to the 1917 revolutions, and Thompson created an imitation of this myth vaguely attached to the history of England. This is more a work of the imagination than of reading of evidence, but it was seen as a rescue of history from the grasp of the ruling class, and people wanted this.

Christopher Hill, *The World Turned Upside Down.* The suspension of censorship during the 1640s and 1650s allowed bizarre material to get into print as never before, and Hill here studied the Far Left of the time, factions miles outside the revolutionary government. This was the recovery of a lost world. The Levellers, Ranters and Diggers became part of the imaginative world of Alternative poets. Kevin Brownlow made a film about the chief Leveller: *Winstanley.* The Ranters were foes of reason.

R.D. Laing, *The Divided Self;* Laing and Aaron Esterson, *Sanity, Madness, and the Family.* Haunting suggestion that the medical profession was systematically letting down the mentally ill, also in some way a critique suggesting that the family has a design and this design needed to be completely changed.

John Berger, *Ways of Seeing.* This may not have been more rational than John Michell but it exerted a cult fascination over a number of writers. It is from a TV series and the author did not bother to add bibliography, notes on sources, etc. for the book publication. This suggests that it has no connection with the past at all. The lack of reasoning or evidence may have contributed to its popularity.

Joseph Campbell and R.F. Hull (eds.), translated Ralph Manheim, *Papers from the Eranos Yearbook: 3, Man and Time.* An anthology of different versions of the occult, the lost knowledge, hidden patterns. Jung was popular at the Eranos gatherings but they reflected something much wider than Jung.

Henry Corbin. *Avicenna and the Visionary Recital.* Probably accessed via the Eranos yearbook. Corbin, a scholar of Islamic mysticism, was a minority interest but ideas like *mundus imaginalis* and ta'wil keep cropping up in poetic texts.

C.G. Jung. Jung's ideas are important but his books are unimpressive.

(The Club of Rome) *The Limits to Growth*. One of the books which everyone read about pollution, the consumption of natural resources, etc. These ideas were everywhere and the TV series *Doomwatch* was a lot more popular.

Germaine Greer. *The Female Eunuch*. Just a sample statement of early feminism; not very scholarly, but very effective as polemic.

Theodor Adorno, *Prismen*. Example text from the Frankfurt School, held at the time to have solved the connection between society and art (even if this doesn't seem very plausible today), and much read at Cambridge.

Raoul Vaneigem, *The Revolution in Everyday Life*. One of the great Situationist works.

Mircea Eliade, ed., *From Primitives to Zen*. A reader of religious texts, mainly non-European.

Raymond Williams, ed. *The May Day Manifesto*.

I feel upset because this is just a drop in the ocean, faced with the complexity of the intellectual milieu. Suppose you could walk into a bookshop in 1975. You might find 3,000 different titles on the shelves, perhaps many more than that. This is too much to recover. However, the number of books which any individual, i.e. one who writes poetry, has read is far smaller. Yet – each poet has read a different subset of the books available. The advent of mass higher education devalued both the weight of any individual's knowledge – because too many other people had it, and the weight of any single work of scholarship – among so many. Actually, the whole economy of information was changing. What we may be seeing is the conversion in the university world of complexes of information into objects of consumption and forms of competition. This means that the underlying pattern of ideas is a key way into reading different Seventies poets.

We can sidle into the bookshops of the time via an original exhibit, the blurb of the Paladin paperback series. This is taken from the 1971 edition of *Mysterious Britain*, by Janet and Colin Bord. "Open your mind and extend yourself […] Our titles are intended for those who want their curiosity aroused, their imaginations stretched, and their brains stimulated [...] Our books deal with love, death, drugs, revolution, art, sex, war, psychology, archaeology, biography, sociology, travel, science, anthropology, literature, philosophy, films and much more." (What *more* could there possibly be?) Could we say that any volume of poetry which didn't cover those alluring subjects was just not up to the minute? The phrase *mind-expanding* is drifting just beneath the surface of this shimmering come-on. Dare we recall that the subtitle of *2nd Aeon*, Peter Finch's great Underground magazine, was *poems of the exploding universe*? It's cosmic, man. Knowledge is becoming interesting, child-centred, attractive, boundless, and academic dullness is looking like blocked-up self-esteem. *Flying Saucer Vision* came out in the Abacus series, which was a kind of second-rate Paladin, junkier but perhaps for that reason less inhibited and more revealing. Abacus put out the *Poetry Dimension* series of mainstream poetry, adorned with dazzling erotic-psychedelic acrylics which could not have been less like the contents. The selling point is that the people who repress any new social possibility are the same ones who decide whether knowledge is valid, and so forbidden knowledge is an asset and a way of evading social control. However, a phase implicit in the small print is that alternative poetry may become a fringe knowledge, and may be just as wrong as Neoplatonist cosmology and just as closed out of historical memory as Robert Fludd and Lodowick Muggleton. It would follow that my attempts to recover small press poetry are like recovering radical tracts of the Civil War period.

GAMES

One of the great texts published by Paladin was Huizinga's *Homo Ludens*, which presents game playing as part of the psychological make-up of mankind and especially as basic to culture. (It seems that Spengler was the major influence on Huizinga.) This idea was expanded on by George MacBeth in his poem *Lusus*, one of the vital works of the era. One of the prejudices of people who were growing up in the Sixties was that play was fundamental to learning, consumption, and culture, and that nothing *had* to be the way it was. The prospect was of aestheticising the span of human knowledge and building it into poetry. The industrial growth of the universities created an unfading pressure to find interesting intellectual methods or areas of learning. Some part of Seventies poetry was taking drafts of what was being found – the search was often successful, and this is a much larger process than just poetry. Typical for these interesting thinkers was the moment of structural insight where two disparate frames of reference are illuminated by the same underlying pattern. This corresponds in poetry to montage. The big story here is possibly that young people, faced with apparently endless years of education, didn't like tired and disillusioned voices and urgently wanted teachers who were enthusiastic and made unusual connections. Was the education system populated with bored and demotivated people? Yes, sadly, and the same is true of the poetry system. The argument is also about making jobs interesting – not the division of surplus value but doing tasks that "extend your mind" rather than grinding you down over years.

I have been looking at a list of 30 new poets arriving in the 1970s, trying in vain to find common points among them. I think there is a separation between them and the poets in Mottram's 1974 catalogue (who had already got some way into their careers by then), but it is delicate to define. The new generation was profoundly aware of the revival. There was a lack of belief in the present, and so in autobiography and in the means of recording experience which we can sum up as realism. The focus is steadily and collectively on the future. But the new poets were free of dogma, so that they knew there were a million possible futures and so no single one could acquire density – move from a vapour into a solid. This poetry was unsustainably light – free to move into configurations of disturbing originality and unusual intricacy. The idea of a learning environment comes to the fore – sequences chosen for their ability to generate new propositions (rather than to confirm moral truths or to record stories embedded in social institutions). The poems propose, rather than a new society, a game-like rehearsal of the building of new relationships, roles, ceremonials, or myths. Showing the poem and the society as things that can be generated leads the reader into radical positions through fascination rather than through anxiety or force.

Losing interest in restricting the poem to actual experience and memory, the poet wishes instead to take a hypothesis and feed it with the data it needed to grow. This made poetry a form of theorising, an exercise in intellectual beauty. The game idea meant that there were infinite possibilities, each tied to a unique set of axioms, and that writing poetry meant exploring the implications, finite but unforeseen, of a particular set. The sense record is a mere storehouse to assist the search for pattern.

POEM = DATA + PROCEDURES. This is a "caption" summary of the position of semiotics on poetry. It allowed an opposition to be drawn between legacy procedures, which seemed natural as well as traditional, and ones derived from speculation. The latter could produce series of completely new results but were unfamiliar to a reading community. The reliance on legacy procedures was seen as generating monotonous and sterile poems which were cranked out in vast numbers and which denied consciousness. Because society too was seen as a generable thing, we could add another slogan: SOCIETY = RULES + OUTCOMES OF PAST MOVES

A tip-off may be the poetry of Denise Riley, which struck everyone as a contradiction of what was around it – thus bringing to light what the unconscious characteristics of the time were. So, the poems in *Dry Air* were descriptions of real experience, recalled emotions, did not gesture towards an idealised future, did not evoke exotic or ancient cultures. A dry air expresses incredulity, and the charms being unwound are those of male left-wing intellectuals. Obviously, this contrast is just a hint.


FRINGE SCIENCE PART 2

There were from an early time courts which were bored and wanted entertainment, and a profession of wonder-workers able to tap vast resources from them. Those who produced 'theatrical miracles' for the Courts in various countries are in the ancestry of Cecil B. de Mille movies, rather than science. Their temporary structures were often more elaborate than permanent ones. In 'The Alchemical Cupboard', Benveniste has that amazing paragraph: *& Fludd awakens Paracelsus the skin Pythagoras to Kelly your Dee names Lully who turns Bruno Dellaporta the axis*, etc., in which he names 20 mage figures in one sweep. People who thought that UFOs had proved the existence of alternative energy (or alternative physics) which could be tapped through ley lines, declined during the 1970s. This occult knowledge was attributed also to the mages of the past, from Pythagoras on. For me, a key moment in the development of the Western magi theme is when the idea of an alternative physics was disproved. Blake's attack on Locke and Newton did not succeed. Eric Mottram's *Local Movement* (1973) is about a tract by William Harvey which was not published until 1959. The title, *De motu locali animalium*, is related to *locomotion* and refers to the movement of animals, which is governed by the nerves. Harvey had discovered the circulation of the blood but failed to resolve how the nervous system worked. Eric slides from this to Duchamp's 'The Bride Stripped Bare by Her Bachelors, Even', also about desire and (frozen) movement – a montage. This is certainly an important feature in 70s style, and it works especially for poets trying to put the past together in a new way. The link between Harvey and Duchamp is weak, but Eric is setting out elaborate intellectual patterns for us to act out speculation and re-connection as we wish. He does not have a thesis – all the possible relationships within the semantic field are significant and "in play". *Local Movement* has material also on mages Robert Fludd and Giordano Bruno, and Fludd was a friend of Harvey. Harvey is not actually a fake, but recall that people at the time, post 1968, expected magi to have genuine "lost knowledge". The design of *LM* is compelling, but the way it is written is confusing and unconvincing. Montage is hi-tech that doesn't work every time. If we find Mottram talking about Robert Fludd, you are expected to wheel out your detailed memories of reading about Fludd in Paladin (Yates) and perhaps Thames and Hudson (Joscelyn Godwin). Allen Fisher and Sinclair also soaked up an astonishing amount of damaged knowledge – Bad Science. Fisher and Eric Mottram, notably, included lists of "resources" in editions of their poems, which do give us indicators of where to look for source ideas. They are just lists; grasping the connections between those sources and the poems takes a further layer of analysis.

## Origins of the Land

The idea of spatial poetry is key for the '70s generation. Jeremy Hilton edited a special issue of *Joe DiMaggio* (#11) on the theme of place, published 1975. He wrote, in *Poetry Information* 18, a follow-up responding to criticism of it: "I do think it is significant that the five books which in my view gave our poetry the most important push to an exciting presence around the 1974 period" – he cites *Place: Book One, Ivan12man*, Temple's *The Ridge*, Owen Davis' *Voice,* and Torrance's *Acrospiral* – "however different they were, had all very much a geographical energy-source." Hilton cites also Mottram's *1922 Earth Raids* and Sinclair's *Lud Heat* as place works that came out just after his anthology. He had taken part in the *English Intelligencer* project, and there were other poets also inspired by Olson, such as Fisher and Sinclair. There was the wave following *The Sleeping Lord* (composed 1966–8) and its Anglo-Welsh parallels; this would include *Soliloquies of a Chalk Giant,* by Jeremy Hooker, and *Charged Landscapes*, by Philip Pacey. We can go on to suggest some of the reasons why the idea attracted so many poets.

One, decentralisation. Narratives featuring the elite in London, with the alternation of power between different fractions of the elite as their real theme, were to be replaced by narratives taking place outside central London. Peripheral nationalism had a structural hunger for such a shift in location. Because ideology was a synthesis, the collapse of ideologies led to the collection of local knowledge to fill the gap. This could even be a form of bleakness, of objects silent once shared symbols have flown away.

Two, the evolution of documentary. This involved the displacement of a self as the centre of the poem. Poetry was driven by a hunger for patterns. Because most factors are effective over a short distance, taking on more factors makes a place emerge as the subject. As long as you keep the cameras running, the outcome was a description of a place. If you fix the camera so that moving figures vanish or blur to a shimmer, what fills our picture is the immobile – which as it turns out is a place.

Three, a wish to eliminate the static viewpoint brought an interest in journeys. This may have been protest at the static quality of English society in several ways. The journey mode involved the description of places, as what was changing during movement. The idea of nomadism became something of a cliché – it was not a symbol for commuting, but a rejection of the village as a conservative symbol.

Four, anti-narrative. A widespread loss of interest in series of events fired the actors but left the camera running so that it caught what wasn't changing and what wasn't connected to any events at all. Historians were abandoning events in the search for structures, preferably researching provinces rather than states. Writers became more interested in finding the rules of the game than in playing it. If you look for stable structures by preference, place is important because it is one of those.

Five, dethroning man the overlord and moving into an ecological viewpoint. This began with the degradation of the landscape you were looking at. Extending the gaze to the land made man seem very unimportant.

Six, a sense of places as stores of memories of past lives. This drew on a Gothic form-world but also on an aspect of Blake. His project centrally involved the migration of the key events of prehistory or mythic history from the Mediterranean to Britain, and a mythic version of particular places in Britain. This was a feature of Blake which could be imitated.

Seven, materialism. An interest in human life as shaped by material obstacles and economic endeavour led to an interest in the physical environment, as the oldest site of factors in production and exchange. The implication, that human volition was not the central thing, was part of a Marxist project of sweeping away illusions.

I can't define the difference between new landscape poetry and old – there is an invisible wall which everyone knows about but they can't consciously define. Certainly I can't say that Peter Levi or John Holloway didn't know how to write about place. The difference may be that in the new world the earth is seen as a will indifferent to humans and with the agency of large processes; this is de-aestheticised and de-humanised when compared to the humanist poets of a slightly older age-group.

Are we talking about literal space? Spengler locates the differences between civilisations in the way they represent space, which is passive to any conventions. So you would be looking at the difference between an Egyptian painting scheme, possibly on walls, and a Western European one. This is *not* the same as contrasting Egyptian geology with Western European rocks and soils and so forth. Humans build mental maps to guide them around. If we imagine a poem as being painted onto an object, then acts which distort the object will reshape the poem, into a new geometry. The fascination with non-western visual patterns is part of a wider interest in the geometry of transforms – perception flowing off its original grounds and becoming subject to wilful doubling, flipping, stretching. The interest in mental maps may be less a homage to Spengler's cultural criticism than a psychedelic flashback. The interest in landscape may be less of a literal geography and more of an unbinding of the large-scale space in which the poet is embedded – isolating a matrix to create new patterns.

Poetry as a visual art

One window is the story of poetry as a visual art and the dramatic instability of the rules of visual imagination in the time. Cold War propaganda had come unstuck and people just weren't taking pictures literally, they were thinking about how they were constructed. The image cracked and the process of ideology became visible – in all its complexity.

Dismantling propaganda was populist, anti-authoritarian, vital, universal. But post-pictorial poetry could simply be puzzling and like a broken TV. This artificial environment can take a visual form, where the interest was simultaneously in enjoying and critiquing such waves of stimuli, with the two features closely intertwined: the artificiality of society, which rapidly suggests that particular skills were also needed to construct a new society. I am writing an IOU for an unwritten book on poetry as a visual art. There was a new regime for consuming images which took the glut of audiovisual data as a new social mythology on which poetry could surf. Images thus became objects and the content of abundance.

Spengler actually wrote about modern art and described it as a disaster, a symptom of civilisational decline. This was a hint that conservative critics would define as decline what was actually an advance into unknown territory. Another view is that the habit of going beyond the borders and developing local specialised variants is characteristically Western, as opposed to breaking out of it. Spengler built something like this into his definition of Faustian man. Equally, art historians have been inclined to identify the craving for competitive personalisation and stylisation in painting as starting with Mannerism, soon after 1600, and Cubism as an innovation which belonged in a *series* of innovations. A model of seeking commercial advantage by differentiating staple products also seems relevant and within western traditions. A model whereby all the excitement is beyond the settled border, where there is a fixed opposition between young rule-breakers and middle-aged rule-makers, and where the new territory is populated by the young who compete against each other by means of conceptual and technical innovation, is profoundly Western. The link between economic growth, technical innovation, and legitimacy, was fundamental to electoral discourse in the post-war era. To be non-Western, one would have to scrap the idea of innovation. Spengler's idea of Faustian Man was partly right.

The factor of competition is significant for this realm of going beyond. Going beyond *other people* was part of it. An in-crowd poet of the time needed, not just an ideas complex, but also an obscure American poet to serve as their guru, and a critique. A modern poet needs a sense of time which grossly defines the artistic rules within which a personal style can be developed. Developing a version of the current position of the moving curve of English-language poetry probably also implies a critique of their predecessors, and *in the 1970s* probably also a critique of the productive cognitive assumptions which held up public language. The unstable segment of poetry is this area of assumptions and rules. If there is a status competition, of course someone has to win it. The competition made itself visible as a scatter of cairns echeloned in space by how far into the unknown they got – shipwrecks in the interior.

# Rite- and Fore-time:
# the Liminal as a Form of the Sublime

Many conservative critics reject modern art for its desacralisation. The tenor of these attacks is that artists are swept up by possessive individualism, the unqualified pursuit of appetites and the reduction of experience to local and real configurations. Actually it doesn't seem that poets are guilty of this. Modern poetry is not based on aggressive consumption. The condition is more that with the social exit from Christianity there are no collective symbolic structures suitable for achieving states of *communitas*. Artists are concerned with the wider life of the group (not just their own appetites); with reflection (as opposed to pleasure); and with ideals (as opposed to passive registration of the real and finite); and with intuition (as opposed to data won by means of instruments, and strictly 'real' and public). The attacks by religious conservatives often seem to be shells fired at something that doesn't exist.

However, modern poetry has largely abandoned the literary means (stories, symbols, shared patterns, salvation schema) of Christianity. The question is then how it can achieve its goals in words; and how the audience assimilates writings using a symbolic code which is, necessarily, unfamiliar and (initially) unshared.

The Scottish anthropologist, Victor Turner, offers in the concept of liminal processes an overall theory of modern British poetry. *Liminality* derives from the rites of passage described by Arnold van Gennep: it refers to the state of people during the rite, when they are outside social structure. *Limen* is threshold, a space between two states. Here there is neither economic purpose nor conflict of interests. Here social oppositions, such as those of class, are deleted; one enters a domain of timeless acts and objects. Turner's theory shows its event cycles starting with a change of status; this expresses his debt to van Gennep, who made his "rites of passage" start with just such a change. The conflict is opened by a formal breach, (stage 1) a moment where an overt violation of social norms signals dissatisfaction. This leads into a state of crisis (stage 2), which is liminal because it is outside the learnt patterns of the social order. The liminal state includes rituals and is an autonomous stage (3). A procedure of redress (stage 4) is set in motion, which may involve the rituals or (of especial interest for us) a contest of strength. Finally, the matter is brought to a head, and the conflict ends (stage 5) either with reintegration or with a permanent rift which might be a migration or one tribe becoming two. Other useful terms are *field*, which is the set of actors in a social drama, not only those taking part in it but also anyone who influences it; in the case of a poem, this might include all the audience, even if the overt actors are only the poet and the reviewer; and *arena* which is the social or cultural space around a drama. The example Turner gives is of the territorial divisions of Iceland, which defined in various ways the scope of action of the events described in *Eyrbyggja saga*. Social dramas are "the time axes of fields". A *field* is the more dynamic, less stable, version of an arena; the field is essentially a grouping of human beings, while arena is the broader "space" in which they move. The arena also includes "territorial and political organisation". Liminal forms are undifferentiated and plastic; as opposed to the forms of social life, which are differentiated and stable. Phonology lends itself peculiarly to this form of analysis, because it's obvious that there is an original column of air which is differentiated by the action of the teeth, the lips, and other parts of the vocal tract. At the apex of the tree, the universal specification of utterance is word (word) … (word), i.e. a word followed by one or zero words, followed by one or zero words, followed by… Any actual utterance is more specific and less universal; corresponding to the way in which a named vowel is more specific than the archivowel, and any named word is more specific than the idea of a word.

Humans like to organise rituals in which they pass out of the categorisation system. 'During the liminal period, the characteristics of the liminars … are ambiguous, for they pass through a cultural realm that has few or none of the attributes of the past or coming state. Liminars are betwixt and between. The liminal state has frequently been likened to death; to being in the womb; to invisibility, darkness, bisexuality, and the wilderness. … In this no-place and no-time that resists classification, the major classifications and categories of culture merge within the integuments of myth, symbol, and ritual.' At the liminal place, we reach *communitas*, the bonds of which are 'undifferentiated, egalitarian, direct, extant, non-rational, existential, I-Thou(.)' It 'is a spring of pure possibility, and may be regarded by the guardians of structure as dangerous(.)' Where power relations are dissolved, the powerful recede into the shadows, and inferiority comes to the fore as 'a value-bearing category that refers to the powers of the weak … fostering continuity, … the wholeness of the total community, positing an undifferentiated whole whose units are total human beings.' The way to the liminal place is a pilgrimage, and pilgrims, like the heroes of quest stories, are liminal characters, outside rational purpose and social structures. Liminal symbols are indivisible substances, often semen or milk, or 'running water, dawn, light, and whiteness.' The rites in the liminal state possess flow, a key concept owed to Turner's associate M. Csikszentmihalyi: it is 'the holistic sensation present when we act with total involvement, a state in which action follows action according to an internal logic.... Flow is experienced in play and sport, in artistic performance and religious ritual. There is no dualism in flow. ... Flow is made possible by a centring of attention on a limited stimulus field, by means of bracketing, framing, and often a set of rules. There is a loss of ego, the self becomes irrelevant.' The limited stimulus field would often mean, in poetry, the repetitive sound structures of metre or the object in which complex symbolic meanings are closed and drawn into tension. Without these focal fields, poems which aim for the sublime can just leave the reader feeling rather dizzy and sleepy. There do seem to be rules whereby sublime topics are mixed with physical, limited experiences. (Quotes from *Image and Pilgrimage*, edited by Edith Turner.) We can see Simms's journeys across the Great Plains as pilgrimages.

Because human cognition likes to use oppositions to distinguish qualities, many cognitive frames can be used to symbolise the deletion of oppositions. I presume that the recitation of liminal objects and verbal forms is adequate to trigger a liminal psychological state in the listener or reader. Of course, the moments where this triggering fails are also of concern to us.

We apparently have here a coherent description of the overall goals of British poets: they want to make a statement about broad social relations, they want to transcend the oppositions of class society, they want to achieve a flow where there is no duality of consciousness, they want to offer communitas, they want to express values which contradict the values of the power elite and the everyday where they hold sway. We are not going to dwell on the whole feel, but rather on the tangible elements of the boundless, which we can identify more crisply. However, the whole feel must follow – that is the point of entering the boundless.

These anti-values are expressed in anti-language. The linguist MAK Halliday talks about an *antilanguage* as one in which all the values of the dominant language are reversed; a value system in which those who are the losers in conventional scales of value can express themselves without simultaneously degrading and denying themselves. We find this in dialect and patois writing, in poetry of simple syntax; and at this point we discover underground poetry as a form of anti-language. To adapt this thesis slightly, the mechanisms of control in (any) society do not produce a population who all share the dominant values; instead, a scatter of responses produces a split population, with a party of opposition on almost every topic. The dominant group expel the oppositional beliefs from most of the public means of utterance, and they are distributed through the private or unofficial realm.

Every symbolic scene can incite dissimilation, the rejection of the offered behaviour pattern. Individual behaviour is a complex where strips of assimilation and dissimilation alternate.

Both represent specific neurological skills. In reading poetry, dislike is as important as liking. To define dissimilation, we would have to say something like: this behavioural tune, which I have modelled and which is therefore inside me, is not going to be part of me, and I am going to eject it. An interesting ambiguity affects such acts of denial; the denial is dependent on what it denies, and so socially conditioned, but it is emotionally charged, and so belongs to the personality. It is pointless to assign denial to either of two groups who deny each other. Clearly, we have a "moves rule" such that move 7 of party A is conditioned by move 6 of party B, and conditions move 7 by party B:

B6 > A7
A7 > B7
B7 > A8

There are problems in assigning particular British poets, or poems, either to anti-language or to (official) language. That is – raising the judgment that poet X is conventional to the level where it is a conventional judgment (commanding wide assent) is not a straightforward task. No-one ever admits to being conventional, conservative – and in line with official opinion.

In a sense, each line starts as a liminal thing before it is written, and subsequently enters time and finitude. This seems fanciful, but the sense of probability and unforeseenness is of the greatest aesthetic importance. If we wish to experience the unbounded through poetry, the arrival of the personality, which we recognise because it repeats itself, is tragic. Repeatedly, we watch the closing-down of potential as the pure arbitrariness of the unwritten poem, infinite and free, spirals downwards and inwards to become a specific form of phonemes, locked together as words, which are locked together. The fact that all poems go through this destructive spiral, minimising something precious, suggests a necessity.

By listening to a voice, you can measure the body mass of the speaker. Speech is loaded with information relating to the speaker. It is natural to associate style with projecting information about a self. That is pretty much the opposite of what we have been talking about as de-differentiation. In the Seventies, we are seeing an opposition between poets using style as an extended self-description and ones who resist that and whose style is aimed at an equally primary goal of information processing. Its features are related to the goal of marshalling, assimilating, and sifting incoming information. Using the variable features of language to propagate a personality is a heedless reflection of a society based on possessive individualism. The radical poetry of the period can be considered as the anti-language to the inescapable language of advertising, which tries to define every act as a projection of the personality. The manic extension of possession can be suspended by a counter-principle. We can look in poetry for the negated and repressed of the everyday.

Turner speaks of a juridical contest (over status) being fought out through the withdrawal to the liminal zone. The poems themselves could be the ritual enactment of the contest, although their status as ritual is unclear. The text is rightly read as a test of strength. The test that resolves the disagreement takes place at the stylistic level. It invokes unwritten rules governing witness credibility and moral prestige. Any poem is a pleading concerning honour – an assertion of the writer's ability to write which runs as an ordeal or a suite of formal tests. You can't fact-check an apocalypse. The question of where the information in a liminal text is coming from has no obvious answer. Reading it as a sort of failed realism is itself bound to fail.

I originally expected the study of long poems to supply mythical accounts of social rules, which I could use as a vehicle for talking about perceptions of social structure. But they really didn't sustain this – what they seem to be aiming for is a point outside social structure, from which it would be possible to talk about how society works; but they do not go on to write such a myth. We find the juridical element of Turner's work especially helpful here – quite possibly, the poets are concerned about the value of their poems as testimony, and are drifting into the uncoded, impersonal space so as to devalue criticisms that start from their subjective, partisan, limits as witnesses. So: every time a critic says *your account is biased because* you're middle class, male, come from Yorkshire, belong to a political party, are loyal to a group, etc., the poet would be responding by evacuating the personal elements from their testimony, and moving to occupy a point which is external, shared, and so safe from rejection. They then speak as the judge rather than as a witness, prosecutor, or defendant.

The escape from the confinement of a first-person narrative, with its partiality and its unstoppable rhythms of appetite, is both necessary and fraught with danger. Identification is the primary act in consuming literature – and it is easier to projectively identify with an individual. The exit into group identity offers a space which is much larger but more weakly charged. The Christian poet strove in former times to write about the whole parish, as the connected community within which the consequences of actions were made visible and so the moral laws could be justified. Problems (of uncertain origin) with creating characters in verse led to a deterioration of this full external space, so that by the mid-20th century Christian poets were suppressing their own selfish feelings but not completing the cycle to show the life of the community. This incomplete exit into the liminal produced something grey, featureless, dominated by phobias, abstractions, and omissions. It struck a chill down the spine of many readers. A simple response was to withdraw, back into the personal. This tended to trap poetry in the sociologically real, caused fruitless arguments about not liking people and the rules of social sympathy, led poets into a commodification of the personality, and blocked the way into a truly mythic discourse. That is – it also aroused widespread opposition.

There is a grey sludge underneath consciousness. Any liminal art has, therefore, the problem of acuity. Emptying the immediate data of consciousness, switching off the rhythms of practical life, can simply leave a pool of infinite greyness – where every memory is literally accessible, but nothing is sharp. This plenary vagueness may be what we experience during nights of insomnia (and indeed insomnia is the theme of two large-scale liminal poems, by David Gascoyne and Ken Smith). This is where devices of acuity like the limited stimulus field and the myth come into play. The myth deploys things like a hero, like risk, fear, and danger, to produce a focus – an area of heightened intensity, where each moment is irreversible and unique.

Evidently language offers us a set of qualification processes by which primal (but concealed) objects of meaning are developed and divided. A sentence can be seen as an apparatus which qualifies its head-word or words; if you accept this, it is immediately possible to extract an unqualified and prior state, by negating the qualifiers. Not only syntax, but also the classification system ordering vocabulary, offer us such trees: where we have a word *animal*, it is prior to all instances of real animals, and there is a branching structure which subdivides the animal kingdom into smaller and smaller groups. Also in the realm of phonetics, we can envisage any vowel as a variation on an undifferentiated general vowel, any consonant as a variant on a primal consonant, any word as a variant on a prior schema, the primal word. There is a functionally adequate link between the combinatory lexical possibilities offered by phonology and the distinct lexical items requested by the shared classification structure.

The avant-garde tries to give us early objects. If there is a slope, down which we find increasing precision and decreasing potential, then the avant-garde poem is high up that slope. It is quite logical that those people should write sound poems (without recognisable, formed, words), and visual poems (made of shapes which are not letters). They see these objects as moments from a stream of boundless, undifferentiated, energy – fossils from an early verse of Genesis. The passage into articulate discourse is seen as *damage*.

When you get to the top of the tree, you have the minimum of oppositions – and you are, symbolically speaking, in the void space, at the beginning of time, outside the world of property, surrounded by 'generative' objects which are about to become sheep, cows, birds, houses, metal, grass, and so on. Fairly obviously, this realm is also populated by people who have no characteristics – although they also have the complete set of possibilities. At this moment, any acquisition of characteristics is also a loss of potential. On the way, deleting characteristics to increase potential might be an important aid to locomotion.

As we said, the unwritten poem is itself a liminal space – every line you actually write reduces its possibilities. The journey (or psychedelic flight) to the void grounds is made practicable by opening up textual pragmatics – the rules of conduct by which the writer creates the text. The act of suspending these is not simply a way of irritating and bewildering the reader, but an attempt to climb to a plateau of potentiality where a new set of rules can be consciously chosen. It is a structural metaphor for redesigning society, and for a landscape where a creation myth, recounting the origin of institutions and social groups, might be staged.

Turner identifies as typical liminal genres of art frenzied dancing (to the point of exhaustion), creation myths, calendar rites, apocalypses, and law codes. The place where the creation myth takes place (telling of the *heuremata*, the inventions, and the *arkhai*, the 'firsts' of every thing) is also the place where epistemology lives, recounting how knowledge came about from ignorance. Poetry has, not with all units but at least with part of its effectives, moved from myth to epistemology. A fight has taken place, at the arrivals wharf, between those interested in the origin of society, how it reproduces itself in its members, and those whose interest in epistemology is from the first anti-political and individualist. The latter group is not at all interested in the social origins of identity. (The calendar rites in question are New Year rites – sited in a liminal time between the end of the old year and the start of the new. These rites may resemble creation myths because they involve the re-creation of every manner of thing, after the destruction of the old things the new ones are drawn out of the pre-form void, and recitation is often the means whereby this is done. Healing incantations often resemble New Year rites because the creation of a new and sound limb resembles the bringing to life of a new world at the turning of the year.) The apocalypse may fit into a cyclical knowing of time as the final decay of the old year. Part of the Twelve Days legends may be the prowling of monsters – beings of incomplete form because the days see the arrival of fully formed objects as the recitations gradually impose true shapes. Biblical scholars have for long drawn parallels between Genesis and Revelations, where the one is the repetition and undoing of the other.

The distinction between local and non-local can be applied to an amazingly wide range of objects and perceptions. Thus, we can say that underdetermined sentences correspond at the level of social semiotic to eternal objects at the level of things. The vocabulary of liminality allows us to discuss Prague School notions about the indeterminacy of poetry, to put it in a larger context, and to explain why it is a quality which fulfils an aesthetic appetite. The more indeterminate a sentence is, the closer to being liminal it is.

The word *water* without any qualifiers, in absolute usage, shows us water in its eternal form – as part of the liminal world, where everything is lifted above change and damage. The notion that indeterminacy is attractive because it offers a greater range of possible moves may be wrong.

The wilderness is a liminal place. The place where property boundaries do not exist shows the deletion of social oppositions – it belongs to everybody or nobody. This already suggests the possibility of re-interpreting the socialist beliefs of most of the significant modern poets as a (misplaced?) aesthetic impulse: instead of a vision of a way that the economy could be arranged, permanently, for everyone, in the future, it could be a loyal description of the features of a liminal state, experienced in the present on a pilgrimage or in a work of art. This would irritate most of the poets beyond measure – but you can't really separate a vision of the way you want to live from the symbolic experiences you enjoy most in art. The beautiful poetry was an experience in the now-time – and not mortgaged, in any way that could involve a bailiff, to a permanent future which seemed imminent in the 1970s. Socialism was arguably an authentic vision native to poetry but not really of any use in politics because not based in administration, material interests, conflict reduction, finance, or anything really.

The idea that social arrangements should be completely non-aesthetic is not very attractive. Perhaps we could relate certain features of recent poetry – its inhibitions about writing in a directly political way, for example – to the over-familiarity of basic socialist ideas, which had been in the air since at least 1840.

Collecting information progressively makes knowledge of any object more detailed; but we have to explain why poetry can become de-differentiated, why poems would have as key elements of their composition the horizon, where there is no colour and objects are indistinct. For them the realm of precision, of dimension, is partly edged out to make room for the random, the blank, and the non-finite. The eventual outcome of encroachment and enclosure is that space becomes like an object, solid and detained by its owner: movement and wandering cease to be possible. Laing describes in *The Divided Self* the state of someone who has internalised urban space in terms of ground to which the owners have restricted access. The culmination of such learning is a paralysed mind, one which can no longer imagine a space which it is allowed into, which has fallen out of social space into a no-place. It is an urban layout in which the public space, the paths and plazas, have vanished or closed up. He described the dense grid of territorialised space which really exists and which liminal space is the negation of. The idea of culture is surely to create a space open for all, where paths lead off in all directions and there is no area which is not a path. In poetry, deterritorialisation was the watchword, and nomadism was a fascination. In Prynne's TEI account of the Mesolithic as a vast nomadic age underlying the Neolithic, the mobility may be an allegory of the principle of change commended by Marxism – and the idea of property follows from a sedentary mode.

Hubert von Herkomer, the English painter who lived at Bushey in Hertfordshire and staged poetic dramas in a private theatre there, identified areas of emptiness and indefinite forms as essential to the sublime in stage design. The links between the spatial arrangement of paintings and the visual imagery underlying poems would repay attention. These visual precepts draw our attention to the conditional use of the liminal – the formless patches occur *within* wholes of organised form. Perhaps, just as the liminal gives a source of the sublime and suggestive, so also the spectrum band of the sharp, definite, and classifiable is necessary to let the liminal release its energy.

The aesthetic which moves towards the indeterminate and the featureless is the diametric opposite of one which privileges the unique self of the poet, egocentricity, and autobiographical experience. However much we admire the artistic project raised to mythical level by Pater, we must recognise the wider forces taking 20th century art in just the opposite direction. The gap which Rudolf Otto pointed to in the horizon of Western art, the sense of the void, is no longer a gap: Western art, untethered from classical models, has reached out to new methods. Modern art has on many fronts progressed by emptying out the manically hypertrophied realistic detail which filled the art of the 19th century. Modern poetry is full of liminal imagery. Its writers have always been able to recognise the threat posed by photography and documentary, and to distinguish the values precious to poetry which excessive actuality obscures or contradicts.

A SUIT AT LAW

Turner first developed all these ideas to explain field observations in Central Africa. He was a pupil of Meyer Fortes, who was interested in law in tribal societies, and the liminal thing is actually a form of anthropology of law. He started with the conflict resolution process but this could take the form of withdrawal to an uncoded space by an entire class of people. How this cultural custom observed in what was then Rhodesia could explain forms of art in Europe is not wholly clear to me, but it was Turner who made the connection. When anthropologists were looking for social customs as sources of harmony and stability, Fortes was looking for social conflicts that would tell a different story. Perhaps conflict is normal and the stable order is a fiction. You can't observe it. The number of things you can't observe is not limited in any meaningful way. Disorder is actually what you observe.

Turner's stages of conflict are crisis, breach, liminal state, redress, and reintegration (or separation). Fairly evidently, the creation of an Underground in poetry was a breach. The Underground exists within the confines of a liminal state to the extent that it cannot take part in the business of society or official culture until the original crisis has been resolved.

The poem is not of itself a social conflict, but a suit for status and attention which is both for and against the audience, whose approval it is seeking. The opposition traditional in jural procedure is not necessarily there. However, it tends to return, because it is perceived to make the experience more integral and complete in itself: the poem is felt as partial without the conflict. This restitution of unconscious norms is of great interest. It justifies us in defying explicit evidence to treat poems as latently conflictual even where they make no reference to the opposing party. If we look at the support discourse, we find sound poetry being described as a challenge, as a denial of something; although that something is, like everything else, missing from the sound texts.

Poetry which looks at the code rather than at the utterances made using the code is like the judge who controls the law-code itself and applies it to acts, culpable or otherwise, which it defines. If we ask why reflexivity is attractive, part of the answer leads us back to the liminal world. The median term between poetry and sociology is law – a superlatively verbal skill, based on a concept of equity which goes back to a Bronze Age liminal concept – the *isotes* of which equity is a translation. *Isotes* appears in the *Parmenides*, in the space between philosophy and myth. *Aequus* reveals a spatial metaphor – it is a physical quality, that of flatness. Indeed, as a noun, *aequor* also means the ocean – what is flat and spreads indifferently, which is fused with itself. One of the offspring of law, historically speaking, is sociology – law expresses as norms what sociology uncovers and recovers, descriptively.

This exposes the possibility that sociology is a secular version of the sublime and liminal. The attempt to depersonalise the reported experience by filming it from the universal point of view can end up as something turgid and bland. However, the romance of poetry with sociology (which starts, possibly, not with Charles Madge and Auden in the 1930s, but even with the Georgians and their preoccupation with poverty, their sidelining of the poet's personality) was inevitable – a phase that had to be survived.

## LIMINALITY AND PSYCHOGEOGRAPHY

MacSweeney spoke, in an interview with Eric Mottram in 1974, of the contrast between an industrial and dockland city like Newcastle and the moors inland from it, pristine and uninhabited. This opposition generates his work *Black Torch*, where the striking miners go out onto the moor and form a camp, where they can live by fishing and catching animals. This is a foretaste of a juster society, based on shared wealth. The boundless terrain of the moor is also a symbol of a return to a time before coding – a time before the law of property was made, as the miners are suspending the laws of the land, brushing them aside to build a juster settlement of affairs. You could get to the moor from Jesmond Dene, the part of Newcastle where Barry lived, and where I visited him, in a few hundred yards. You didn't have to trek to Alaska. In West Yorkshire, the early mills ran on water power, and so were built as close to the hills as possible – the factories were as close to the bare tops as they could be, and this is the landscape where Hughes grew up. Imaginative space is generated by experientially learnt oppositions.

Physically, the connection between the ocean and the moor is fairly clear – they are without boundaries, they are populated by wild (ownerless) animals you can catch, they are not owned by anybody, social rules do not operate there for lack of people, you have to accept the laws of nature. One could even add that they are cold and windy (since moors tend to be high up). They both become increasingly prevalent as you go north or west from southern England. So, they can undertake the same symbolic charges. Both are examples of uncoded space, *espace lisse*, as described so powerfully by Deleuze and Guattari in their work *Capitalisme et schizophrénie*. Because language is a whole apparatus of coding, it is not surprising that attempts to reach the liminal state have set in train a large-scale rethinking of language – and that its result, what we call the avant-garde or the underground, often seems like the removal of linguistic coding; the recovery of pure space as the fully empty.

In two of our poems (*Marimarusa* and *Malcolm Mooney's Land*), the ice appears as a primal substance, the origin of language and concepts. The common ground is that ice is mere substance without shape or colour or heat. This qualifies it as a liminal substance proper for the place of origins, where everything is formless and yet about to acquire form. It resembles milk, water, light, etc., as classic liminal substances. Because the world is seen as growing ever less coded and more archaic as we move north and west, the ice-pack is a proper site for a creation myth. Thawing (cognate in Germanic languages generally with the word for dawn) is the return of colour and vegetation to the world, out of the timeless condition of winter – a re-enactment in the now-time of the fore-time of creation.

If we look at various works of modern poetry, we see, not only that there is a location of the undemarcated wilderness in northern Scotland, but also that there is a chain of additional locations of it which heads further west and north. By the time we have passed through Greenland (Francis Berry) and the Beaufort Sea (Aklavik, in Prynne's poem 'Aristeas'), and the shore of Alaska (as recalled by Tom Lowenstein, who did fieldwork there, in his poem), we are willing to accept that this logic takes us one step further on: to the Koryak people of north-east Siberia, and the origin of the Crow myth. If there is a relationship of degree between two terms, in a current system of classification, it is possible to extract the distance between them, redefine it as a repeatable operation, and use it to construct a third term. This can either be invented, or ascribed to a real thing which roughly fits the bill.

Perhaps all scales can thus be used to generate fictional but comprehensible values; and literature is often derived by *over-fulfilment* of rules within familiar sets of language and social customs.

The structural logic by which the undifferentiated ice substance is adopted as a symbol of the timeless and of the origin of language and organic cells is familiar from the work of Turner. The sea was a place of exile in the Irish tale of the children of Lir and corresponded with the forest in the Sweeney tale – which was a source of outlaw imagery appearing in works by Ken Smith and Barry MacSweeney. The area of liminal substances allows narratives outside the realm of the social.

Because the wilderness takes on wider dimensions, within the British Isles, as you move north and west, a projection into the remote north and west could appear, psychologically, to the audience, as a trip into the most intense wilderness – the most liminal place. I would offer this as an explanation for the fascination of the Arctic. There is a double shift whereby that direction means an increase of upland moors which are uncultivated and therefore undivided, and of uninhabited tracts; and, further on or deeper in, means the Atlantic, a desert waste of ocean sprinkled with windswept islands and, perhaps, with ships. A simple additive logic takes us from {Northumberland as wilderness suitable for poetry} to {the Arctic as super-wilderness super-suitable for poetry}. Land without field-marks differs from land organised as private property in the same way that the primal aleph differs from articulate language.

Let's look at some poems of the time.

This stone polishes him.
It wipes him gently amber from the fingers up.
This stone is a powerful blade to set
The king free. His vine ropes hold the house
And his knotty hands. There are bands
Of silver sweat dripping his face away.
His wax face weeps amber tears. I collect
The stones for a necklace that will talk of him.
His words take my neck in their hand.
          (Nicki Jackowska, from 'The King Rises',
                in *The House That Manda Built*)

Casting a spell the hands, two sets of four

Dark into a mirror a charging bull
the *prisci theologi* that
'This is my body' denies
'the power of the keys' locked out.

Gold into sea light
yellow to blue embodies
arsenite of copper
and red burnishes trilogy:
a toad.

What price this 'indulgence'
without visibility, magic
and the square root of minus one
boastful of being different from predecessors

rings of iron in blue gold
not freeing nor sound
knot disguising slavery or death.
The laws *are*: but who handles 'em?
too many gates for the city.
        (Allen Fisher, 'Erase Muse' from *Shorting Out*)


knots on a weather vane spur on the burgee
windknot against sea goddess
wind tendrils    wind feelers
antennae of long keels
strike water lightly
knots of honeysuckle
of convolvulus grasp
contractions of coil space
bean stalks wave for a hold
slow each night a scarlet flower revolves
the rotation of lilium
magic lines in each wind
Vinland a knotted horn
calls out of dream without map
sound of small waves in sedge
in sand and beyond sands to plough
their harmony of lace cells
keels needle Ocean to a head chart
to hold any thing
make longitude flicker
but never to float across film of tropics
where flower latitudes break firm coils
where crabs leap on hot sands
        (Eric Mottram, from '1922 Earth Raids')

Liminality may not be the ideal pattern for explaining these poems, this kind of poem. It would be interesting to think of other descriptive models. I would draw attention to the time-sense, the interest in analogy over reportage, the exit from literal biography, the interest in the unknown. The poems still have elements of documentary, but they are on the way to becoming pure pattern. They do not have reality as a makeweight, a way of reducing instability. As the interest moves away from literal time, it often loses finite verbs, because those carry tense markers; and poetry in general moves towards the state of a picture, which is pure pattern and does not know internal change. In the dissolution of social roles, any human knowledge is within the poetic realm except that which locates a person with a specific hourly wage and weekly rent.

The Mottram passage follows the theme of knots (knot, 4 occurrences). This starts with Viking sailing, where the nautical term "knots", a measure of progress during a day, comes from, and goes on to talk about twining plants, also forming knots. Convolvulus, bindweed, winds itself around other plants. The real topic is dissolved out of a specific time or substance, and emerges as an eternal form. The sequencing which gives difficulty is the move which lifts the poem into a timeless and liminal space. Visibly, Mottram's poem has no signals for the concept it advances; syntax, conjunctions, punctuation, summaries, are all missing. The metre is not used to supply emphases. The *doxa* on this blankness dominating one channel is that the lack of labelling gets rid of the expected path to follow and that this is preparation for seeing a real-life situation without the paths, so finding an alternative outcome. Most people who hear this proposition don't think it works. Because the sailing is 'without chart', (like flying blind) and the tendrils of the plants also feel their way out blindly, the theme may be of navigating in the unknown, without reference points. We know that Mottram read *Mental Maps* (by Gould and White), and their title could be a gloss on the phrase 'head chart'. If this is significant, the question is why there is no explicit statement about it. At the time, this deletion of any "internal prose" was a way of defining your poetry as purer than other poetry.

There are a number of evocations of the liminal state in the poems we have been looking at. What we seem to find in poetry is a resort to liminal objects and actions which is persistent but also incomplete and unregulated. The move towards things as they were in the beginning is governed by an unconscious impulse and has no whole schema to guide it. This is hardly surprising in a society which has a belief in spontaneity instead of collective rites, and which has replaced the pilgrimage with the summer holiday. It is no secret that the liminal breach with existing scales of value takes the form, in some of these poems, of a nervous breakdown.

## DIDACTIC LABYRINTH

It's not clear to me how these liminal states reached these poets. I suspect they were latent in cultural material which was available to anyone who was a persistent reader. The source question is not really a problem. Because liminal patterns are so clear in *Marimarusa* (1947), *Night Thoughts* (1956) and *Out of the World and Back* (1952/1958), it is not puzzling if the patterns were available for Tony Lopez or Martin Thom in the Seventies. These structures will travel. They can even give us a way of linking the poetry which came after the great revolution of the Sixties to what came before it. If we look at Andrew Young's poem *Into Hades*, we find it starts with the poet's death; having crossed out of life, he comes back and experiences the moment of creation. Time no longer moves forward, but only swings – from age to youth, from youth to age. That is, he sets the whole thing in a liminal space. His other long poem, a sequel, has him as a ghost travelling in time. (They were published in one volume as *Out of the World and Back.*) It is unlikely anybody in the Sixties read these poems. The imagery is spooky, paradoxical, almost psychedelic, but there is no real drama. But there seems to be some layer of imagistic thinking where they meet modern poetry and both buy from the same warehouse.

Andrew Young is more or less missing from the memory record. I was amazed when I first read his poem although it seemed less populist, more traditional, the second time I read it. He made a radical departure and this is an era when Christians could only write good poetry by breaking out of their entangling traditions and inventing something new. So, it wasn't Christian poetry which fled the scene but only a version of Christian poetry. As Christian poets reacted creatively to the decline of the inherited forms, secular poets could share part of the journey. Young's poem is a kind of apocalypse, and could be compared to some poems by Henry Treece.

Turner spent a lot of time describing pilgrimages as a form of the liminal, as a purposeless journey where function vanishes and distinctions of status between the pilgrims fall away. As this underlines, Christianity had moved into existing (pagan) notions of liminal space and defined them pervasively as penitential. This seems at first glance to be a definition which modern poetry has rolled back, in the pursuit of the hedonistic and secular. However, that may not be so. In the Seventies, there was a current of opinion which saw the social breakdown as opportune, and saw the structures of capitalism and patriarchy (and militarism, imperialism, you name it) as being forms of knowledge which needed to be unlearned by those who were occupied by them, and specifically through an experience of art. Rather obviously this is a penitential view of art. The bourgeois goes in, finds his prejudices overturned, and comes out cured. Yes it hurts yes it works. This was so much, for example, the intent of feminist artists for men. So, the idea of the wilderness as a didactic labyrinth may not have disappeared quite as our script says it should.

We can see the Seventies underground poet as out on the moor, far from the built-up zone; outside society, and denying social roles; peeling back the shared order to the origin of laws, and laying down new laws; oversetting inherited hierarchies of social power; reciting myths. They were in a liminal landscape. They were in secession from authority – literary as well as political, and they set that authority aside *in toto*. Most of the new poetry fails if you apply criteria of realism and empiricism – the whole book of rules had shifted. Although we shouldn't lose sight of all the poetry which used an older rule-book, liminality is obviously worth studying as a figure capable of generating, not just many variants, but entire literary works.

Using mythic material from foreign and archaic societies is clearly clutching at straws; this material will only work if drawn on parsimoniously, with the real work being done by myths organic to the poet and to the living society which will consume the poetry. In the absence of collective myths, such supra-personal material has to be developed by artistic research and then taught to the reading public. Inevitably, this involves delays before the work is understood. As this implies, now is a good time for assessing the recent past, for example the 1970s. The committed readers can now explain what was strange and unseizable then. The fit to Turner's schema fails strikingly at a number of points; which isn't surprising, since he derived it from fieldwork among the Central Bantu (Ndembu), a society with no known cultural past in common with us.

Turner began by studying Classics and was a Forties poet. After a not very well organised 20-year search, I found his poems in the pamphlet, *Preludes*, linked to the magazine *Opus*:

Girls in silk and satin
Quilt the amber floor,
Each has a sombre Satan

To breathe into her hair.
Green light changes
To charnol blue,
Singers with metal fringes
Chant and mew [.]

# Blink and it's There – the Future

The lack of identifiably political poetry is one of the features of the British scene, already identified by Lucie-Smith in his 1970 anthology. None of the public events of the decade are recorded in poetry. Try and find out from poetry about Wilson's loan from the IMF in 1976, when the balance of payments was capsizing. Poetry is not written for that. Raymond Garlick's poems about pro-Welsh language demos are an exception (and Edwin Morgan wrote a poem about the protests at the 1971 Miss World contest). Yes, they're really good. Certainly poetry is not much concerned with stocks and shares, ownership of the means of production, prices and incomes policy, profit levels, union politics, or class consciousness. There was an idea of cool which screened all that out.

Even conceptual art has more of indolence and stoned leisure games than of political aggression. All the same, the tonality of the '70s milieu was unbelievably far Left. There was a post-'68 consensus among the new poets. Of the poets in *A Various Art*, it has been claimed that the whole Cambridge School is Marxist. But I am pretty sure that several of these poets were Right of centre. If you read *AVA*, you are getting a lot of indolent coolness and not very much political fire. If the poetry doesn't tell you whether the poet was strongly on the Left, there is clearly a problem of ascription. Are we looking at Left poetry, or non-civic poetry written by people on the Left?

Poets certainly did not want to work in a factory, or stuck in any other situation where freedom was sold off and life was predictable, at various scales. There was a recognition that society had constructed machines to make people behave in predictable ways, and that stored knowledge had simplified and stylised its reports on human behaviour, protecting and burying old limits. The lure of modernity and of poetry was centrally that it abandoned these restraints. If you saw a billion possible futures, the plan of selecting a single one, and unifying a whole political faction around it, was nugatory. If the future was uniform, it was not also free. Poets were entranced by the future, but no two of them were seeing the same future. This was not privatisation, but it had the effect of drawing people into private worlds. Even as you ask people to think collectively, you are imagining a future state in which they will share nothing but the institutions. Essentially, the future isn't collective. This multiplicity was the subjective content of the poem, not just of the future.

The radical future meant more of prosperity and personal choice – it could hardly offer less. There was a legacy Left art which was a realisation of anonymity and squalor. Marxism couldn't deal with a non-alienated present; the new Left poetry is free, it is intimate and so deals with small groups. It looks much more like the stories of ads than like '30s socialist art. The '70s style was rather, *where we're going to is great. You will be a great person. And we're going to have a real good time together.* It did not contain masses or stone statues or moments deserving of statues. The question for poets was how you get from the shimmering and overloaded surface of daily life, with its short range and constant repetition, to the deep structures of property, enclosure, and inequality. Freedom and pleasure occur in the short scale, and the deep patterns negate consciousness.

Lifestyle is replacing class. The choice of style is based on the pleasure principle. You have to attract people into the future through pleasure. Argument and anxiety don't fit into this. The new life is all about consuming, not producing. But more central than acquiring objects or food is socialising. You are the product – other people consume you. The poet starts by being your friend. So the poem is an invitation – as well as coming from the good place, itself, it invites you into a changed lifestyle. Intimacy is everywhere but does not take everyone. The question of how to behave towards/around other Leftists within the (neo-capitalist) present is more about manners than social theory, but is something which fills poetry. Capitalism was selling itself through 10,000 ads and they were all inviting; socialism adapted to this by also becoming attractive, taking the loneliness out of experiment.

In his 1974 reportage, *Soft City*, Jonathan Raban wants clothes to record people's economic status. He sees his Balzacian project, of linking what is visible to what is (socially) real, failing because people are dressing up all the time and not carrying out rules. But this spontaneity is also what people were capturing in poetry – they didn't want to record their income, possessions, etc. as the core of a documentary poetry. They wanted to record feelings and ideas, as they evanesced. The scale of the future dissolves, scatters as flakes. It stops being like a block, a solid monument made of time. It becomes more like a series of 30-minute TV programmes. Freedom is never traded in. Raban explains why his text is unconvincing by saying that the life of the city is mainly seized by illegibility and incomprehension. People do not know each other and the signals they give out lead to short circuits, fake conclusions. But this is also a key result: poetry is the interruption of this illegibility.

The basis of *Soft City* is that "cultural identity" has separated itself from economic identity: the people he sees do have a job and a domicile, but this set of relations, while it yields stable information for sociology to use, is devoid of subjective content. This is the soft city, while the world-order of property and money and the price of labour remains hard. The feeling of ease got thinner after 1974. It was impaired by the effects of the oil price increases and the UK's humiliating resort to a loan from the IMF. Money became more central because it was in short supply. The styles relate to temporary identities and not to permanent sociological posts. The cult identities were not connected to the realistic and long-term: having a job was not like an identity, it was a thousand times less interesting. It was repetitive, constrained, other-directed, designed to avoid the unexpected. To blend daily life and self-expression was possible for a few selected people. The nightmare was always that the hard economy would re-assert itself, and that the nineteenth century enclosure of wage levels, rent levels, and the demands of completing work tasks, would take over again. Then, the liberated and groovy people wouldn't find you groovy and liberated. You would be back in the basement. After 1974, the problem in the Underground was more that people who saw the future disappearing could become doctrinaire Marxists (or whatever), abandon the idea of freedom, and subject you to loyalty tests in which it was proved, recurrently, that you were the reason why it had all gone wrong.

Raban says "The freedom of the city is enormous. Here one can choose and invent one's society, and live more deliberately than anywhere else." This answers the question of what '70s poetry stands for. It does not connect to a social class, or even to a political platform with law projects and so on. Its components relate to cells which are much smaller than that. They are invented, as Raban says – the city is soft, the interstices are 90% of the space. Reality is dull, under-specified. Cultural life is there to offer narratives of belonging. You can't refute a poem or a lifestyle. But the poem loses validity when it crosses a cell boundary.

The loss of inevitability dissolved too that other fixed pattern of monumental scale, that of a reproducing self, storing and obeying childhood conditioning. Indeed, the whole point of the "soft city" was of deprogramming. The replacement was flimsy at first, and this is where you get into the realm of the experimental in poetry. If behaviour loses the quality of inevitability, a new role arrives for *theory*. Poetic innovation mirrored a proposed innovation in political arrangements.

How would conservative poetry lead to a new society? Stylistic choices can express endless variants in structure models of human personality and social institutions – this is the pay-off for dissolving the rules of how to record experience.

Are the underground poems blinks of the future? does the future refute them? Is it the Refuture? where is the society for this new language? Is the new thing the future of poetry? The key to the new lifestyle was how the children turned out. This separated a real idea from something merely to do with how you dressed. I don't really want to answer this because too many people have too many feelings about it. Maybe someone should write a book about it. Where the Counter Culture turned people into drug addicts, their children probably aren't so keen on the Counter Culture. On the whole I think the children are super-enthusiastic about the New Left/ hippy thing. Actually family relationships are too complicated to let you separate out an ideas layer from everything else. I don't think experimental living produced monstrous offspring, even if they weren't bearers of a new society.

## FEMINISTS

Authentic sources are hard to find. We recovered a tape of this 1977 conversation, recorded on cassette in a launderette.

*Verity*: Well, Wanda-Sue, you said that Peggy had told you that feminist poetry was steadily getting better. Poems have come out from Judith Kazantzis, Denise Riley, and Liz Lochhead that stand up. Poems founded in an exalted fantasy state which came straight out of reading revolutionary calls to arms weren't convincing. A different society was on its way but you had to point at it by writing poems founded in real experience. The exciting future had to take place in a kitchen, a living-room, in the park, to be something you can live rather than some kind of allegorical mural.

*Wanda-Sue*: As you told me last week, Verity, the arguments couldn't be made in poetry but once people have grasped the basic ideas through seeing them in magazines or hearing them on the radio, basically through prose, then they are available to poems as a kind of shared footage. Is this launderette phallocentric?

*Verity*: We are going to give up contestatory demos because they are a kind of symbolic war in which the temporary possession of territory becomes unnaturally important and you antagonise the other side in order to win. The only way of winning in democratic politics is to persuade the other side and have them march off side by side with you. By using a language which is full of equity, we set up truths which will be accepted by the group. The idea is to change the norms, not to dramatise being a rebel and a political failure. The language needs to be common enough to become the sound which people hear inside.

*Pelargonia*: As Lynette explained to us last year, because the Left is based on tolerance, community, and reason, and women have those virtues in greater abundance, women can take over the Left and guide it towards feminism.

*Wanda-Sue*: I understand feminists are competing through their children, though. There is a whole swarm of post-feminist children being used as advertisements for the mother's ideological brilliance. I met some in Clissold Park last week.

*Verity*: They will need books to read. I visited the new radical bookshop in Mare Street last month. Is it true that the whole extent of existing books and films has to be scrapped and rewritten? What about music? Or town planning?

*Wanda-Sue*: The whole mass of literary history records male taste even though so many of the readers are women. The idea that a critic represents what the reader will feel relies on the critic being empathetic and sensitive. Men who are retarded when it comes to empathy and became scholars to avoid listening to other people are not in the best state to do this.

*Verity*: All that formal verbal activity is based on a metaphor of competition. Then the male who won the competitive display of language gets to own the territory. And they can attract a woman and install her on it. That is obvious. From WON to OWN.

*Pelargonia*: What is this competitive thing? Why is it men want to go further and faster than each other? And why is it only the last inch which counts, not all the land you have crossed, where people could live?

*Wanda-Sue*: It's based on Spengler, I think. He defines Faustian man as going right to the edge and being unable to stop before a natural boundary is set.

*Verity*: So, he is a streak spread over a thousand miles. Whenever you want him, he's not there. Whenever something happens, he misses it. The history happens without him.

Feminist poetry is not going to use freaky language. That defines a way of losing that makes people forget the point of speaking, to record experience and find out what is right and who behaved badly.

*Wanda-Sue*: The whole avant-garde academy collapses if someone arrives who has a different way of using the territory and a different ecology. I don't get whether the problem with the territory you leave behind is that it is devastated or that you don't want to share it. I can't really believe that the whole history of culture has been reduced to scorched earth by the act of living through it.

*Verity*: By the time you get to where there is only you, there is no-one to talk to. Jessica is starting up a course in Male Studies.

*Wanda-Sue*: Is she really going out with him?

*Verity*: No, she likes him but she's a political Lesbian. She was just helping him with some Adorno. At the consciousness raising group last night we talked about the programme on TV on Tuesday and how it was really exciting but they had male characters who were kind of scientist-activists and the female character was the secretary and wanted to make coffee for them all the time. Malacia said that you had to have dramas showing secretaries because so many people actually are secretaries and you shouldn't broadcast to them that they are insignificant and only people who have degrees and high-powered jobs are worth watching. Lenore said that objectively the secretary was alienated and showing her acquiescing in it was humiliating. The job made her switch off 90% of her intelligence and in some sense she actually wasn't there, she was sleepwalking. Ragwort said that if you didn't show characters who have been marginalised and alienated then you couldn't show how society works, as those processes really are how it works. Luci said that the key thing was to avoid nailing people inside their roles. You should show a process of becoming, so that people can imagine the outcomes being different even if the narrative did record people doing stupid jobs and becoming stupefied. Blodwen said that she was wearing an especially nice fuchsia poplin mini-dress in that episode.

*Wanda-Sue*: I think women readers of male writers are like secretaries. They are sensitive to every wish and ignore the faults because the faults could cause pain. They gather up the words and solemnly store them as if they mattered.

*Verity*: Is empathy due to being in a weak position where you have to guess other people's arbitrary wishes and moods? Could we give it up once we have won?

*Pelargonia*: Blodwen explained the new goddess thing they have in her raising group. Apparently, the Mother goddess is the most powerful force in the universe and basically all women are part of her. They plan to free the inner goddess and basically worship themselves.

*Wanda*: Is this megalomaniac narcissism blooming in Stoke Newington?

*Verity*: Blodwen explained that all culture was really about promoting your ego via various accessories that match your mood.

*Wanda-Sue*: Blodwen never was the sharpest knife in the drawer.

# Long Player:
## The Long Poem of the 1970s

Long poems were a feature of the 1970s. In the Sixties, there were few long poems, but in the following decade there were at least 80 significant ones (with *Crow* and *Mercian Hymns* leading the way). This is so many that explaining their rise is close to explaining what happened in Seventies poetry. The stalls of the time were full of A4 stapled-photocopied books which always seemed to be instalments of something even larger. The magazines were full of "extracts from works in progress" which were only partial disclosures of a glimpsed but unimaginable whole, only sequences of a few frames from an energy wave running on the idea that history itself was changing all the time. The open project seemed to give the poet a better chance of controlling this rush forward – and so expressed a revolutionary faith in guiding the wave of change towards a better society. The impulse came largely from the USA, where open poems taking decades to write seemed to raise the stakes of poetic art.

Compare the move of popular music into albums of around 1968, the neglect of and even scorn for the three-minute single and its sugar-rush. Stereo outfits and albums replaced the limited but perfect sound-world of singles played through a transistor radio. It may be the greater subjectivity allowed by the album forced poetry to go deeper in order to compete. The semantic context of short poems appeared to the new sensibility as shallow, conventional, and frustrating. My impression is that the short poem is an adaptation to external pressure and hostility. The idea that a shorter poem is better is a stage towards the idea that no poetry at all is best, which was the direction of travel of the mass media. People who hate poetry give you five minutes, grudgingly, to deflect criticism, and you fit into the slot. The long poem is a seizing of autonomy, a protest against the marginalised and numbered conditions of the poem in the media.

Since reviewers were unable to judge the complete works from the instalments, it is appropriate to revisit them now seismic activity has stopped. There has been no comparative study of these impressive poems. The period is sunk in mystery. There are no reliable anthologies, no textbook, no consensus. Few of the poems have been reprinted since the 1970s. Their extent pushes us back from confident conclusions; this constellation of undefined relationships between poems continues the novelty and uncertainty of the relationship of parts within the poems, which offer themselves as suggestive nontransparent spaces. We certainly have to ask how the impulsiveness and immediacy, which conservative critics wanted to be typical of the new poetry around 1965 to 1975, are borne out by the sustained effort and structural insight which a long poem demands. Here is a list of the poems we are talking about.

A READING-LIST OF LONG POEMS FROM THE 1970S

Hugh MacDiarmid, *Direadh*
J.F. Hendry, *Marimarusa*
*(These publications have been separated because it is unlikely that any part of them was written after 1970. However, it would be irrational to exclude them, given how often these poets have been passed over by survey anthologies.)*

Peter Abbs, *For Man and Islands*
Asa Benveniste, *Tabelli Linnaei*
George Barker, *Villa Stellar, In Memory of David Archer*
Anthony Barnett, *Fear and Misadventure; Mud Settles*
Jack Beeching, *Myth of Myself*
Francis Berry, 'The Singing Dome'
D.M. Black, 4 narrative poems (in *The Happy Crow* and *Gravitations)*
Euros Bowen, *Siâp rhyw brofiad, Ecsodus*
George Mackay Brown, *Fishermen with Ploughs*
Gerard Casey, *South Wales Echo*
Barry Cole, *Vanessa In the City*
Andrew Crozier, *Pleats; High Zero*
Allen Fisher, *Place (4 volumes); Long Shout to Kernewek; Sicily; The Art of Flight; Shorting Out*
Roy Fisher, *The Cut Pages*
Eddie Flintoff, *Sarmatians*
Ulli Freer, *Rooms*
Raymond Garlick, *Notes for an Autobiography*
Paul Gogarty, *The Accident Adventure*
W.S. Graham, *Dark Dialogues; Implements in their Places*
Paul Green, *Arthurian Cycles*
Harry Guest, *Elegies; Miniatures*
John Hall *Days; Couch Grass*
Lee Harwood, *The Long Black Veil*

David Harsent, *Dreams of the Dead*

J.F. Hendry, *Marimarusa*

Geoffrey Hill, *Mercian Hymns*

Jeremy Hooker, *Soliloquies of a Chalk Giant*

Ted Hughes, *Crow, Gaudete, Cave Birds, Adam and the Sacred Nine, Prometheus on his Crag*

Emyr Humphreys, *Ancestor Worship*

John James, *Letters from Sarah, A Former Boiling, Toasting*

Philip Jenkins, *Cairo*

David Jones, various poems in *The Sleeping Lord and Other Fragments, The Roman Quarry*

Judith Kazantzis, *Queen Clytemnestra*

R.F. Langley, *Matthew Glover*

T.S. Law, *Referendum*

Peter Levi, *Christmas Sermon; Canticum*

Antony Lopez, *Change. A Prospectus*

George MacBeth, *The Orlando Poems; A Poet's Life; Lusus; Winter Light*

Sorley MacLean, *Uamha 'n Oir / The Cave of Gold*

Barry MacSweeney, *Black Torch*

Brian Marley, *Bargain Basement Sonnets*

Alan Massey, *Leechcraft*

Roland Mathias, *Madoc*

Matthew Mead, *The Administration of Things*

Christopher Middleton, *Anasphere: le Torse Antique*

Edwin Morgan, *The New Divan, Instamatic Poems, Memories of Earth*

Eric Mottram, *Local Movement, Tunis, Elegies*

Ulli McCarthy, *Horsetalk*

Walter Perrie, *Lamentation for the Children*

F.T. Prince, *Dry-points of the Hasidim*

J. H. Prynne, *News of Warring Clans*

Kathleen Raine, *On a Deserted Shore*

Tom Raworth, *Ace*

Peter Redgrove, *Love's Journeys, Dr Faust's Sea-Spiral Spirit*

Jeremy Reed, *The Isthmus of Samuel Greenberg, Stratton Elegy*

John Riley, *Czargrad*

Peter Riley, *Linear Journal; Tracks and Mineshafts*

Colin Simms, long poems on the American Indians, including *A Celebration of the Stones in a Water-course, Parflèche, Carcajou, The Compression of the Bones of Crazy Horse*

Iain Sinclair, *Lud Heat, Suicide Bridge, Red Eye*
Iain Crichton Smith, *From the Notebooks of Robinson Crusoe; The White
    Air of March*
Ken Smith, *Tristan Crazy; Apocrypha from the Western Kingdom; Fox
    Running*
Nathaniel Tarn, *Lyrics for the Bride of God*
Martin Thom, *The Bloodshed, the Shaking House*
Edward Boaden Thomas, *The 12 Parts of Derbyshire*
Gwyn Thomas, radio or TV poems included in *Cadwynau yn y meddwl*
Anthony Thwaite, *New Confessions*
Gael Turnbull, *Residues: Down the Sluice of Time*
John Wain, *Feng*
Jeffrey Wainwright, *Thomas Müntzer*
David Wevill, *Where the Arrow Falls*

These are the good ones – there are others which I do not greatly esteem.


## At the Turning of Two Ages: David Jones, various poems in *The Sleeping Lord and Other Fragments* (1974)

Although a great deal of Jones' work was published after 1970 (*The Roman Quarry* includes further long poems), it is unlikely that the poet, born 1895, composed much after 1970.

Therefore these poems are not within our purview and do not help to answer questions about the literary mood of the 1970s. They were probably composed after 1952 (date of publication of *The Anathemata*) and up to about 1970. He tried to find a sense in history, although as a victim of war neurosis, after being in the trenches for four years, his view of human life had a pessimistic undertone. He was formed intellectually in the 1920s, when there was a peak of disillusion with authority and radical individuals could exit into a new culture. His rich location of sights in a mesh of fabrics and signs belonging to a moment in time follows a condition of being lost, a mind piercingly conscious but outside any historic situation at all. The solution for Jones was a revived Christianity, to guide government, in line with Christopher Dawson and Saunders Lewis. This also involved Welsh nationalism, interpreting Wales before the Normans as the ideal Christian society. Catholicism did not have a general vision of history, it had a theology and a sacred history and limited ideas about the legitimacy of certain dynasties: Jones integrated a few sacral moments into a personal Catholic system, which was visual and ritual (so unlike *history*). Jones was the greatest poet writing in English for some decades of the mid-twentieth century, and his use of montage (to relate moments of the present to ritual time) was influential for several people (notably Gerard Casey and Jeremy Hooker). Because of this use of montage, and because he saw the West from outside, he fits in with Seventies poetry. Jones' poetry reaches such peaks of intensity because he sees human memory as bound in one vast pattern.

### Seven Shades of Sunlight: Euros Bowen, *Cylch o Gerddi* (1970)

The title means a cycle of poems so we should expect the poems to be linked in a greater whole. I am not convinced of this, they read like unrelated poems of a similar style and tenor to me, rather than a cycle. I have seen them referred to as concrete poems, but that is not so; the poet in a note on the dust jacket refers to them as *cerddi teipograffeg*, typographical poems. The typography has spaces indenting certain lines, which the Note advises are to show pauses and divisions (*toriadau*). This is not concrete, and the words are organised in sentences like any poem. So this does not fit into our scheme. (A poem in the volume *Elfennau is* a concrete creation.) The poems are of high artistic quality, belonging to Bowen's second phase, much more lucid and less full of primeval symbolism than the first phase. The difference may be emerging from the influence of Dylan Thomas, but that is controversial.

A poem called 'Siâp rhyw brofiad' clocks in at 11 pages and so fits our parameters. The title means "the shape of some experience". There is no definite article. This is like *Uamha'n oir*, it is *cave* and not *the cave*. I read the autobiography of Euros' brother, *O groth y ddaear*, so "from the womb of the earth", but again it just says "from womb of the earth".

There is a rule which says you can't have two definite articles in one phrase. So just maybe we have a resemblance between Welsh and Gaelic here – where otherwise they seem as remote from each other as English and Latin. Geraint describes an extreme lack of money in their family. Their father was the clergyman for some Nonconformist sect for people who had no money. So Euros left school at fourteen and went to work in a munitions factory. Later he worked for a bit catching rabbits. But then he went back to school. So it was that he went to Oxford, but he was born in 1904 and he was up with people who had been born around 1912. He began composing poetry in 1946–7, almost as a by-blow from protesting against the atomic bomb.

*Siâp* is the English word *shape* and I have never seen it used in Welsh before. I suppose that *llun*, a more common word that means shape, is being avoided because it also means picture, and perhaps *siâp* has a narrower semantic field – as loan-words usually do. *Siâp* is vague, *experience* is vague, but they are not as vague as *some*. This vagueness does not point to the theme of the poem, which is undoubtedly about peace and its correlatives, faith and friendship. It takes place in an allegorical landscape; the objects are all natural but none of them is secular. The statements deal, primarily, with equivalences in a cosmic symbolic matrix, rather than propositions about condition, size, function, and so on.

The collocations of words are often phonetically motivated (translations here are my own).

> Crows of the wind on an empty tree,
> snatching and challenging
>                       above the stumps of the earth,
> thoughts in the clay
> about what will come from the shape of the tree,
> and the hush of two hands holds
> on the long sky of the hill,
> the moon of the clouds making the valley pale,
>                                           the treeless hills
> and shelters of the vales:
>
> A prophecy
>         is in our sympathies from now:
>
> prayers and the form of the place's myths went
> from their green satiation
>                       on swamps and moor
> altogether free
>                 into the path of the darkness.

The tree looks like two hands. It is bare but will bear fruit. Its shape refers to the wood of the cross, from which salvation will come. The (polytheistic) myths leave the land because the Covenant has bound the faithful to the single God and dispelled them. *Dwylo* just means two hands (*dwy* + *llaw*) but in this case it appears that the two hands belong to two different people and are clasped as a symbol of amity. I counted 19 occurrences of *dwylo* or *dwy llaw* in the poem. Hands – isn't this like *hands across the ocean*, a typical Forties clip phrase signifying help, kindness, unity, in the international sphere? The birds as symbols of peace lead on to a lake where the furies of mountain streams have become pacified – another deluge that gave way. I am not sure if these are real crows or the wind ripping at the tree as if to eat its carcass. The word *darogan* appears five times and means prophecy. I do not otherwise find prophecies. The poem has a set of key words which repeat. Of these, *rainbow* appears only once, nonetheless the rainbow as God's covenant, Genesis ch.9, is clearly the centre of the poem, the point about which everything else is organised. It is not autobiographical and not a reflection of sensibility. The flow of the poem is governed by sound, a secret pattern of phonetic doubles which involves endless curves of tension and endless fulfilments. So, we have a poem by an Anglican priest using Biblical imagery – this sounds like a turn-off but there is radical originality which is an adequate counterpart to the legacy. The crows of the wind may refer back to the doves which Noah sent out. That would imply that the tree is an olive tree. The poem is rather more about peace between nations than about the wrath of God sending a new Deluge. Repeatedly we see adverbs which mean "from now on" – the poem must refer to a Kairos, a special moment in time which divides history into before and after. What time is this? Probably, a double moment, sacred and secular – once for God offering a covenant and once for peace spreading across the earth now, that is in 1970. Where the poet says hours, the point is that human destiny is unfolded within time, along a calendar line.

> From now
> with the prophecy
> the two hands are climbing,
> the two hands are wings
> of the seven shades of the dew
> > stiffening into the look of the land
> past its awareness
> clear (is) its raiment on the covering of the earth,
> high flight above the swarming
> brown of the soil
> in a gesture of desires

The next page refers to a rainbow, so the covenant of the lord could be the prophesy in question, and then the poem is about peace. The reference to the seven shades of the dew is a cryptic reference to the refraction of water in the rainbow, a typically cunning Bowen positioning. The seven colours of the Covenant cover the earth in the guise of dew, and bring its fruitfulness – the green satiation.

I can't write about *dwylo* without thinking about the panel in the Sistine Chapel ceiling where the hand of God touches the hand of Adam in the act of bringing him to life. This intervention is echoed in the rainbow which is the Covenant. An earlier poem in *Cylch o gerddi* is about the painting of Moses, also by Michelangelo, also in Rome.

I have translated a word as *grey* (moonlight) and *brown* (soil) but it is the same word. English divides the spectrum up differently. I am wondering if *profiad* is a sort of screen word hiding *profedigaeth*. Both come from Latin *probare*, test (English *prove*), but *profedigaeth* is a religious word meaning the believer's faith being tested by the hardships God sends (English word *tribulation*, exactly) and *profiad* means more the human testing of the truth of ideas, empiricism in fact. It is a secular word and I don't see that *Siâp* is a secular poem at all. But *profedigaeth* would take you straight to Noah and his Flood, the tribulation par excellence. Possibly this would be too obvious for our poet, the pleasure of the poem is in seizing the connections, which must be latent and delayed. I am also wondering if *siâp* refers specifically to the rainbow – and the hands clasping look like the rainbow. It is also possible that *enfys*, the word for rainbow, used once, contains a cryptic reference to *bys*, finger, basic for *dwylo*, the two hands.

The poem ends with "the fever of being born", and a paragraph on the miracle of mortality. I think *marwolaeth* could be translated as incarnation here – not the opposite of life but of immortality. "Tissue and nerves" (*gewynnau*), the soul is bound into the sensory world but this enables it to hear the messages and see the symbols. The poem is not just about the Covenant but about incarnation itself – the biological process as the precondition of redemption. I am going to try a different way of translating here: "Clucking quickly a crack in the bow and the rapid disvesting of two hands descending over minutes, by hearing, from the blue depth, from the back and the width of the burning light, thick bareness along the sensitivity of the skin, beating of Icarus, beating along the energy of the wings' wax, then a lodging in a swallow of dust, and its boiling of embers, in fear of the left-hand earth the road a ditch would go down into the rapid depth." This sentence is about mortality, and precedes the immortality which follows the protection of God, shown by His covenant. The flyer is held up by the hands of God, and when these let go it is like wings melting. He is divested and falls.

This is a poem of controlled variations within a Biblical story which offers a satisfaction of our basic needs and pushes us up against the hindrances to fulfilling those needs. A relaxation of the solemnity of *cynghanedd* rules releases something which deploys syllabic echoing throughout in a blissful permanent memory of *cynghanedd*.

### Pearl Sailing Outwards: Kathleen Raine, *On a Deserted Shore* (1973)

The text is about 150 stanzas long, composed of short disconnected lyric moments, all reacting to the death in 1969 of someone close to the poet. The line lengths are mainly very short, with the first and last poems having longer lines and being more firm or conclusive.

The story is of the poet falling in love with a gay man. The range of possibilities for such a story is quite limited and the extension to such an extraordinary length invokes several risks. It certainly undermines the poet's claim to wisdom, since any romantic advice column would tell you "he is not going to stop being gay just because you fall in love with him". The poem is not rich in events and once you start to realise that its grip wanes rapidly. At the start the loved one is dead and at the 150th stanza he is still dead. He had published a book in which he claimed that his life had been ruined by a curse (which was uttered by Kathleen Raine) in 1957. The shore image occurs only a few times in the text but may refer to a shore on the edge of death or eternity, with the poet gazing outwards – deserted by the dead person.

Literally, the shore deserted by the friend was at Sandaig in Inverness-shire. The oyster, a shore-dwelling creature, features as the origin of pearls; the pearl is a Manichæan (also Christian) symbol for the soul trapped in the flesh. The start has the dead loved object freed "from the weight of earth and the wheel of stars", a striking Neoplatonist image, where the rotation of stars is a pitiless force bearing down on human fate. The text does not describe the course of the affair (if that is the right word) and does not tell you anything about the loved one – he is a vast but featureless presence. In fact, concrete events are almost wholly missing. The poem is not especially interested in the object of these affections, and the idea that a love poem should record the consciousness of two people, giving us the knowledge which in real life we desire the most, is not realised here. The poet is not happy with what the man wanted, had quite other ideas, so was not much concerned to write down what he was thinking or feeling. The fact that he was gay comes from other sources, it does not emerge in the text of the poem. There is no argument and the compelling descriptions of ideas which light up the poet's other work are missing here. There is some speculation about what happens after death, so for example "the earth of heaven is sound" is a notion about dematerialisation and progression towards states of greater harmony which is of interest as an expression of Neoplatonist doctrine. An early stanza has Narcissus seeing his drowning face; this could be a comment on the loved one, a moment of psychology, but it remains a fragment, no context supports it. Unrequited love has also been described as narcissistic and indifferent to the object, so it is not even clear if the Narcissus comparison applies to the male character or to the poet character. Small pieces of information are more striking because the whole is so poor in content.

This is about 80 times as long as most of the poems which Raine published. The folklore is that Raine wrote a farewell of 16 lines within hours of hearing of the friend's death. These 16 lines are the most striking in the whole poem. Raine's other poems are, many of them, wonderfully good, so why was the design extended so far? Part of the answer is that the situation of frustration inclined the poet to pile up thoughts, and that these then ended up in the text. But a lack of purpose and climaxes does not sustain a great length in any obvious way. Length can be a sign of vagueness. The poet strays into expositions of insight into human nature, somewhat undercut by her lack of insight into the loved object. The biographer of her friend describes him as repressed to a point where he was not there, a shell; but also swayed by romantic fantasy. So *Deserted Shore* could have perverse insight, where its disappointing vagueness records the subject and not the author.

### The Green Hound: Sorley MacLean, *Uamha 'n Oir /The Cave of Gold*

This is a poem about 300 lines long which draws on a folk tale attached to more than one cave in Scotland and Ireland. (It is "cave of the gold", but not "the cave of the gold".) The Skye cave is called that because of the folk-tale (and there is another one on Barra). Three parts of MacLean's poem were published in *Chapman* in 1976, two others are in the most recent *Collected*, so 50 more lines, but said there to be 'fragmentary'. *Tocher*, 47, prints a text for the folk song which is in MacLean's mind.

I located a dozen versions of the tale, none of which seems to be complete. A band of men, including a piper, go into a cave which leads far beneath the ground. They are seeking a treasure, or possibly the gift of music. The piper's music is heard above the ground, tracing the hidden route, up until something terrible happens. Only their dog comes out, all its hair burnt off by encounter with a hell-hound of green colour. There is a song, presupposing that you know the tale, in which the piper wishes he had three hands – two to play and one to fight. If the man was still piping, it is not possible for him to speak, and be heard at the cave mouth, but there is speculation that he encoded the message into his piping in some way (or, that his voice was heard coming up through the water of a well). The pipe music possibly holds the monster off – while it lasts. There is a story that the Cave of Gold in Bracadale leads to an exit miles away, in Trotternish. Perhaps the piper was trying to reach daylight through darkness. The hellhound appears as the "green bitch". Hounds sometimes come to fetch souls to hell. It is possible that he has made an exchange with the devil, possibly for the gift of music, so that risk and the keeping of conditions come into it.

The song mentions a harp, so possibly there was a musical competition between the piper and the devil. The piper never comes back. He sings in death: "I lie on my side, my flesh decaying/ A beetle in my eye, a beetle in my eye". The tune of the song is one of a group known as fairy tunes: they have an ethereal and eerie quality and are associated with tales of someone hearing the fairies play them. This might suggest that the piper went into the cave to learn the tune.

MacLean starts by a lament for the piper, without telling the story. The first stanza is directly from the song. Given that he is lost, the poet asks why he ever went into the cave; the poem lists all the fine things he would no longer see, but the story now seems to be about someone emigrating from Skye. The poem asks four times "why did he leave"; the description is of landscapes, of fields beneath the moon, but we inevitably think of the Gaelic language and culture as other things lost to the emigrant. That is, we are not sure if the piper left or the ancient culture and sounds of the land left. The stanzas about losing Skye have a more local resonance – the Clearances. The second part has a second piper in the cave and he has four hands – two for the pipes and two for his sword and shield. His equipment is unadorned and worn by long use, without show. He is aware of the risks of his expedition, but he does not care – he wants to show his art. He does not know what the first piper had said, but he understands the art (of the pipes). He starts to ask questions, and the subject now becomes the value of sacrifice: the poem foretells the wreck of his fortunes and the arrival of a mean churl as the lord. His sacrifice will buy him nothing. The poem speaks of "the grey scrape of Spring" on the land, this is a proverbial calendar phrase and is held to mean the worst time at the end of winter, when men and beasts are scraping at the bare earth to find some edible plants. So as a condition it means "destitution". He hears his culture and his country disputing with each other. He does not know what happened to the piper. A voice in his head says that he is free and does not need to defend his culture. The music is a "melodious rotting", cannot avert poverty and ill-fortune. Now there are two men in the Cave of Gold meditating upon death. One is ignorant and one is without sense. The music creates an expectation that is an illusion, not knowing itself to be an illusion. The bitch put a bond on the piper, so that he did not cease his music. The pipe had the power in the lack of every feature of the dimness of the cave or the gilt of sunlight on the world outside (so music has no sense content and so expresses the *ideal?*). The music did not lose its power while the MacLeods, as lords of Skye, still had their virtue, before the bracken came (inedible to cattle, overgrowing pastures). The bracken, it is suggested, comes out of the mouth of the cave. The two men are both going to meet death but only one of them knows that the green dog is one of the hounds of death. The poem returns to the song, with the piper lamenting that he does not have four hands, and ends.

The MacCrimmons, a family of hereditary pipers, appear, because they were the peak of Gaelic musical tradition – but also because some words (*cha till* etc.) from the famous *MacCrimmon's Lament* also appear in the song about the cave. They were employed by the MacLeods – the poem seems to be about the MacLeods of Skye, both the tenants and the landlords.

The song has the piper listing all the things which will happen before he comes back. This is a figure of speech saying he will never come back. This is a device typical of folk songs: it opens out, it is all yearning and carries us to great heights of hoping and wishing. Yet the facts are already known: the piper is dead, he is not coming back at any time. This device seems to me quite indicative for how MacLean has written the poem: what is at stake is never fact, but throughout the state of yearning, hope, aspiration, in fact high emotion, is the tenor of the poem. MacLean has an extraordinary ability to do this. Reflect – he never says why the musicians went into the cave, he never says that the traditional culture of the Gael is at stake, he never describes what that culture was, he never says why the musicians must die or what kills them. But he has that tense that the song has as it talks about what must happen before the piper returns to the world of daylight.

Twice someone called the Blind appears. This is a specific historical person on Skye, called Donald Munro, a talented fiddler who was a convert to piety in 1805 and persuaded the people of his district to make a bonfire of all their musical instruments, because dancing leads to immorality and because the music kept people from holy thoughts. The poem refers also to the Black Chanter. In legend, this was a magical mouthpiece given by the fairies to a piper after they had cruelly blinded him, and which gave unlimited power over music.

Munro's power was to make it fall silent. The song lyric includes a word which normally means harp: *between us the harp, the harp, the harp*: possibly the pipe is a late element, and possibly (again) someone went into the cave to acquire a harp. Stories where someone acquires a piece of fairy wealth are quite common; they usually involve trickery, so a variant where the trick fails (and the thief never returns) seems quite credible. Punishment for covetousness would fit into the folklore background without a gap. One stanza has "the countryside and the heredity of his people/ crying 'liar' and 'thief'". This is not easy to explain. What had the piper stolen? Yes, it could be the harp, the other-worldly thing bursting with eerie tune, but MacLean never mentions that. What is the lie? He never speaks, and it is a question whether music can lie. Theft could describe the actions of Blind Munro, and of the MacLeod landlords who took the land from the people, under George III. But the piper is neither one of those. Does the journey into the cave represent MacLean's relationship with Gaelic oral culture, and does he feel a guilt either about taking or about not restituting? This is more problematic. The journey seems to be a penance, not something that has any place in Presbyterian doctrine.

The poem is close to folk material and this is distinct from almost all the other poems in this list – though not *Gaudete, Fishermen with Ploughs*, and *Dry-points of the Hasidim*.

Donald Meek has asked for Gaelic history to be considered from a Gaelic point of view. This is on the field of debris where so many writers from outside have completed Gaelic stories or simply invented stories or historical eras out of thin air. Should we apply this to *Cave of Gold*? Parts of this would be some kind of identification with Presbyterian theology, and the right attitude towards folklore, as a thing that yields its wealth when remembered. MacLean was open to European ideas and poets but this poem is not very European, it maintains the values of songs. MacLean learnt the song from a family member and lifts whole lines from it to use in his poem. The original song and tale do not explain very much, and the poem does not seek to correct them – it never completes the story or gives a reason why the piper descends into the cave. It follows the axes of the song. Fact fans: *uamh* is the same word as the second half of Pittenweems.

Can we see a resemblance to Euros Bowen, where both poets are walking through myth? Both make something mesmerisingly modern out of very old material. Both are idealists, not part of daily compromise. And are, finally, ambiguous.

### Cae budr: Gerard Casey, *South Wales Echo*

Casey was born in 1918 (and died in 2002), and this first came out, in a *de luxe* edition, from Enitharmon, in 1973, under the pseudonym of Gerardus Cambrensis. This is a remarkable long poem, heavily influenced by David Jones, a montage of 'memories and echoes' recalling the sights and sounds of 1920s Cardiff. The introduction (by David Blamires) says it is about "the particular setting of Cardiff in the early years of the twentieth century – Cardiff with St Peter's church and the Salvation Army band, the newspaper seller, the businessman and the street gossip, Adam's Street, the Anchor pub, Tiger Bay and the mining villages close at hand." The setting is one specific night but over forty years the physical reality has evanesced into a nebula of echoes:

> flotsam I come
> as to a place much longed for
> as to one much prayed to
> to the place where the streams empty
> but I knew Tom of old … long ago

far back in the storm of the world-flow
he foresuffered all
humped trembling over Esau
bent in flamelight over Tilphussa's spring
gulped the black water
all worlds consumed in everliving fire
And eyeless under Suhir
sang with Shiddeh his bahilowi

The *South Wales Echo* is, or was, a Cardiff newspaper. The *foresuffered all* phrase is a tag from Eliot, and the poem uses the same artistic syntax as 'The Waste Land', which means it is temporally out of place in 1973. It is a line uttered by Teiresias, a blind Greek prophet who changed sex. Tilphussa is the spring from which Teiresias drank, to end his life. Tom gets his name from Tom O'Bedlam, from the Elizabethan poem, but is a Cardiff street singer, a fool, whom the child passes on his way. An epigraph says "Moving towards the Southfacing Form/ Voices off/ in/ A shadow dance for Puppets on Stilts/ SOUTH WALES ECHO/ for/ the Night before All Souls' Day". That night is better known as Hallowe'en. The theme is death, as we gather from the introduction, about the child (who may be Gerard Casey): "And he knows […] that inside the Gaol are three men, of whom two are brothers, awaiting execution, condemned to death for murder. […] as the evenings pass it seems to him there is fear in the sound of the bells too, as, in remembrance of another death, another execution of three, they call to prayer." This is All Hallows' Eve and some of the voices are therefore souls, so that we get excursions into the mystic and the symbolic realms of the cosmos, referring back to Boehme, Robert Fludd, Plotinus, etc. I am not sure about the south-facing form, but obviously Cardiff Bay faces south. (A note refers to the Great Bear, the Pole Star, as 'southward-gazing'.) As John Goodby has pointed out, the poem is like a radio piece, so that many of the parts ask for sound effects. The *bahilowi* is a Somali medical rite, and in this part of the poem it is the Somali community near the docks which is being evoked. *Suhir* is the star Sirius. The word echo is key, as the poem is a string of snatches of sound which certainly evoke the 1920s but also belong by situation to a moment of memory, so that the voices are coming back from great depth of time and are like the dead who wander the earth on Hallowe'en. Echo is also a technical term in Neoplatonism. Its basic meaning is "disembodied voice" and for the Neoplatonists the space beyond the earth was filled with such voices, carrying shapes. (So, "the earth of heaven is sound".) The image of wind is also vital in the poem, starting with the breath which is so short for a miner with pneumoconiosis, and is surely the air as breath: *pneuma*, also the Spirit. The Hallows are souls. The wind is blowing all the souls away, the scene is the border between life and death. The introduction by the author relates the poem to a moment of a childhood (no doubt his) where he was crossing the town to go home on the night before the execution of three men: "The scene is outside 'The Anchor' as evening moves on to closing time." He says also that for the child "the darkness should establish itself as unchangingly central in the consciousness of the child, [...] that for the man [...] the sun should remain centred in darkness" was extreme.

> sightlesse he drownes
> againe he strides the blast
> in teares teares teares

> echo   echo

> eyes darkened at Plwcca halog
> sockets emptied at Cae budr
> smoked out at the end of the way
>         at Crwys Bychan

> *bonfire night bonfire night*
> *three little angels dressed in white*

(The names are places near the old place of execution in Cardiff. *Cae budr* means rotten field – Latin *putreo*. The loss of sight stands for the effects of death.) The style is less documentary than snatches of memory as if from very far away, perhaps in another dimension. Much of the story is in the notes and introduction – Casey had a limited concept of the realm of poetry. The poetry is largely quotes from other texts – he was happier with this. The italics signal lines delivered by singing voices. Of course the sewing of these patches is very precise and is the key to the artistic method. The model is surely a church service, where the words are all old and charged with divine power for that reason. Hearing the liturgy on a given day can conjure up memories of hearing the same words years, perhaps many years, before.

Other information on Casey is that he was interested in occultism, in the learned and syncretistic English form which was promoted by *The Quest*. Casey did publish a large volume, but most of it is translation from modern Greek, mainly Seferis; the classic translations are by Sherrard and Keeley, and they do not have the unliterary features which Casey attributes to them. The translations may shed light on Casey's interests but they are not important as recreations of the original texts. The book includes an essay about religion, expressing a doctrine about the mechanical view of the mind as characteristic of Western culture, to be rejected therefore in favour of Eastern mysticism (perhaps in actuality the line of "Tradition" as promoted by René Guénon and Titus Burkhardt, since a Traditionalist magazine published the two essays). No other original poems are offered. Really it comes down to *South Wales Echo*. At the time of writing the press is covering the allegiance of Steve Bannon, Donald Trump's chief of strategy, to Guénon's Tradition.

### Split by Sparlight: W.S. Graham, *Dark Dialogues* (1970)

Dark is here a synonym for obscure, and the dialogues involve only one person, the other side being dark or silent. The message is not coming through, and the key thing is the acuity with which we or the poet listened out for a message that might get through.

This is a 5-page poem, in the book *Malcolm Mooney's Land*. The whole book dwells within the same themes of the mystery of language, etc., and while readers should be warned that the answers are not supplied anywhere, familiarity with the whole book will solidify the uncertainty that might dwell in 'Dark Dialogues': Graham's uncertainty is of a very precise and steady kind, and it permits reflection rather than confusion.

> I always meant to only
> Language swings away
> Further before me.

Next, the poet addresses language, the night and the sea, admitting that they are metaphors. Europa and the bull appear; as they have riding lights, which belong on ships, they seem to be a ship. The bull swam to Europe, in the legend. He addresses a "you" which might be language, but he says, "who are you", so we do not know. He asks by what right he waylays this "you". He speaks across the vast dialogues, hoping his words will become a place where he can think. The you, the entity that he is "other to", stands still "by the glint of the dyke's sparstone". (Spar, a lustrous mineral, cf. feldspar.) Then we get about 50 lines of memory of a tenement, evidently in Scotland, evidently many years before (the lighting is by gas). The you is still there, and is in the embers: so, seeming to be a spirit of some kind, in a Scottish folk-tale. He speaks of games and moves on to say, "I am their father", that is he is the father of games, which must also be his poems. He himself is made to occur by the words. The next page involves what seems to be lingering outside in the storm, in a forest by some loud streams in Scotland (they are burns); he addresses a you which might, this time, be his boyhood self. He hears sounds from the shore, where he lived as a child, and so he is the shell held to Time's ear. Part IV is about decisions, indefinable but seemingly about turnings, taken or not; "and all/ For a sight of the dark again". The speaker is living the experiences of two people who are not us, a time which is not his. We return to Europa and the bull, who are now possibly in the stars; they turn slowly home. Climactically, over love which has the apparatus of a dock and a bridge, a real sky is slowly becoming light.

The title includes the word dark but each section of the poem includes things that shine, the glint of a spark, the gas mantle, the embers, etc. (The exception is the scene by the Otterburn, which seems to be all darkness and mist.) The last line is about dawn filling the sky, turning the dark over. Perhaps the topography is a point of light in a much wider darkness. The point could be consciousness, which would be a metaphor from the shared stock.

What is the other speaker in the dialogue? The answer might be that Graham studied intensively to become a modernist poet, stripping language of its familiar habits and of the sequels that any utterance entrains, in ordinary daily exchange. He tore language out of its tissue of counterparts. After this, he had a complete language faculty, but deprived of a fellow-speaker. Its energy was such that it created a counterpart, but one which has no words. Another explanation is that this is an autobiographical poem which has gone wrong: Graham, aged around 50, is remembering scenes from this past, but his acuity is such that he finds the consciousness of past Grahams strange, and he does not follow the imperialist-self line of reducing that strangeness – so that he always was as he is now. Instead he leaves the strangeness in place; the memories have real vividness, but of sensory experiences and not of the awareness of one's *self*. The memories reply, but what they say is dark. This explanation is too simple because it does not account for the similarities between *Dark Dialogues* and the rest of the book, which is not about memory.

Poems contain information, but in this one we don't find the answers. That is, the poem poses us on the edge of the unknown. A poem is, equally, standing on the edge of the unknown: the wish for information starts with information we haven't got. Logically, poetry never needs to stifle the need and bring it to an end, it just needs to move us on into the unknown. Graham says, "always language /Is where the people are", Crichton Smith says, "Language is other people"; the verbal echo is connected to a Scottish preoccupation with what language really is. The starting point is recognizable to anyone who can't speak English, but the topic has been developed over a great distance by the poets, and their discourses do not map readily onto each other.

### Journey to Earth: Edwin Morgan, *Memories of Earth* (in: *The New Divan*)

This is not going to get a detailed description but it is a long poem. It is a science-fiction narrative. The narrator, an alien, fingers the tapes from his trip to Earth, which he says changed everything. "I hear that sea beyond the glass/ throwing its useless music away in handfuls". He had to prepare a report so his visit was something like a reconnaissance. Tape 1. On "the north shore/ of the inland sea", the six visitors must enter a stone. It is giving off signals. It is as big as his fist but he shrinks down again and again until he fits inside it. The landscape explodes as he shrinks. After shrinking to sub-atomic size, they travel through the cosmos. They head towards the signal. The clouds move around in disorder, not controlled by the Council as at home. They try to identify the signal, which is coming from the landscape:

> it melts
> at the edges like a photograph in flames,
> throbs, re-forms, faces appear, a flare
> of light on metal, swords ringing, a gold torque
> filled with blood, the high whinny of horses.

Their time and the world's time can never be in phase. The visitor sees another landscape, "a desolation/ of mirages,", perhaps Hungary. More scenes of Earth life. They see a murder camp, filled with people in the process of dying. They are recording everything. They see the people of Earth in an observatory which seems to be on the moon, or a "near planet", and devastated by some collective grief. The screen goes blank. Scraps of language reach them. Then they are in a "void of echoes". They come down over the Pacific and see a canoe. The rowers are tattooed and so may be Polynesians. They are crossing the ocean to an unknown landfall. The signal is still unidentified. The visitors depart and "shake out a few million worlds" from a nebula which they pass. They make their report and are told it is useless because they had identified with the action. They disagree because the question of time past and time present has become insoluble. They plan to change the regime on their home. They prefer compassion and reject order and orders. One of them is growing the spores, perhaps germs from Earth, which carry memories.

### Mordant on Retina: *Myth of Myself*, by Jack Beeching

> Mordant on retina as acid smoke,
> Hot dreams of eremite, or prisoner,
> Degrade the vigil with a Judas kiss.
> Only a lover's bodily embrace
> Tattoos a never-fading cicatrice.
>        (from 'Words and Deeds')

– the vocabulary choice is very precise but also exotic and striking. The theme is "words and deeds", in this stanza fantasy and real experience, but in the whole poem about love. The "vigil" is staying awake late, evidently due to erotic arousal. This is treacherous (Judas-like) because it promises and then lets you down. It is made of smoke. Real lovers, though, make a scar on your skin (or ego) which never fades. (There are love tattoos, on the skin, saying perhaps "Julie".) The word choice is bizarre but the idea is not original. This is part of a section of 11 stanzas within a long poem ('Long poem in progress') in the 1970 Penguin Modern Poets 16. In the *Collected*, it had the title 'Myth of Myself', but was altered: the first section became a separate poem and the fourth section became the first one. Beeching's publishing career is one of the most painful and depressing to contemplate. He was involved in editing some Communist magazines in his twenties and even late teens. He got two pamphlets out in the Fifties but there followed a blank period with his first full-length book only in 1996. A large *Collected* followed in 2001, prepared before his death (he lived 1922–2001). What happened? So the 38 pages in PMP 16 are very important.

Beeching produced four hundred pages of poetry, over sixty years. The question is, how good is it? The surface has an impossibly high gleam yet the processes are conventional – this is genuinely elusive. The version of *Myth of Myself* in PMP 16 is 179 lines long. The first section is set in what must be an Orthodox church, though we do not find out which country it is in. A boy has a strange moment when he is in love with the Virgin, in a painting in the church. The poet is also present and as he turns his head the church spins – an apparent motion. This section of *Myth* describes the experience of mystic but sexual love for the Virgin. The poet is there as a tourist. "His pebble face is blank, yet rosy thorn/ Turns as my turning spins the dome, takes root,/ Sanguine with bud, in dead and caustic soil." The crown of thorns takes root and flowers, and a pigeon, flying across the dome, stands for the dove as messenger of God's promise. This is an affirmation of faith. The second section evokes the death of a boy soldier, through the setting of a school cadet corps; then the poem evokes suburban gardening before returning to the death "within the frozen wood". Section 3 is a dystopia based on social breakdown as the young unlearn basic inhibitions. Civilisation is not passed on. Due to qualities of compassion never developing, the children are animated by technocratic violence. "The seamless garment has been torn to shreds"; the shroud of Christ was *inconsutilis*, without a seam, and the reference is both to Christianity and to the social fabric. "All language turns, though dense and sweet with love,/ Incomprehensible" – the feelings are lost. In the 4th, we hear

> Gold particles, in spectral saraband,
> Throb an erotic motion all day long,
> Dust in the sun, this flesh like gossamer.
> Add word to word, since words, perhaps, are deeds,
> As, knelt in dust, another planted seeds.

We are made of "dust", which in erotic charge shines, as real dust shines in the sun like gold. The flesh is transient (like cobwebs, archaically called gossamer). The dust is light and dances (a saraband) in slight currents of air. This section appears to be a further dystopia; while 3 is about the death of compassion, 4 portrays a social state where only perverse and disastrous states of love occur, involving the erasure of the difference between the sexes and the replacement of people by images. The "words and deeds" opposition refers to writer's guilt but is resolved at the end by declaring that words are deeds (probably meaning the Gospel, in this stanza). The section opens with a line (actually line 6) "Word was a deed, but all the doing's done", in a noticeably 17th century and Metaphysical tenor. The line appears to mean that a declaration of love is an action, but is now inactive: the rest of the stanza describes the disappointment of lovers. An enemy "maims… with caponizing bomb": perhaps the death of sex is due to chemicals in the air and earth.

> Romantic memory is hermaphrodite,
> Haunted by soldiers' as by women's faces.
> An obsequy for ghosts

The ceremony for the brave becomes "A spinal tremor and a public dread." The survivors attempt sex in conditions which sound like David Bowie's "Drive-in Saturday". Smoke and dust are conjoined, as figures of what the hands cannot seize but which capture the eyes and the lungs. Both are symbols of sexual attraction. The situations are heightened, in the manner of anxiety visions, to a state like characters in some Jacobean tragedy; "Is that the chilling face his lovers saw,/ An English mask, its every lust held tight?" Just before the end we hear that by love "Annihilation may be nullified", another paradoxical and metaphysical phrase.

> Crowd to this open, perfume-haunted window
> Myriads of Ariels, free as senses die,
> Waiting that midnight when the mirror face,
> With rigid mouth, comes closer than a flame
> To drink the breath, and cancel out the name.

This appears to describe swarms of released parts of the self, separated from the body as senses give way, waiting outside the bedroom window for the moment when death, bearing the man's face, finally comes to "drink his breath". The spirits are unrealised authenticity, and yet not quite human. The perfume continues the dust and smoke. This is a peak of subjective and highly-wrought poetry which evades reason. For a long time, I had a blank feeling about the poems. The reason I didn't have an emotional memory about them was that they were more technically brilliant than emotionally communicative. My other impression was a feeling that he had spent years of writing all day and every day, learning how to turn 400 words into 100; the concision and clarity of his poems were just unique, they were almost intimidating for me as a writer. There are 3 poems of his in the 1952 PEN anthology, *New Poems*, which was silently an anthology of Left poetry. His problems with publication were linked to his having a group of friends who did not keep control of publishing and other resources. Beeching sharply criticised the Party (in astonishing poems in his 1957 pamphlet) and broke away, with thousands of others, an ex-communist market which turned out to be confused and in dissidence. This group was not short of talent, with Jack Lindsay, Edgell Rickword, and so on, but its loudest members distrusted poetry.

Beeching has a poem in *The New Reasoner* (Autumn, 1957), a collector for ex-Stalinists. The information in two helpful essays in the online magazine *Jacket* says that he was a Catholic. Also, he was living in Catholic countries after 1956. He wrote a history of Christian missions 1515–1914. The pattern of his history books is about imperialism, the overseas spread of Europeans after 1515. It is obvious that these books are not conventional works of Marxist anti-colonialism.

The poems very noticeably bypass the expected aesthetic patterns of the 1940s and 1950s. This is another aspect of Beeching's sophistication. I think Roy Fuller and Christopher Logue could be a comparison – both were, during the Fifties, clearly Leftists working inside the Formalist idiom. This does not seize Beeching but it highlights a contrast – he was much less animated by dramas of doubt than Fuller, and his vocabulary was much more recondite. Beeching was much less worried about the problem of commitment, and in fact wrote much less about being political. It is almost as if the drama is in the vocabulary choice. The subject area is moral interpretation of human behaviour, individual or social, often with character as the focal point and the thing which is being tested and judged. Evidently these statements would hold for the majority of poets using the Formalist style. This leaves as a puzzle why he did not get published more in the period, say 1950 to 1980, when people committed to this style were in charge and many such books were being published.

The 1952 anthology includes a poem about paintings, evidently of the 1650s or thereabouts, of Roundheads and Cavaliers. Its point is that today we have war propaganda, which is bad, whereas the paintings are realistic and unexciting. In PMP 16 we have a poem about a painting, evidently 16$^{th}$ century, Flemish, and by a Protestant, about a woman pinned to a wheel. It may be the cadaver of a woman. This is a display punishment. It suggests to me that Beeching likes to work from a picture, and that this gives a static quality to his poems even though it allows for distantiation and for the impressive level of control and precision which his poems consistently show. In the poems, there is a movement from detail to generalisation. There is not a tracking of a process in history, of history as made up of changes. The great Catholic art of the Mediterranean countries, produced by an ancient belief in "visual instruction" (for a largely illiterate flock) used static visual images as basic to spiritual (and aesthetic) process. Beeching had a pamphlet out with Key Poets, who were owned by the Communist Party: *Aspects of Love*, 1950. *Myth of Myself* bears a certain resemblance to *Aspects of Love*, the title poem in 24 parts, which is also autobiographical, and highly emotional, but also made of parts that have no obvious fit, and talking as philosophy and not just direct emotional memory. Two poems impressed me especially about Beeching. The second is 'Weathermen in Hiding Play Jazz', in which fugitive members of the illegal American revolutionary organisation meet to play jazz ("Their mythified explosion blew up the pathos cry/ Of all who stood nearby. They abhor a private tower/ For its long green perspective"). The first is in *Truth is a Naked Lady* and is about forty murdered Jewish writers. Undoubtedly this refers to the night of August 12, 1952, when thirteen ex-members of the Jewish Anti-Fascist Committee were shot in one night, on Stalin's orders. Five of them were writers, so I am unsure about the figure forty. But in any case, this is a devastating attack on Beeching's former Communist Party colleagues and on the facts they so often wrote out of history. It is part of a series of anti-Stalinist poems grouped together in that 1957 pamphlet – the next one is about tanks and very clearly refers to the "fraternal intervention" in Budapest in 1956.

The closest poems to Beeching, in our dataset, are late poems by Jones in *The Sleeping Lord*, for example *The Tribune's Visitation*. *Myth of Myself* apparently finds the collapse of socialisation so that the young have no values, and the collapse of gender roles within sexual relations, leading to vacuity and perversity. What strikes me is how Beeching can site these vast changes at a precise time in history, around 1945 to 1970. This is similar to Jones' description of a moment in around AD 32 as the turning-point: the *Tribune* poem is set just before the Crucifixion. Jones also saw a cultural break in around 1920, making the past unreachable. Western Marxists, in the late 20th century, were addicted to the idea of crisis and the idea that you are about to lose what you love. These panic-inducing stimuli were indulged in by artists. I think we have to accept that most of history is not part of a crisis and that few changes are clear and irreversible. This casts a light on the process of *pictorial reduction*, where history is compressed into a moment and everything loyally turns around that turning-point. This process involves genius and falsification at the same time. Beeching liked to work from pictures. He says "All language turns, though dense and sweet with love,/ Incomprehensible": this obviously did not happen and is not an account of post-war history, but it is so saturated with feeling. I have to ask if this enhancing of melodramatic moments is also part of poems about individual lives, in the early part of the century, and if a feature of modernity is that poems no longer believe in destiny, revelation, turning-points, and irrevocable loss. In the Seventies, the mélange of different generations shows in high contrast the older poets (such as Raine and Barker) as melodramatic and the whole group born since 1920 as low-affect.

### Didactic Labyrinth: Iain Crichton Smith, *From the Notebooks of Robinson Crusoe* (1975)

Donald MacAulay's introduction to his 1975 anthology *Modern Scottish Gaelic Poetry* says there are two kinds of poetry being written in Gaelic, and it is the "intellectual, modernist, written" poetry (and nothing else) which he anthologises. There is a phrase "the famous five (*an coignear cliuiteach*)" to refer to just the five poets he selected. (The phrase may be due to Donald Meek.) Four of these were Hebridean. Obviously the twentieth century also saw quite a few people writing poetry in the folk or Gaelic manner, not usually destined for print. Obviously, again, a number of poets in the written style have arrived since 1975. Smith is one of these *modern* poets. MacLean stood up in defence of village poets (*baird baile*) in the introduction to his collected poems. An open question is whether MacLean differs from 'local poets' because the poem is more intellectual and recording of argument than one of the songs could be, or because of some European influence.

MacLean's local model for argument and self-doubt would be Evangelical sermons (as documented especially by John MacInnes and Terence McCaughey). Following up MacAulay, you could say that Smith and MacLean wrote poetry which notably has features in common with the folk poetry, and that reading an amount of the village bards is helpful to getting with their more developed work. For example, in part VI of 'The Cuilinn' MacLean uses the phrase "chunnaic mi" (or *chunnaic mise*), "I saw", 17 times in a row, as he narrates the history of the oppressed; in 'An t-eilean mun Cuairt', a poem by the North Uist *bard baile* Angus MacLellan (1879-1962), we get the equivalent phrase "chì mi" ("I see") 18 times in a row, as he evokes the island viewed from the sea ("I see islands and bays/ Lochs grey green sloping tranquil/ The bay of Loch Euphort smooth for sailing/ Which taught sailors when young").

The theme of *Notebooks* is how it feels to be an exile stranded on a remote island and feeling society and its patterns of behaviour dissolve, so that the central figure falls into a different world, which he can live in but not imagine.

There is a problem with writing about this because Smith (1928–98) removed a large part of it when preparing his *Collected Poems*. About 80% of the material in the original 1975 text has been removed from the *Collected*. Some of what was removed is about Man Friday, and the motive is likely to be fear of being criticised, and dishonestly interpreted about the relationship between the imperialist and the colonies. By writing about it I may be slighting the author's wishes.

The poem has quite a simple structure, but on the other hand it has an unusual intensity – it has the quality of a nightmare, in fact. It throws you into a total situation, one where normal life has simply stopped. The experience is of being an actor who has stepped out of the film, who can only see it as a film, even if for others it is reality: the lead figure is on an island where food and shelter are available, but his consciousness is taken over by the memory of what life in Europe was like:

> I do not pace up and down in a hospital waiting for the doctor to
>      tell me about my wife and whether the haemorrhages have
>      stopped.
> I do not hear the crazy white-haired violinist scraping in the attic.
> I am not feverish with love.

I do not phone my sweetheart at midnight from a squalid bar, nor
do I see her raising her shadowy lips to her lover's, behind a
closed curtain.
I do not stand by a stretcher watching the pale mouth hardly
breathing.

*Crusoe* fulfils the model of the poem as didactic labyrinth. I deeply
regret the shortening because the strike of the poem, the size of its
founding catastrophe, depends on the length of the work: the extent of
time before we return to normality. The length is essential to the strain,
the pull on us as human ropes. Like other such labyrinths, it works as
a brain gym. Loss of memory is a gain of acuity. In that maze, you can
extend to the limits of your energy; you leak out into the emptiness,
your warmth is diluted but also you are filling it with pattern.

When Smith writes about an island, even a fictional one, he is
talking about the Hebrides, because most of his poems are about the
Hebrides, one way or another. This is a poem about language and where
you have Man Friday not knowing English, speaking broken English,
this evidently refers to the experience of a Gaelic-speaking child going to
a school where the teacher was only allowed to speak English and where
on the first day he understands nothing at all. Crichton Smith went to
school circa 1934. This was the experience of every child from Lewis, in
his generation and for seventy or eighty years. What Smith knows comes
from exile. Recognising the impact of this moment of forced migration
must bring us closer to the experience of other children going to English-
medium schools who had little or no English. Crusoe is rescued from
his island after thirty years, but even this might correspond to the life
experience of many islanders, going to sea, or to teach as Smith did, and
returning to their native place after thirty years away. The Gaelic area is
thick with people who have lived far away for many years. My grasp of
the history of the Gael shows Highlanders coming to Glasgow to seek
work, sleeping standing up in Waterloo Street because they could not
afford rent at first, and at first not knowing any English. Of course, they
took labouring jobs. This is what the Man Friday passage is about, you
go to a foreign place and find that you are dumb and a servant. I really
wish the passage had not been cut.

Island, what shall I say of you, your peat bogs, your lochs, your
moors and berries?

The cry of your birds in the fading evening.
Your flowers in summer glowing brightly where there are no
    thoroughfares.
The perpetual sound of the sea.
The spongy moss on which feet imprint themselves.
The mountains which darken and brighten like ideas in the mind.
The owl with its big glasses that perches on a late tree listening.
The mussels clamped to the rocks, the fool's gold, the tidal pools
    filling and emptying.
The corn that turns from pale green to yellow, my scarecrow rattling
    in the wind.
The smoke that arises from my fire.

This is very beautiful. The peat bogs are not what you would expect on a Pacific atoll. Crusoe seems to be stranded somewhere west of Skye.

Smith then says "language is other people". I wish, again, that W.S. Graham had known this. It would have answered all the questions he was so elaborately asking. What is language doing with us, well, it is the trace of other people and of how you fit into their subjective worlds. Crusoe is without other people and language is breaking down in him. This is also like saying, if you go to Lewis and everyone is speaking English it is like being deaf.

The poem is about ordinary things but made poignant and strange because they are only being imagined. It doesn't have a thesis but instead a point of view, of someone hidden behind a sea. This is also like a child encountering the everyday world and not yet understanding it. The fine details are less important, because people are compelled by the subject which the poet is wading into. The more compelled they are, the less they are interested in your refined wishes and perceptions and the more they are interested in their own reactions and in working out what they feel. This is the most productive area for poetry. Smith is noticeable for not having a personal thesis or set of preoccupations. That is, he returns endlessly to a set of themes, but these belong to a whole population, that is the Gael, probably of his generation, and not only in the North and West but in any part of Britain, and *his subject is other people and not an idea or fantasy which he owns.*

Although he kept saying the same things, reading his *Collected* involves mulling over the brilliant poems which you favour and which aren't there. Since you have an island, ours, where millions of people belong to a different ethnic group, you might well want poetry to help people to imagine what it's like not being part of the majority. This indeed might offer the learning which reviewers are short of. I don't want to say that the experience of non-English-speaking groups in the Highlands or in Wales is very similar to the experience of groups reaching the UK mainland as immigrants. Human cultures never resemble each other very closely. Welsh culture is not strikingly like Gaelic culture; this was wishful thinking. The differences are a huge area of information, and information is the raw material of literature.

There are many problems with certain *Collected Poems*, and so much material is lurking in the original issues. There are about six or even ten of Crichton Smith's long poems which don't fit into our period. He thought his best work was 'The Deer in the High Hills', 1962. Other people think the best one was 'Shall Gaelic Die?', 1969. Quite possibly the long Gaelic poem, 'An Cànan', from the Eighties, is his best. Two sequences of lyrics from the Seventies could fit into our project.

### Iain Crichton Smith, *The White Air of March* (1972)

This presents as sixteen sections of which each one offers a scene characterising Scotland and the memory of Scotland:

> This is the land God gave to Andy Stewart –
> we have our inheritance.
> There shall be no ardour, there shall be indifference.
> There shall not be excellence, there shall be the average.
> We shall be the intrepid hunters of golf balls.

(Stewart was a singer popular on television in the early Sixties. He wasn't a *bad* singer, but his material was comic or sentimental.) They might occur to anyone thinking about Scottish politics, and because they are half-way towards abstract thought they are also part-way towards clichés. They are not specific to Smith, they are recognisable and fit into the SNP's cultural argument, but Smith's personal emotional emphasis may be sarcasm. The oscillation between feelings of sentiment and idealism, and a revision which sees the stock images as having lost their truth and so leading the people to failure as a society, is the axis around which the work rotates. He raises themes of exile, the heroism of warriors in the past, the bitterness of exile, the Cuillin mountains on the isle of Skye, green dollars. The Cuillins are mentioned in five sections of the poem and the literal meaning of the word excel, to surpass in height, is embodied in their height. "The Cuillins tower / scale on scale./ The music of the imagination must be restored / upward" seems like the nucleus of the poem, its centre. When I first read the poem, 40 years ago (my father had a copy of the Penguin book it appeared in) I read section 13 as a serious record of Gaelic antiquities, with Smith wearily recording information which he had salvaged as the society was dissolving. In fact, it probably stimulated me to study Anglo-Saxon, Norse and Celtic at university, to get closer to the ancient civilisation of the outer north-west:

> [...] contained in the 'Book of the MacMurrows',
> 'The Annals of the MacMurrows' and much matter significant
>     for scholarship
> including the first use of the ablative absolute in a categorical mode
> with animadversions upon the umlaut, the Dawn of the Present
>     Participle
> though in one or two places the record is unfortunately blank.

Today I can see the whole thing is a spoof. He says the MacMurrows are a sept of the MacMorrises, but the only trace of a MacMorris I can find is Jamie McMorris, a comic Irish warrior in 'Henry V'. 'Morrow' is a variant of *morchaidh*, the word for seafarer, also surviving as Murphy, but there are no MacMurrows. The conclusion about the MacMurrows is "enough I think has been said to show their importance / to the quality of our civilization, our language, and the perpetuation / of our culture, our literature, and, if I may say so, our Cause": the question is what exactly makes Smith sarcastic here. Is he sad about the ignorance of the modern Gael, which means that they will accept almost any junk about the past of their own ethnic group? Is he criticising the quality of regional scholarship, with pedants having forgotten how to talk and having long since left intellectual curiosity behind? Or is he obliquely lamenting the loss of historical memory, due to illiteracy, the unemployment and dispersal of the "living memories", and the destruction of manuscripts in the 17th and 18th centuries? He does not specify. No clan left "annals", there is a sort of chronicle of the MacDonalds but the annalistic form belongs to monasteries and these vanished long ago in Scotland (there is a set of annals of Iona in some form). The "book" refers to a collection of the panegyric poetry of the chiefs of a given clan, the ones that weren't just lost. There are several of these in Scotland and quite a few in Ireland, for the Burkes, MacSweeneys, etc. There is no ablative case in Gaelic, so evidently no ablative absolutes. There is a verb-noun which could be called a participle, but it is not marked for tense, so the term present participle is meaningless. The point may be that Gaelic scholarship is mediocre, it is to real scholarship what Andy Stewart is to popular music.

March is the month of sowing (and belief in the future). But the text refers to white sails and the air may be a brisk breeze carrying the ship: "March breeds white sails". The relationship between the sections, the tier where we get from primary images to an intellectual pattern, is not made explicit. Syntax and conjunctions are not used to make an argument. This is typical of Seventies long poems. We must add that Gaelic folk-songs also are mainly paratactic, do not say "therefore" or "because of" very much, and express much of their meaning in symbols. Smith's poem resembles *Y Dŵr a'r Graig* and *Ancestor Worship*, in our list. Each of them contains the scenery for a nationalist self-celebration but two of them show a sort of disgust for this emotional script, at least in the form in which it is proposed. Gwyn Thomas' poem (the commentary for a television film, in fact) is happy with the idea of a nationalist reverie, although it is sad in tone. Both Smith and Emyr Humphreys are full of ambivalence, which does not keep quiet. Smith writes

> The hedge buds,
> puts out white flowers.
> The sails fly seaward,
> the rocks attend the keel.

The group white/sails/new Spring is the core of the poem, I think. But the bit about the rocks predicts disaster, touching on an old Gaelic proverb about the ship being young and excitable while the rocks are old and cunning. There is always the possibility that distaste for the legacy set of associations and feelings will provoke the creation of new symbols, new feelings and a new politics.

The succeeding section is about William McGonagall, from the Cowgate in Edinburgh, a mid-19th century uneducated poet of legendary banality. Smith tries to rehabilitate him:

Baffled, beaten, buffeted, scorned, despised,
You played 'Macbeth' to a theatre of villains.
You swung your sly cloak through gaslight
a devotee of Art.

It is fair to say that in no country are people more cynical about the
common icons of the national past than in Scotland, or less able to create
new symbolism which can appeal to a wide consensus. I said Smith's
themes were not personal; by groaning at the banality of public life, he is
articulating public opinion in Scotland, not creating a hermetic cell where
he escapes from everyone else. In the 1970s, changes in voting patterns
and in constitutional arrangements were on the agenda; devolution has
since 1999 changed many things, including history teaching in schools.
He is describing the condition of a nation without a State, rather than
of an individual who has dissolved out of a nation. Fifteen proposes a
kind of animist transfiguration set on the Cuillin mountains, a trance
of optimism in which everything old is shed. This seems like the end,
but there is a section Sixteen. "Minotaur of guilt / coiled at the centre,
vivid." The word *excellence* heads the last two sections, an optimistic
resolution. The poem concludes with "In the white air of March / a
new mind", evidently led by this excellence. (*Ardour* does not re-appear.)
This is one of the passages where the imagery is clearly original and
not quoted from a nationalist romance. It is difficult and elliptical,
arriving in a succession of fits and starts, a kind of coda where the rules
are broken; the breakdown of structure could be a sign of incomplete
patterns bursting into awareness as the old ones break down.

If we say that this poem makes none of its internal structure explicit,
that it demands a radically new collective symbolism, that it does not
describe the changed world but asks us to imagine it, we are saying
that it has the qualities which readers dislike in political poetry of the
Seventies. Smith was not a Marxist student, but he did ask the reader to
imagine something he does not describe. We can make a generalisation
here: the poetry of the time asks people to imagine how society should
be organised. Someone who has no energy for that can bypass the
poetry. The poets never describe the new society and we judge them by
how intelligently they use public imagery to stir up memories and set
them free from pre-programmed connections.

*mallow scent on twin pulses*: **Eric Mottram,** *Tunis* (**1977**)

This is a poem of 15 pages, a typed copy mimeographed and stapled. The subject is the region which includes Tunis, and the atmosphere is one of warmth, relaxation and sensuous enjoyment. Mottram wrote a large amount of poetry (maybe 4 or 500 pages), much of which is too obscure to recover easily. He used montage insistently and didn't pause for long enough to make each brief scene clear. It is as if he felt that if he had more jumps or lapses of continuity than anyone else then he was more modern, and this meant he had won the poem. *Tunis* is much more artistically successful, simply because he does not have a jump cut every few lines. Instead, the camera stays with the idea of Tunis all the way through, the title tells us what is going on, and various travels into differing themes converge in one pattern. *Tunis* is almost disturbing because it is so good and suggests that some of his other poetry could also be good if you could grasp it before it jumped away into culture-historical abstruseness.

Topography is a wonderfully permissive topic, it lets anything in but if you miss a page or so it is just as if you had been neglecting to look out of the bus window for five minutes. My guess is that the order of the book is irrelevant: the various elements of ancient history, geography, and vegetation are all fascinating but you can take them in any order.

The poem starts with the tale of an Egyptian King, Necho, sending a sailor (Hanno), to sail around Africa and finding that Africa (called Libya in the source) was surrounded by sea. The word for red/purple is Canaanite, a trace of Phoenician merchants coming to North Africa.

*Qart-hadasht* means "new city" and is Carthage, and they sailed further, to the Tin Islands, seen as Cornwall. Page 2 gives us the overthrow of Carthage, and a catalogue of Syrian and Carthaginian gods. We move on to more contemporary pictures of the land south of Carthage. While the presentation is modern and unexpected, the content is factual and so not invented by Mottram, it could belong to anyone.

> through later music
> up from the world's centre sea
> sea of descents into what pregnancy
>                         is afforded in which the dreamer
> awakens to a body
>                 to be cultivated

                              mallow scent on twin pulses
            vetch and sweet peas twine her wrist
                              their stems climb Mediterranean caves
            a sea-purple hibiscus rambler
                        long stemmed fire geraniums
            thrust up into orange trees whose white heads
                              drench closing air

This reminds me of Erich Arendt's Algerian poems. Page 13 gives us 'A Night in Tunisia', the famous Dizzy Gillespie number, escorted by 'Bags' Groove'. Mottram sees this as an old dwelling of mankind, soaked in the relics of ancient culture:

    punic        cufic        arabic
                              marble scripts      the walls aflame
          cold alphabets
                        men from cities write
                        repetitions in crystal walls
          through glassless space

I have never had strong views about the scattering over the page in this layout. It looks as if handfuls of blank space have been inserted into the poem. This does not affect the sound of the poem. What is it for? All I can say is that the blanks halt the forward motion of the poem, but because its mood is being on holiday, where we don't have to arrive anywhere, and because where we actually are is very pleasurable, slowing it all down is possibly benign.

    With *Tunis*, the line of sense jumps constantly, but if you have a tourist-level knowledge of North African history it is easy to follow. The poem is seductive because of its warmth and dissolution of responsibility, and the frequent arrival of new and pleasant sensations.


**Madness of the King: John Wain, *Feng* (1975)**

The long poem *Feng* tells the Hamlet story from the point of view of the usurper, given his original name (from Saxo Grammaticus's book) of Feng. *Feng* is in 17 parts and totals about 2000 lines. Wain says in a brief note that he was interested by the theme of madness in power because of its relevance to many situations in the 20$^{th}$ century. Feng is "the sick and hallucinated person who seizes power and then has to live with it".

Shakespeare's version is about Hamlet feigning madness but afflicted by doubts; Wain's story is about the madness of the king. The story belongs, arguably, to a series of narratives about nervous breakdowns, in which poetic imagery and hallucination take over from political logic and an isolated but eloquent figure is unable to continue with a social position, with its interlocking roles, and lives out the social process as fictional and irrational. *The Graduate* is a classic example of this, but the Theatre of the Absurd in general tells such stories. They often show uncontrolled indulgence in sexual activity or violence as instances of pre-social energies, released because social inhibitions seem as ridiculous as other rules. It is ambiguous whether the resort to poetic logic, and to the processes of symbolism and metaphor, is part of a similar regression. It is also ambiguous whether this regression is a way out or part of a dangerous loss of control. Feng has an image of wings which attach to his body and fly with him; they are also his madness. (Horwendil is his brother, whom he murdered.)

> I was content to hate Horwendil secretly, but the wings were not
> > content
> they dropped from the quiet clouds to snatch me from my dull
> > content
>
> making me act the revenge that till then was an unregarded dream
> making me kill and seize power, forcing me through the doors of
> > dream
>
> never to wake. The vision I made in secret is now my world:
> there is nothing outside it. Only the dark at the edge of the world.
> > (p.53)

The condition "there is nothing outside it" sums up a whole situation. But Feng's ambitions are not different from those of many political chiefs; the story exposes the raw desire for power, the wish to be first among the few, which is normal in elite politics. In the final poem, Feng anticipates his own death and commits a sex murder:

> The wet trunks stood
> erect, forming a guard. They were so still,
> and she, all flowing and suppleness.
> Her haunches…!
> I was not chasing her. My blood was moving
> with the same tide as hers. The rain that touched
> her skin, touched mine.
> […]
> My feet on the turf were sharp and shapely hooves.
> My brow was branchy. Pride came smoking out
> in twin clouds with my royal breath.
> To mate!
> (p.55)

The metamorphosis from man into deer echoes quite a few other poems of the era, *The Book of Herne* by Eric Mottram for example. The aesthetic of the poem is one of shock images, flowing on kinetic energy. Feng analyses his feelings but this does not give a way out, his feelings have dissolved into mania. His actions are surrounded by mystery and the events of the poem remind one of the horror films of the time. However, there are long passages of detached reflection which take us out into another world: Feng cannot make his social being follow down the path his intellect has gone down. He has reached a higher plane but cannot live out this awareness – this is perhaps the classic experience of adolescence. This is especially true of poem V, 'A Circle of Stones and a Nude Blade':

> Is it I who am free, and the animals enslaved
> to their rigid patterns, those unbreakable laws engraved
>
> on their nervous systems, so that to disobey
> cannot occur to them? I, whose dismay
>
> at this fertile and comely den-partner no bear
> or wolf would agnize?

The final poems see the king become a beast, so reaching a state of perfect unity and lack of consciousness which complements the states of doubt, nausea, and exalted insight in which he spends the earlier poems. In poem VIII he has what appears to be a slipping into the mind of

Shakespeare, and watches a long series of scenes played by other people. He can only see these by becoming a ghost. Everything significant is visible but he cannot take part in it. This is like a drug trip and it connects with Seventies Underground poetry: which one can often see as a re-enactment of the history of society, without participation, by an onlooker who is not in control of the sequence of events. Feng is not concerned with a law code because he is the king and above the law. His crimes have the force of acts of state. His condition is one of the variants of the liminal – the uncoded state as nervous breakdown. The poem unfolds through immeasurably powerful concrete images:

> Today I saw the footprints of an elk.
> I was repelled. A stag is stag-sized, but
> this monstrous shape comes out of a bad dream:
> too big for the trees, too heavy for the grass.
>
> This parody of a man, an elk in armour,
> a bad giant, hides his heavy skull
> in a heavier helmet.
>      It is as if
> he wished his animal brains to simmer slowly
> in that great polished pot, until he might
> eat them with absent-minded relish, then stamp on
> guided by instinct and the forest breeze.

Large stretches of the poem, though, have Feng speak in 20th century language. This is an expression of the basic Absurd situation in which he finds himself: he apparently has knowledge transcending the local, wholly anachronistic knowledge, but it does not help him. He cannot switch off the madness. The poem is stretched between poles of intense physicality and complete abstraction plus detachment.

There is a possible link between John Wain and Tony Conran (1931–2013), as signalled by the letter to Conran in *Letters to Five Artists* (1969). That discusses at length the ferns which loved the rainy climate around Bangor and which I presume grew in Conran's garden. Conran's early work (say 1951–67) was almost entirely "social poetry", messages to named individuals and often relating to calendar events, such as weddings. This may have influenced the form of *Letters to Five Artists*. The Conran letter is based on a strong series of symbols about the old rocks of Bangor, the thinness of the soil, the continual rain, and the ancient nature of the ferns:

> And the fern holds on,
> rooted in any cranny, green and curling,
> its form a patient embroidery, a scroll,
> one of a set of variations on
> a form basically as simple as an egg
> and full of possibilities as a hand:
> it grows, it climbs, it unfolds,
> not to be questioned, permanently there,
> younger than nothing but the rocks and water.

Their tenacity and ability to develop complexity from simple forms are "why you love them, o master". The analogy is:

> intent on your page of cool petal and stone,
> assembling grain by grain in the dispersing weather
> a soil firm enough for your unsentimental flowers:
> enamelled, regal, giving to life their master
> the strong homage of art, which cannot show
> love except where love is. Their glowing patience
>
> mellows the air of your steep house, that stone
> ledge where you perch above your century's weather[.]

Conran's romantic mediaeval poems (based on figures from the Mabinogi, often) may have influenced Wain in venturing into a "romantic Middle Ages" with *Feng*. John Holloway is the other *New Lines* participant who showed radically different ideas and the capacity for changing what he was doing.

### Gael Turnbull, *Residues: Down the Sluice of Time* (1976)

This poem reminds me of Guest's *Elegies* because it is about how life is lived and what is beautiful and which we can get access to. We see about sixty individual scenes – the key is the transition from one to another which suggests a vast complexity dwelling behind it. We surrender each image only to give way to an imaginable landscape of unrestricted variety. The theme is the variousness of life so the images don't really relate to each other except through the figure of the poet explaining them all. The effect is exhilarating.

> and near the head of Chapman Cleugh, in the
> neighbourhood of Nether Clogg, lies one – but
> neither his name (nor the names of those by whom
> he died) is known
>
> > where the wind is keen
> > even in summer
>
> a weapon called the Galloway Flail: the handstaff,
> tough and durable ash, five feet in length – the
> soople (that part used to strike the barn floor) made
> of iron, three feet in length and with three joints –
> one stroke could shatter a sword (or a skull) to bits
>
> stroke upon stroke – day break, day
> break – threshing the world for seed,
> the reaper sun

(Soople in English is *swipple*.) The stanza about graves (referring to Walter Scott's *Old Mortality*) ends with the word wind, and wind is necessary to winnowing, which is the subject of the following stanza, which shows threshing corn and runs-on to the sun threshing the world. Some of the frames have these clever run-ons, but not all. Why is the sun threshing the world? Threshing makes the seed jump out of the husk. I think the sun is making seeds – like fruit, like pollen – jump out of plants, and this could extend to seasonal mating behaviour of animals, governed by the sun. The poem starts with the stars and with needfire, a seasonal rite where a new fire was kindled and shared around the village. The moments are a bit generic. One 'shot' is about the battle of Catterick (late 6th century?), immortalised in Aneirin's long poem *The Gododdin*. The week before I read this, I had read a poem of Euros Bowen's (the first in *Cylch o gerddi*) which is about the same battle. There is a problem in using stock footage. The residues are moments so vivid that they stay in the mind – the poem is composed as a series of vivid memories. The sluice is just a general term to evoke a water course – a sluice being an artificial work which fills and empties. Residues in a real sluice would have to be cleared by dredging. Three of the scenes are about violence, old age, disease – Turnbull was a doctor so these were cases he treated – the poem includes scenes which are not at all comforting because it is about the breadth of experience. Some of the descriptions are very beautiful:

> and at midnight, cold and old, in
> the absolute of their vastness, far,
> the stars are strewn in the dark:
> a precipitate of shimmers, mica seeds,
> of milky crystals, hoarfrost grains,
> a dust of spicules, flaring glints,
> a spume of shivered silver, diamantine
> flecks, an archipelago of quivered light

Why are there two residues poems? They are very similar in style and continuous in terms of content. The length is either 20 pages or 20 plus 5.

The whole resembles in theme a Thwaite poem in *Confessions*, number XXVIII "The spectrum smeared on the narrow paths of snails" etc. Behind the poem is the ghost of a doxology, of the world declaring the glory of God. There is a verbal echo of Euros Bowen's poem in the key phrase *till skin and sinew quake* – the words skin (*croen*) and sinew (*gewyn*) appear at key moments in the Welsh poem. The poems are pictorial. They could be a series of slides being projected. I am raising this, not because I dislike either the visible world or sets of pictures, but because this was an area of stylistic shift during the period. Bowen uses visualisation as a ground for allegory – an older mode. Both Thwaite and Turnbull visualise scenes or objects as a basis for the poem in a way which is sensuous, no longer allegorical. They are poets of the nervous system. Both *Residues* and *Confessions XXVIII* are virtuosic – you can't improve on them. But the Seventies saw a current where visualising was seen as too literal – much as artists were making conceptual art and not valuing the sense record, or even visual imagination, any more. I am wondering what happens when the reader is not seeing any picture at all (is this the cue for them to leave?).

### How the Alans got to Alençon: Eddie Flintoff, *Sarmatians* (1978)

In early times, the expanse from Hungary to Afghanistan (roughly) was populated by tribes speaking Iranian languages. The area is known as *l'Iran extérieur*. Thus river-names Don Donets Dniestr Dniepr Danube include an Iranian root meaning 'watercourse'. The most prominent groups (or hegemonies) were the Scythians, Sarmatians, and Alans. During the breakdown of boundaries and long-distance movement of armies in roughly the 3rd–5th centuries AD, some of these population groups moved to central and western Europe. Flintoff's remarkable long poem 'Sarmatians' (1978) records how the Alans reached Alençon:

> eyes on the far horizon
> to still newer distribution-plains, *uaran faz,*
> under the green edges and ridges of the Caucasus,
> whose peaks we named as we passed, *Elbatiy Hokh*
> the Squatting Mountain, *Aday Hokh*, Grandfather Hill
> out of Asia across the lush hush of Russia,
> the crane crossed Ukraine, numinous and luminous Rumania,
> below the carboniferous Carpathians, across the flat Banat
> westwards across the wastelands, up into polar Poland
> along the long frozen strand of the cobalt Baltic.

Under Frankish rule the settlers turned into French peasants like everyone else. The date is the 440s, when the Huns were pressing the Goths (and other groups, perhaps the Sarmatians) out of the Black Sea steppes. This is merged with the destruction of the Emperor Valens by an army of Goths (with a contingent of Alans) at Adrianople in 378. The poem introduces itself as a dream, so that the account of capturing Rome is not real. The pattern of internal rhymes is compelling – I guess that, in the quote, *uaran* rhymes with *newer*. It is likely that the rhymes show the influence of Colin Simms and that this story of the Sarmatians migrating is influenced by Simms' American poems like *Stones in a Water-Course*.

### Stretch, power-leak and dispersal: Roy Fisher, *The Cut Pages* (1971)

This was published by Fulcrum in 1971 and republished jointly by Oasis Books and Shearsman Books in 1986. The 1986 edition has 38 pages of text. The introduction says that the text was written at the end of a long period of stress in the poet's life and was a way out of it, of "dissolving" damage and patterns which had missed their exit step. The exit period saw six projects being created simultaneously, but Fisher records that up until that point in early 1970 he had been blocked since 1966. All six were concerned with "dissolution of oppressive forms, 'purposes' and personal identities". He rigorously kept a diary as a way of steering through adversity, and there was a volume of diary from which he cut the unused pages because the used ones were full of psychically adverse material, a cluster of memories which directed him to being unable to write. There was a strain in opening up the freedom of association splashing everywhere, which is usual in modern poetry, and the need to avoid the familiar and sterile and yet organic lines of association which he wanted to leave. "The aim of the improvisation was to give the words as much relief as possible from serving in planned stations[.]" The text "could have anything it asked for." He does not say anything further about the project: we are not justified in finding a biographical theme, or an argument, or a method of gathering information to answer questions. On the other hand, there is a unity of tone which we are justified in naming as the concept of the piece, along with the plan of dissolving verbal and emotional patterns which had become tedious. Did these patterns have an attraction? Yes, as that is the only way they could have repeated enough to become tedious. Improvisation can mean anything you like. Of course, Fisher was a jazz pianist and knew about liberated music – but the kind of impromptu music which jazz produced, at every stage up until the revolution of "Free Jazz", by the Ornette Coleman Double Quintet, observed all kinds of rules even if it was unscripted. This is an area of the first interest: the older jazz musicians had to keep time with the other musicians, and indeed with the dancers in many situations, so their freedom had to stick to the paths. We can view the equation of familiar verbal collocations with unpleasant emotional patterns as the basis for a radical openness, which blew off most of the audience; and reflect that the poets who liked familiar verbal patterns did not tie them to emotional pain and depression. Is there a basis for evaluating the revolution in poetry in a single way? Surely it is possible for someone to link happiness and security with old linguistic patterns and as a consequence to associate modern poetry with *unhappiness*? *Cut Pages* was just about the most advanced poetry happening in England at that time: most readers probably wouldn't even have known what it was for. "This method made for rapid changes of direction": it is kinetic and non-affective. Is this actually a unified artistic statement or a large set of discontinuities? Although moving rapidly down many different paths, the piece has a dimension: as, if we looked at a honeycomb, we could see the average diameter of the cell. This would allow us to recognise the text, if we saw a fragment of it. The cells could be repeated indefinitely, whatever different things they contain the thickness of the walls and the diameter of the cells are structural constants. The link with a state of irresolution and distress is significant: as I am arguing that these were key factors in Seventies art. In this state rapid changes of direction are the only way of proceeding – and perhaps the decision process, that is a way of making moves without reflection and study, is the anatomy of the text, the element we can retain as a way of describing it.

Coil  If you can see the coil hidden in this pattern, you're colour-blind

> Pale patterns, faded card, coral card, faded card, screen card,
>    window fade

Whorl   If you can see this word and say it without hesitation you're deaf

> Then we can get on with frame

Frameless    Meat-rose, dog-defending, tail-ruffling

Dodge

The Redcliffe Hotel? Forget it.

Coming in on the curve. Cross under the baffle. Dropped through,
    folded in the flags

Street work. Across purposes and down flights. Only male shades flit

The first moment gives the impression of a psychological project, the project in fact of the scientists who devised the colour blindness test, which could continue – but the work immediately moves on from that moment of rationalism. The poem is autonomous, not a versification of a pre-existing achievement of psychology. In fact, though each new moment gives a flash of opening out and pattern recognition, the structure of the text is the change of direction. Is this biography? Well, closing and opening frames is an area of cognition which is human, carried out by humans – and part of their biography. What it is not, is part of a story about emotions or human interaction. The opening image about colour blindness – a variant which sheds light on the physical basis of perception – does have a thematic value: the poem is going to be about opening and switching frames, something equally basic to perception. The possibility of defining frame switching as the spine of the poem is to be found also in *Residues: down the sluice of time* and *Bargain Basement Sonnets*, within our set. It is difficult to say whether this is a collection of disconnected themes recorded in the same notebook or a portrait of a connected mood with different episodes. It is on a borderline. The brain can associate things which are not structurally bound – they are aspects of a place, or a virtual place, and do not need to cause each other. The question is more of where a frame edge intervenes – where we empty our minds and stop associating a set of ideas. We can call it a set because the parts are printed together. The aggregate can be evocative in spite of a lack of connective logic. This can be compared with Guest's *Elegies*, where the different images do not link to each other, but seeing a series of fascinating images throws us into a susceptible state where we see patterns which arise spontaneously. The power of a frame is to bind images which have independent lives. The composition follows the frame.

The poet proposes a form of melancholy which sees blankness as covering infinite space and newness as a flash of life which lures the brain out each time into Awareness. Is the text-puzzle a precursor of the book's function? "If you can see a shape in this frame…" We sit before an eyepiece through which we see 300 discrete frames and try to describe each one. In these essential wind-blown fragments, we can never pause and nothing is literally true. They are analogies to explain things never yet seen. The proposal is that the new is only there in peripheral vision, that if we stay forever in the unfocused area we will never fade to what is old.

> Once the hiding place had also swallowed up the last of the pursuers into its winding and blind ends, the pursued ones started dismantling it around the pursuers, who were thus driven in deeper and deeper, like hares in the corn

Strangely, this reminds me of poems by R.F. Langley. Freedom is hard to attain. "Free Jazz", that epoch-making 1961 stretch of total improvisation, was released on CD with the rehearsal as a second track. It sounds a great deal like the master take. How do you rehearse freedom? Well, that's what you've got, a tape of the rehearsal. And Ornette sounds like Ornette, his tone and even the line sound like his older recordings. Removing the sound of your own voice is a serious task. *Cut Pages* is radically unlike Fisher's other work, even if some of the moments involve descriptions of machinery and man-made structures which are statistically much more common in Fisher poems than in other English poems. It is a poem without justification, it endlessly rolls the dice and gives the stakes away. I like it a great deal but it is not a project Fisher wanted to follow up. How you combine the planned and functional object-units of those engineering structures with the radical improvisation of *Cut Pages* is a difficult question. The moments feel tooled and efficient but are really improvised and insubstantial. It is an imaginary labyrinth which looks very much like Birmingham.

> Enamel panels passing, as if of use to the adjacent effort

> Bluish network of flicker, running across the dark fluid surfaces,
>     finding them

> Stretch, power-leak and dispersal. Then a radial diagram of the
>     next order

It is as if someone were dreaming but what they dream looks like crane parts or panels of switches. You have two takes of 'Free Jazz' but there are six Fisher poems or groups begun in 1970 and which share the same idea of openness and dissolving fabric and structure. I am wondering how you can define liberty as the dissolution of the personality when so many people see liberation as allowing their personality to occupy a larger space and influence or take over a wider range of decisions. Dissolution – Fisher was really unwilling to reproduce states of mind, at that point in 1970, and self-recording is exactly what was in the main notebook which he discarded. Raworth says something similar, in that strange moment of *A Serial Biography* where he talks about the abolition of the self. Empathising is the founding dogma of modern poetry; *Cut Pages*, like Raworth's poetry from at least *Ace*, does not permit it. The cognitive networks or fusillades on offer are not affective, point away from the self. Both works rushed forward without justification and it would have been easy to lose arguments about their value. But that is the task, to identify how good such poetry is, how many poets wrote it, without ignoring the arguments in favour of empathy and humanism, in favour of the shared appetites which constituted the poetry world, as a group of people who liked the same things and didn't like abstractions and cold orthogonal structures. Fisher found his way to this poetry but it doesn't follow there was an audience for it.

What is left when you get rid of the self? What is it which speaks?


### Top Cat: George MacBeth, *The Orlando Poems* (1971)

This would only be interesting if it turned out that MacBeth wrote about a marmalade cat who travelled through all eras and countries and Ted Hughes was so chafed that he composed *Crow*, about his own animal which had no dimensional limits, as a riposte to it. Alas, extensive archival research has revealed that *Orlando* is a parody of *Crow*, which came first. The name comes partly from Virginia Woolf's time-defying hero, partly from Kathleen Hughes' series of books about a cat named Orlando. Orlando is partly an echo of *orange* and perhaps also a reference to Orlando, Florida, near the orange groves. The strange thing is that MacBeth and Hughes were both preoccupied with animals, just in different ways.

MacBeth was a dandy-poet and his hero-cat is, like many things in the Sixties, kinky, spoof, spontaneous, serial, groovy, obsessed by clothes. The work has merit as an example of extreme loss of inhibitions – MacBeth is ignoring artistic strength just as he is ignoring consistency and plausibility in describing his aesthete-cat. A poem has here become instantly accessible, like goods in a supermarket. He wrote more than a thousand poems. This was surely what happened in the Sixties – a large part of the public got the idea that they could write poems without effort, and this faith has remained bright. It is hard to disagree without using words like *strict* and *restricting* – unpopular words. We can even see a parody of the academic poet of the time: who was committed to a version of Existentialism in which experience was limited by the body and authenticity resided in observing those limits punctiliously, shedding all knowledge except direct experience. Orlando's liberation from the bonds of Time is a critique of this. Beyond people whose imagination favours virtuous substances, like wood and stone, there is a space for people whose imagination lingers on structures made of cellophane, polystyrene, and marzipan. Faced with the problem of advertising being less authentic than poetry, one could make a dialectical riposte and write poetry which is less authentic than advertising.

The *Collected Poems* preserved 4 of the 40 poems in the volume. Would it have been better to throw away the last four? Yes.

### "fishing, standing in rays of sunlight, malice": George MacBeth, *A Poet's Life*

This is a narrative or vérité-diary which narrates a week in the life of someone who would seem to be MacBeth. It is based on a trick: the poem shows the lead character as narcissistic, frivolous, short of inhibitions, dandyish, and simultaneously the style of the poem is narcissistic, dandyish, lightweight, etc. When someone shows themselves in such an unfavourable light, we tend to believe them. Having fallen for that, we accept the validity of the poem. This is ingenious. And we can accept a weekend break in which we say farewell to the authenticity which was such a feature of the most tedious poetry of 1975. The poem shows him at no point engaging in the study, profound compassion and empathy, experiment, theorising, which we might expect poets to carry out, heavily, in their own diary-poems. Instead he reads his own entry in *Who's Who*, thinking about listing his hobbies as "fishing, standing in rays of sunlight, malice". He sees success as a competitive game rather than as an exchange in which he pleases the public and they like him. No, he is only interested in visible success and in the visible humiliation of rivals. He undercuts this (how do you *under*cut vileness?) by quoting a review which says that his poem *was transformed by fright wigs and plastic incisors*. I guess a fright wig is one with hair standing up as if in fright. The point that his effects are cursory rather than graphically convincing is hard to fight off. The poem starts:

> By the fire one might see him reclining
>
> on a white Indian carpet. Beside him, some books
>     and perhaps a peppermint cream

convey the mood. It is evening,
although the curtains remain undrawn, and the poet,
        as poets will, is obeying
        the urge to compose. He composes:
*today I got up at eight, felt cold, shaved,*
*washed, had breakfast, and dressed.* We observe him

sucking his pencil.

This is a fantasy of being observed and, even though it sounds like a TV advertisement, it is somehow an authentic piece of inauthenticity. After failing to think of a poem, he starts to watch *The Avengers*. In part VI, he washes his hair. Unusually, he records himself vanishing into fantasies. You would expect a poet to be authentic and so to believe in the life they lead; this regression into fantasy can only come over as shallow and narcissistic – other people do not seize his attention. This lack of engagement may resemble the attitude of alienation which feeds into critique and resistance, but gets there quicker. The jacket (the *Collected* 1989) says "No-one writing now has worked harder to combine experiment with traditional writing", and this may well have been written by MacBeth, if he was as preoccupied with image as *A Poet's Life* suggests. I am tempted to rewrite – this also shows shallowness and lack of engagement, sorry – as "if you always take the easiest way out then you will write several poems every weekend in the style of the last book you have read."

I still feel that his best work is in the ludic poems of *A Domesday Book*. In the Seventies he wrote some terrific poems, like *Lusus* and *Homage to Arcimboldo*.


### Glass burnished by autumn: Harry Guest, *Elegies*

This contains six elegies, is about 540 lines long and was published as a pamphlet in 1980 prior to collection in a volume (*Lost and Found*) covering 1974 to 1982. I am classing it as a Seventies poem because I want to write about it. Elegy has for some literati an association with Gray's 'Elegy in a Country Churchyard', which implies prescriptively a tone of moralising regret, of wistful reflection. However, the meaning in Roman times was nothing like this.

*Elegiac* therefore has no specific meaning, although something epic or satirical would not normally be called an elegy. 'Elegies' is a minimal title, it gives away nothing about the poems before they start. The first describes how there is a gap between a bounded area, enclosed and marked, and a place as felt by humans; then a house by a lake where the poet spent summers as a child in a house (present day?). Two paintings represent two 'illusions' of a path and a stream. The poet's wife recalls a house, now torn down, replaced by a road: her experience of it showed no foreboding of "a wind with dust and fumes". "In theory you can walk around any lake": the circuit of knowledge seems susceptible of completion but the gaps in knowledge are inexorable rather than merely chance arrangements of perspective. The second starts with the curve of a bowl in which locality is (still) present, although a style has become nameless and international. Yet "geology cannot be flouted", chemically affecting things, so that "soil round the roots of the plum-tree still / matters when fruit is eaten miles from the farm". A series of images illustrates the effect of time, and real things which resist rational analysis are where "This is the interchange / of faith and belief." A comment about the status of poetry leads into discussion of how the concepts *house* and *apple* are different for each reader because of their different sensory experiences, another example of the limits of the visible. Five describes a barrow interment, empty because "the skulls have gone", to a museum. Its stone slabs have been washed clear by "five thousand years of rain". The poem describes a ferry and how well it is made, leading on to a statement about how art "joys in its own structure", its cladding in the sensuous. Making money is the least important part of life. Another ghost story. The poem continues to a moving description of love and family togetherness, to attack naturalism and say that even a thousand years ago people "have known of life what we know", new knowledge is not central and what we know for certain is little. Six describes a track leading to a house (undescribed), where what we would call a poltergeist was active, and invisible creatures carry out visible actions.

> If you treat the symbol
> as a screen before an object claiming the thorn
> indicates protection or the ruined barn
> the failure of the old ideas you reduce the painting
> to a work in code.

The theme moves on to a discussion of the invisible being translated into visible images and how reality is broader than a prose paraphrase. A description of a winter scene, then of a woman 'silent in the white room', evidently a ghost. The moat is frozen. "If we are patient / there won't be time for questions at the end": meaning, if we are attentive to all the signs we will understand our role as brief appearances of a reality, as we move out of sight.

Throughout, the poem is beautiful:

> The starting-point may once have been a rose
> or a rose-seed or, as you watch through glass
> burnished by autumn, one petal falling
> and striking the thorns as it falls. An age
> of lyricism can be said to have ended.
> He stands there, flushed and starlit behind the mirror,
> uttering cryptic phrases, for instance, "The well
> is fed by a spring on the highest point of the island"
> and the reflection laughs back with Arcturus
> studding the bare shoulder.
>                               ('Fourth Elegy')

The beauty is partly the *serenity*, a depth of time which rides out momentary instability and returns to itself. That might also be true of the movement through 540 lines, where we are at the end more or less where we were at the beginning. The gain is perhaps a feeling that return is possible. A census shows the ghost appearing in Elegies 2, 3, 4, 5 and 6. Perhaps the word elegy refers back to Gray and the ghosts remind us of that grave-yard. I should clarify that the relevant passage in Elegy 3 is "Others depicted the blaze of recognition in the inn / as the travellers grasp the fact that they've been walking / along the edge of two worlds" – the reference is to a '40s film (*Halfway House*, Basil Dearden, 1944) in which some travellers are, indeed, in an inn from which they can go on to the after-world. The travellers are therefore ghosts in some significant sense. As with the Forties cycle of plays or films about being "between two worlds", the subject is glimpsing the larger patterns of life, and drawing a boundary to it shakes it into a new state where we can think with it. It could be that the overall theme is time, so that a ghost is like a picture, as both stay constant through time although everything else changes. Transience appears as another aspect of temporality. Guest is writing about daily life being lived in a way which none of the other poems under review is. That is, arguing about life, pursuing a political line, instrumentalises daily experience and pushes it to the edge of the page. Moving beyond dispute is the precondition for Guest writing great poems. You can't write such a poem about a life after crucial political changes, because you can't observe it or give it existential thickness and refinement of shades.

The group of Elegies is a zone of high sensitisation where the various images form patterns with each other but do not come down to a single pattern, the assembly is not defined at that level. This is very powerful and evocative. The line of argument is constantly less important than the sense of life being lived, the offer of a passage of time which is opulent, beautiful, and tranquil, and which encourages thinking about experience. The ideas are not a dispute; nothing is being refuted. The poem offers us entire and coherent cognitive positions. The group is written with wisdom about poetry and about what affects people, rather than from some external knowledge project.

### Pink Pavilions: *High Zero*, by Andrew Crozier (1978)

It was suggested to me that the title refers to both *Striking the Pavilion of Zero*, by John James, and *High Pink on Chrome*, by J.H. Prynne; the book is dedicated to these two poets. The theme, for this commentator, is of reproach to those two stalwarts of the Cambridge Communist Party. When I interviewed the poet, he denied this – he had Prynne and James in mind as poets he felt close to. Zero remains, reassuringly, a low figure. In fact, the two poems at the start and end of *High Zero* are transformations of two poems from the named works (by Prynne and James, respectively). The seven-line poem which completes *High Zero* is a reprise of the seven-line poem 'May Day Greetings 1971' which completes *Striking the Pavilion of Zero*. Similarly, a 20-line poem starts *High Zero* and answers the 20-line poem which ends *High Pink on Chrome*. Crozier mutates Prynne's lines –

> The float is criminal; access by
> blood spread, dimercaprol 200 mg.
> Dead right you are as you bleed
> for what you see and what you do.

into

> It would flout its law saturation by
> the contents spread anecdotally (BAL).
> Shored up together as you breathe
> you hear the brain stay tuned to you.

The 'tuned' bit must refer to two people in a bed breathing to the same rhythm. BAL is 'British anti-Lewisite', an antidote to a poison gas (also connected to breathing, I suppose). All that seems to be a keynote is the reference to the sun looking "as if it were a lamp of earthly flame", which the cultural context (of the two poets mentioned) suggests to us is the introduction of phenomenology: the relation of perception to the physical limits of the perceiver, the law that the qualities of new perceptions are detected by what they resemble, the use of known quantities to describe, by means of a reference frame, unknown quantities.

The sun is too bright ("over-exposed") to see clearly. "But / in shock, rare gases leave their stain to / burn its bright sign on everything.": the gases are neon and its relatives, within bulbs, fluorescent.

Apart from the first and last poems, the work consists of 24 24-line poems, and as this implies there is a grid structure, with horizontal relationships between poems being as important as sequential ones. The poet has explained that he wrote all the first lines, then all the second lines, and so on. He was interested in the quality of visual art whereby all parts of the work are simultaneous, a total set of relationships; the poem is related to the conceptual art of the time, interrogating the physical nature of the medium of art and using arbitrary processes to produce results outside conscious control. The first poem includes lines which appear in the 24 central poems as well as being a rewrite of a 20-line poem in *High Pink on Chrome*.

The fourth stanza says "The evolution of the principle optic/content is an illusion." "Principle" is some kind of weird pun; there is an allusion to a quote from J.D. Bernal, in the 1930s, remarking on the limits of human perceptual equipment, and how a range of new senses would complete our understanding of the universe. Again, the point is that we are limited by our biological equipment: we are biased towards the visible because our eyes are so acute, but what we see is not simply "the world" but only what light (from the sun) bounces off, and information in other spectra we simply pass over. This is also a version of Prynne's

'The development of the main body cavity / is more obscure'. *Optic content* could just mean being happy with what you see.

"And for ever and a day runs on / at arm's length, held with scents/ too vivid to see: beneath / the reckless apex of that hope." I believe this refers to the continuing experience of life, within reach of the dense clusters of nerve-ends; invested with hope. The existential situation of the poet is limited in space and accuracy (by the limits of perceptual equipment), but indefinite in time.

The poem is obstinately domestic, physically sited in the poet's home; it refers frequently to phenomenological themes, and the static quality of the setting may relate to the exhibition of physical limits, which the movement of the perceiving organism tends to blur, since after all we move to overcome the frustration of standing still. The skin is the margin which decides you from now on. The theme also involves continuity, in fact circularity: the seasonal cycle is "the whole spectrum / in a retained sequence / beginning nowhere". While this is a more thorough description of the sun's course than a momentary one, it is also the mapping of an infinite figure. (I thought the "high zero" is perhaps the apparent circle described by the sun, but Crozier denied this in interview.) The other poets talk about the origins of English society, but Crozier denies the existence of an origin, and of a "before". His world ends at a horizon. The movement of the discourse is from one voice to another, "I have *High Zero* as a kind of theatre in which certain knockabout characters can be rapidly led on and led off", although there is also a cycle of observations, i.e. of solar light.

Gases are a repeated theme (for example, the fluorescent bulbs, BAL, and air bubbles on the stalks of irises in a vase). To be sure, anything visible is part of the investigation. There may be a reference to the chemical senses (based on osmosis), which other animals rely on so much more than us, but I can't confirm this.

Does weather affect mood? I suspect that there was a course of events whereby an interest in geography and myth, in a group of poets associated with Prynne and Crozier in the later Sixties, moved on to the space around the body as the site where geography envelops humans. So an interest in geography as a factor in English culture moved on to a recording of intimate scenes, focusing on air and light. This chronicle of hours and days answered the question about "the influence of climate". Merleau-Ponty was brought on stage as someone who was reflecting on the state of the observer as an influence on the observation. The interest in gas may reflect interest in the air around the body, as the milieu to which the body adjusts, and which we draw inside the body with every breath. So, when we read

> In the time it takes
> a beak to probe a grass's root
> or a heart-beat to lose its echo
> within the automatic illusion of memory
> like glass, the sound sharp and clear,
> too brilliant to the touch: within
> the body cavity: unequal pressure
> across the surfaces keeps up
> the polished moment with its smears
> of iridescent after-image

The tone is lyric but we may also reflect that "lyric" could be defined as "the description of sensations inside the body" and that this is a phenomenological poem which continues the lyric beyond simple sensations like hot and cold. Embodiment is profound and infantile at the same time. Evidently we feel emotions as nerve messages from the body cavity, where the viscera are, rather than from the arms and legs. A very early tract on geography is called "peri aeron", concerning the airs, i.e. on climates. The release of sweat as gas, and the dissolving of oxygen gas in the blood, are processes close to how we feel – happiness and comfort are close to our identity as gaseous processes. Space is all around and how we feel is where we are. The shapeless nature of fluids and liquids is in opposition to the definition of shapes and relative sizes by light, which the poem also describes; perhaps the transition from the unbounded to the bounded is the subject matter, with the implication that it is never completed. We can perhaps divide intellectual English poems of the period into those concerned with the origin of knowledge in light and those interested in the origin of categories in language.

One section (that beginning "there they were surrounded / by their infidelities") describes a street demo, seen rather scornfully ("consciousness raised like a / speculative loan"). The politics of this are fraught, but the moment was clearly one where most of the former demonstrators had themselves become disillusioned with the effectiveness of their exhibition of principles. Philosophical poetry is better at exhibiting a symbolic truth. The proposals belong to "the list of recurrent solutions / to problems of the modern world"; cyclicity is here seen as negative, whereas in the rest of the poem it is (apparently) reassuring. Section three also includes references, apparently negative, to the transformation of values.

Two sections (the 10th and 11th poems) seem to deal especially with the use of arbitrary measures which structure consciousness in the way that verticals and horizontals structure the space of a painting. A regular beat inside the nervous system allows one to time incoming signals: their periodicity is faster or slower than the beat. The echoes of footsteps allow us to measure the distance of the person who is walking: at any moment, there is only one echo, but we "hear" a whole series. Perception is different from the model, which is an intellectual thing; it relates the pause between the sound and the echo to a distance. Experience is thus structured by our models as much as by primary perception.

Crozier gave an interview in about 1972 where he describes what looks like the arrival of conceptual procedures in poetry. The atmosphere of *High Zero* is intellectual but also instantaneous. The arbitrary limits of the work demand the ability to make impromptus. By taking on very recent poems by Prynne and James, the poet rejects the recession into deeply internal processes – and upholds the evanescent, social nature of conversation.

Construing a conceptual work as though it is an autobiographical one is a classic way of misreading everything. Not only Crozier, but also Allen Fisher, use formal procedures to guide their poetry. I have had discussions about the possibility of publishing collections of procedures, in order to get across to readers the idea that poets may not just be remembering things that happened to them one day. The purpose of using procedures may be too complex to explain – let's just say that it was in the air in the 1970s, and it was hard to resist trying it out.

## Allen Fisher, *Long Shout to Kernewek*

This was composed in the early '60s and so has no bearing on our theme. It is listed because it was published during our period. It records a very early stage of Fisher's development as a writer. The theme is Cornwall (kernewek means 'Cornish') and it adduces information about history, topography, etc. The language Cornish is also referred to customarily by the adjective, so *Pana yeth yu Kernewek? what kind of language is Cornish?* The title could therefore mean long hail to the Cornish language. Fisher then spent ten years engaged with the conceptual art movement and his conceptual powers were utterly transformed. It was published in 1975.

### Waste as Signal: Allen Fisher, *Sicily* (1973)

This includes no discursive passages and it would be reasonable to say that it can't be read. It was one of four works, not very verbal, which were carried out in the mid-'70s outside the large-scale work on *Place*. "C. *Sicily*, covering system, process, printing and writing." The programme is printed at the start of the book. (My description simplifies significantly, sorry.) Step 1 was to take extracts from existing texts, books or magazines, and cut them up. The cutups are reproduced – four strips torn are laid side by side to create new running lines across the set. The next steps transform this inorganic assembly. An operator picks key words and ticks them, then selects words that seem to go together. Using a typewriter and carbon paper, new text is created which uses the ticked words and is apparently coherent. This is retyped to remove the gaps and so on. At this point we have a realm of language which was not produced by a human mind and is full of patterns which are non-personal and reflect, if you like, the unconscious of language or the Noise of the social machine. The copy I saw printed the waste words as well as the output of the "ticked" words, so you have the process being shown as well as the output. This could reflect a long debate on documentary film, where you see the finished film apparently capturing unmediated reality, but you start to ask about any film that was exposed but edited out, and perhaps ask for a showing where you would see everything and the selection process would be foregrounded.

The title *Sicily* comes from a source sentence about the Mafia giving the US Army control of Sicily in 1943. Part of the project was to recycle all the waste generated by the process so that it is incorporated into the final work. The book is partly on yellow paper which may relate to lemons as the key product of Sicily, but anyway several colours are used. Fisher worked, then, for a building materials merchant, and was very interested in waste and waste technologies. Allen said "*Sicily* has another aspect to it […], in that it was decided at the start of writing *Sicily* that, which is a poem written using very complex mechanisms, mainly mechanical, was that it wouldn't allow any waste. So the words that are being engineered and brought about had to be used. As the process involved a whole range of photocopying, I ended up producing a whole book of waste. Waste products from the writing of *Sicily*. It's almost unreadable. And that's been made evident by the fact that it's green ink printed on green paper, and yellow ink on yellow paper and so on. That business of waste, and letting the waste stay, and making use of the use of waste in some way or other, has a kind of, there's an ambience of the period, in the Seventies, to do with the early ecologists[.]" Also, "That business of waste has always interested me and I did work in waste management, for a short period. The company I was working for were running out of new ideas, and they started to develop ideas to do with waste management. I got very intrigued and interested. They for instance, produced a chimney, a concrete chimney made from the ash of volcanoes and suchlike, and it was very good for very hot chimneys, when you were trying to burn haystacks for instance, hay bales, and hay burning has a very high thermal capacity. It burns very slowly, very hot. So most chimneys you put it in would just fall apart. So you have to produce a special chimney for that kind of burning. There was a time, more in Scandinavia than in Britain, where an interest in burning waste in warehouses that would then heat the warehouse." So the printed object *Sicily* makes a statement about recycling and the process of generating product and waste. The text is so to speak a support for the write-up rather than *vice versa*. The end-output script is a point where language becomes subject to mathematical processes and in fact such processes emerge as basic to natural language.

Conceptual art has a free quality, that is the output is designed to facilitate thought and debate. Not everyone regards thought or debate as good things. *Sicily* can help me think about the selection process in culture. Obviously, every sixteen-year-old reels out the piece about the literary canon stifling diversity sixteen times a day. If there were 6,000 books of poetry published, in the UK, in the 1970s, it is worth thinking about what happened to ones nobody read. You read a book on someone's recommendation, but someones didn't read everything. There are pipes where new information can enter the system, but their diameter is limited. Reading the "waste" (and we could spend hours devising more accurate lexical terms for the non-selected, left in the ground, nihilated, underground, etc.) could produce deeply unexpected results. Evidently my career as a critic has been based on pushing into view poets from the realm of invisibility, but I only read what people suggest to me, not the whole lightless mass. We can imagine an alternative strategy where I would have picked books not on quality but at random, and where I would analyse them not for aesthetic merit but for formal properties, or how they staged ideology.

### *Musky glasslight forms pool*: **Allen Fisher, *The Art of Flight***

The title is a translation of Bach's treatise 'Die Kunst der Fuge', since "fugue" literally means "flight". The printed vision (1976) is incomplete. There is a tape of a performance of the entire piece, which involves four tape-recorders; the overlay of multiple voices is essential to the intent of the piece, which explores the way attention works when there are multiple areas of stimuli needing to be processed. The link between a central dominant self and perceptual environments tailored to be simple and easily subdued is what is to be revealed by the polyphony. The text however is about the perception of light, and the cover shows a photo of rhodopsin cells in the retina. The sleeve note on the tape says "'Flight' is fugue, folly, and fancy. The work was composed between November 1974 and July 1975." An example is:

> Full beams     beams on coastal water
> blue now green breaks screen the yellow
> absorbing the blue     announcing our joy;
> their herald of disaster, the yellow inside
> blue-fall beams sight as green sheen
> by the beach. Threads silk into dew
> musky glasslight forms pool.
> Halobium photosynthesises
> the raying sun in the form of
> electro-chemical gradients.
> Protein wilts pool shattered white light
> where large particles haze-close sun.
> Vision revealed in foggy opaque […]
>                    (from XXV, 'Bacteriorhodopsin')

A note in the programme statement *Prosyncel* says "The *Art of Flight* offers opportunities for four voices (on tapes) simultaneously and continuous readings incorporating ideas from Terry Riley, Steve Reich and George Crumb. The lyric content is concerned formally with the uses of light and dark in science and literature (with of course religion)."

(The named people were composers using "systems" processes.) The print issue is called *Paxton's Beacon*, partly because it only includes half of the pages of *Art of Flight* (as you can tell from the numbering), but also because Joseph Paxton designed the Crystal Palace, a glass building "using the structures of water-lilies in Chatsworth". The glass let in multiple rays of light and it became a beacon when it caught fire in 1936. The illustrations are from Isaac Newton's *Opticks*, a plan of condensing light from a lighthouse, and the colossi of Aboo Simbell inside the Crystal Palace. The issue with focus and semi-focal areas is perhaps how knowledge uses models and reaches its credibility within those models, a feature of which is the removal of ambiguity and so the creation of a clear focal area – in which undivided attention can thrive. A knowledge-model is supposed to relate to reality in some way, so at some time the model must make the transition into a real world of multiple overlapping patterns of stimuli or event. Political policies are justified in terms of models which are tried out, but which are then tested by a selective attention to witnesses and to areas of effect or impact.

Selective attention is arguably quite important to social power and to how the official record is constructed. *Art of Flight* has a simple programme in cognitive psychology, a preparation for more complex set-ups later. Perhaps the key movement in *Art of Flight* is when the number of tracks builds up enough that you can't follow all the voices – that handful of missed grip where you can't seize it all any more. The concept of inattention as something flowing, alive, affecting every line, is significant for the time. A definition for thinking about what you don't know could be philosophy.

The weight of the word *fuga* could be that it is a line of music which runs away from you.

## Digging for wasp-grubs: *Change: a Prospectus*, by Antony Lopez (1978)

This is one of the famous A4 stapled photocopied productions of the era. Several of the poems are prefaced with hexagrams, and the overall design nods to the *Book of Changes*, used for divination (with yarrow stalks). The cover shows a sky full of birds migrating. So our state is one of wondering about the future. In 1978, this meant wondering about the transition to socialism. The poems can be used for divination. They use simple syntax like translations from classical Chinese.

There are 20 poems (to a total of about 160 lines), which, although there is no explicit articulation between them, all relate to the theme of revolutionary change. Poem 1 describes birds migrating. Poem 2 describes a journey for which there is no map and the problem of coming home. Poems 5 and 6 describe the exploitation (of everybody, presumably) by the Church and the landowners, while telling us that the primary producers can see, not only the parasitical upper classes, but also the future.

The book is as it were a negative image from which we have to develop the real subject of the poem: we are about to put out to sea, and the memories we have of life inland are drifting away from us – the real point is life on the further shore, which the book never reaches. The real subject is a pristine, radiant, featureless circle – the future society, which it is our task as readers to imagine. The lack of explicit, classifying discourse leaves us with complete freedom intact. This is a moment of perfect balance where we can sum up our true wishes and our true understanding of how the world works. We could describe the language of the book as a deliberate withdrawal from the historically particular and from categories; everyday experience is being peeled away so that we can see time yet to come in its full extent. Because the new society will be so different from the existing one, the resemblances will be only the most basic and unchanging elements of human social order – this is how the timeless gets into the poem (although this withdrawal can also be defined as a *liminal process*).

The third and fourth poems discuss coinage, a theme which appears in a number of poems of the time. Perhaps the idea is that something went wrong with the invention of money, the whole commodity circulation system being imperfect at mediating between needs and productive forces. There may be a pun on change (small coins) and change (political).

Poem 7 is a report on a text whose true form cannot be recovered and which may not have existed, as it was a living thing: 'many variants of this text are extant / each records a stage in process'. This is an attack (one of hundreds in modern poetry) on organised knowledge: where government and corporations (and the professions?) rely on formal records as valid memory, to attack the documents and their relation to the original event, is to disqualify the authorities who control social process. Along with the attack on the pricing mechanism, this composes an attack on the information by means of which society reflects on itself

– exposing the arbitrary under the rational.

Poems 14 to 16 describe simple, Neolithic skills:

> weave nutwood hurdles for a sheep-pen
> or daubed with mud a wattle hut
> fire the walls, line the floor with baked earth
> rough cured skins breed fleas and lice
> we know which wood burns with least smoke
> where to dig for wasp-grubs and tubers
> we break ice on the pool and drink
>
> (poem XIV)

and seem to anticipate a society with much less wealth but much more autonomy. (Nutwood probably means *hazelwood*.) This reflects a belief that we are trapped into collaboration with capitalism by false needs which we are taught by advertising. There are indications of seasons changing but not otherwise of the passage of time. The author is probably also thinking of the need for a sustainable economy, because he talks about ecology and pollution in poem 19.

Poem 18 describes the migration to Britain when there was still a land bridge; the migration of the Germanic tribes across the North Sea. This is symbolically the foundation of English society – by a voyage through perilous waters, and of uncertain outcome. It recovers the history of the last fourteen centuries as the unexpected result of a previous collective risk – recalling that humans can launch into the unknown and don't have to just cleave to inherited customs.

## *Manhattan's needlepoint mercury:*
## Jeremy Reed, *The Isthmus of Samuel Greenberg* (1976)

This is a poem in 25 parts. The jacket text explains that the subject is three poets: first Reed and Hart Crane, then the "more shadowy and catalytic figure" of Samuel Greenberg, who died of TB aged 23, who is an isthmus between Reed and Crane. Reed said in an email that he was "mashing Crane/Zukofsky/Prynne". The first poem explains how Reed's "febrilely posthumous hand" was stimulated to write by Greenberg's passion, which pricked "with snow's sensitivity / on Manhattan's needlepoint mercury". The needle is the stimulus

(literally a *prick*) and an indicator; mercury is the sensitive fluid of a
thermometer, that measures the fever of *febrile*, but is also mercurial.
The snow takes up every shape but melts rapidly; it could resemble
needlepoint, which is very delicate (and often *white*). The needle points
are the tops of skyscrapers, as a fever chart. The first thing that strikes us
is the combination of narcissism (Greenberg appears as a link between
Reed and a once well-known American poet, but the isthmus image
claims even Hart Crane as an extension of Reed), and the Gothic:
whoever is the subject of the poems (a sort of compound of three poets,
I suppose) is permanently in an anomalous state of mind where high
pain levels make for super-sensitivity and normal logic is suspended
in favour of something which is supernatural and physiological at the
same time. In part 25:

> Falling, the circle's always contracting
> to an imaginary node. Right foot
> in space, the left bird-hooked to scaffolding,
> a viscous curlicue of nausea
> entrailed in white ribbons about the throat,
> fluorescently shell-bald, to leave swinging
> a mannequin, and make an armed retreat
> into the black pores of an oil cellar.
>                            Dying
> is not the extroversion envisaged,
> but something pain withdraws to a subdued
> release.
> So rare the crisis that the lungs explode
> like swiftly compressed riding fish.
> Leaving total suspension, two red valves
> paralysed by the pistol's butt;
> while outward flashlights on the dummy hiss,
> pitter, and jockey pigeons across street.
>                               ('Exit 5')

Greenberg was not a native English speaker and when he encountered
English literary poetry he snatched up its vocabulary in a way which was
profoundly unidiomatic but also extremely liberated and expressive.
English become an artificial language for him. Although this poet likes
to make rare lexical choices, the problem with this kind of poetry is less

the style than the literal meaning, unusual states of mind. Someone researching ghosts found that air waves of about 19 Hz cause a ripple on the eyeball; Reed in this book is permanently showing the world through a distorted eyeball, a jewel inverting light. An unidentified character is clambering on a scaffolding which itself is gripping, very high up, the side of a skyscraper. The circle which contracts seems to be the impact point which he imagines ending his fall, if it ever starts. (It recalls the splash where Crane struck the sea after jumping from the SS *Orizaba*.) The point must get larger as he approaches it, but in terms of time and possibility it is getting tighter, closing in on him. He is there to hang a mannequin; I don't get what the flashlights on the dummy are (Greenberg was a garment worker so it could be a literal tailor's dummy), but it has torch customisation. They are hot, and rain hisses when it falls onto the glass. A poet hooks one foot to scaffolding to make this attachment, a fake execution. He feels nausea, due to the danger. His neck is naked and white (like an eggshell). He then goes right down, the building is oil-fired and there must be a cellar with an oil-tank in it. The scene is intercut with a death (of a real human). The two valves belong to someone's heart, and we are seeing a cardiac crisis described in a technical way, like a car crash or a boat wreck. Throughout, the body of the protagonists is described in the language of machinery, as if the characters were part robot. This combines with a sort of hysteria, where body parts abandon their nature to act out the emotions of the characters. A blow with a pistol to the midriff would cause the heart to stop temporarily; a "suspension" which parallels the hanging of the dummy. The flashlights are moving because the mannequin is swinging: disturbing pigeons on the building opposite. At the end of the poem, there is a crowd beneath, who think the dangling figure is a suicide, while inside a basin holds "floating red string of a segmented brain", some appalling shock of pain and illness for which the fake hanging is just a metaphor. I am guessing the torches were there to attract attention to the fake cadaver.

There are about 40 volumes of Reed's poetry, as we found out when trying to assemble a *Selected* with four editors (a project halted on the runway). Generalisation must be false in the face of so much raw data. Hesitatingly, I sketch three phases – Gothic, the phase of darkness and distortion, including the reflex of Samuel Greenberg's hallucinatory and neo-Romantic misuse of English words; the *neo-con* phase where the language has that glow of affluence and serenity that art took on as camouflage during the social wreckage and political terror of the 1980s, as the projection of sensitivity invokes shelter and patronage as counter-balance; and the phase of *fanfic*, where the keywords are *glamour, erotica, celebrity*, and poems about Claudia Schiffer fight it out with poems about Elvis. The Gothic phase includes *Bleecker Street* (1981) and probably stops there.

Reed's poems are like photos, each burned into a memory stratum, each a homage to light, the whole a library of thousands of exposures. But what they catch is the subjective reality of the subject, something even more evanescent and more intense than light. The point about photographs is to trap the invisible, not the visible.

As suggested, Reed is close to Barker (apart from them being friends, in the Seventies), and the isthmus can be seen as a continuation of *In Memory of David Archer*. The text shows *Isthmus* as being composed in November–December 1973, so a few months after *Archer* was published. I don't get why Reed never connected with the British Poetry Revival or the New Left/hippie thing, but he had other things on his mind and it seems he made a connection, literary and social, straight back to poets around in the '40s (even the '30s, to be literal), Barker and Gascoyne. Both had that self-igniting mix of surrealism, a Gothic sensibility, moments of intense biographical focus which are imbued with horror, and the setting in a special part of London with rapid pick-ups and also a gallery of damaged people exuding glamour and need. Reed hung out in the same few streets where Barker and Gascoyne had drunk in the 1940s. *Isthmus* was published by Trigram, Asa Benveniste's firm, and Reed published a memoir of Benveniste in 2016.

The organisation of the work does not show temporal progression nor a division into three voices. There is only one voice. The course appears to show that the last 5 poems, so Exit 1 to Exit 5, are about Reed and are explorations of suicide. Before them, we get 'Intake' 1-5, essentially about chemicals:

> Each word proliferates in delusion
> inside failure. My chinese-heroin
> and cabinet .45 placate megrims,
> as sipping blood through a straw to fulfil
> renewed respiration I contemplate
> the red horsehair torn from my sleeping cot.
> In cyanosis my features duplicate.
> Another's eyewhite makes the type-key fall.

My intake of rarefied green-oxygen
revivifies experimental drive.

This may explain the crossover between the mechanical and the human. The reference to someone else's eye points to either Crane or Greenberg, the inspirations of the poem.

Cyanosis is turning blue, oxygen deprivation related to a heroin overdose or to asthma (which appears a few lines later on). This underlines the *rare crisis* of the earlier poem, where the *rarety* means air too thin to breathe, an oxygen deficiency.

The poem describes physiological states in preference to states of mind, and the states concerned are normally the result of violence. We should look past the immediate shock, and ask what caused these wounds. Most probably there is an earlier story of being wounded. We do not hear the story, but to think of it as gay identity in a stolidly heterosexual world, inability to conform in a society which crushes nonconformity and turns it into neurosis, may be on the right lines. The physical forms of damage act as a message, but at the same time they deny dialogue. The mutual investment which allows dialogue is missing – the original damaged thing. The wish to use the body as a set of messages leads naturally on to a later preoccupation with stardom – the model Claudia Schiffer (in *Claudia Schiffer's Red Shoes*) becomes the theme of poems, an idealised and envied body as an *inversion* of Gothic mutilation. The rich array of expressive objects in *Isthmus* evolves into the wealth of covetable accessories in the later poems.

**The skin as an organ of sense: Philip Jenkins, *Cairo*
(part 1, 1978; publication parts 1 & 2 together, 1981)**

The text presents a series of powerful autonomous images, centres of energy. It starts with the description of someone (an I) in a bed, in some psychological state beyond the reach of lucidity and sense. This is "the darkest segment of the film", where "the night / a diamond / hard tonality". The I starts from this blank to construct a world from the available shapes.

Book 1 is continually about the line between nothingness and elementary awareness, which seems to be easy to cross. The figure in bed seems to have a longing for water; this takes us to Egypt, because "It is the moist principle controls all genesis and generation", which is followed by sparse but esoteric information about the Nile. The Nile is simply the principle of all water. This brings us to Cairo.

The third page describes how "In 1974 I wrote a poem called 'A Sailor's Suit and Cap'. This is a line from a song by the Velvet Underground titled 'Heroin': 'Two years after that I began to live it.'" The content of the poem seems to be dreamlike associations of vivid and alien images:

> In 1964, I dreamt that I was sewn into a carcass of meat hanging in a butcher's shop. Inside, I was conscious of colour moving slowly as a succession of projected slides from rich red through purples and browns into black.

> In 1977 at the Vortex, Siouxsie and the Banshees performed a song in which the protagonist mutilates himself before impaling himself on a butcher's hook *anticipating new skin.*

> In the Serapeum at Sakkarah in the third century before Christ, Asar Hapi, the Apis bull of Memphis into whom was sewn the dead Osiris,

> Called the life of Osiris

> Animated by the soul of Osiris.
> (from Cairo, Book 2, 4)

The Vortex was in Hanway Street, I seem to recall. The logic of the three images of a skin, a web of nerves, being shed and acquired is clear but dreamlike. We can see these as the pipe dreams of opiates. Anyway, the power of the images is the principle of the poem.

Jenkins comes from Wales, began with concrete poems, published a pamphlet called *A Sailor's Suit and Cap*, edited an avant-garde magazine in Nottingham, was a fan of punk rock. Cairo was founded after the Muslim conquest and was not there in the Pharaonic era.

An email from the author from 2004 says "Cairo? I've never of course been there. The title came I think from the Cairo Museum, reading about the collection [...]. There were 3 parts to *Cairo* each miraculously appearing 2 years later than the last. I waited another 2 years but nothing came so I assume that was that. I don't know that I can say much about what it's about. Origins? Yes about the state of chaos where everything was an undifferentiated continuum undivided into whatever randomly would be marked off and named. Before agreeing on what we would recognise and give names to, what did we have to talk about? Nothing of course, no language, just a terrible sense of dread." The Banshees song was called 'Carcass'. The division between inside and out proposed by the skin is the start of difference.

A skin is a sense organ and the act of detaching a skin and wrapping it around a body can be seen as the acquisition of a sensory world. It is as if the body were inside an eye. This corresponds to a human form being represented in a picture. The carcass image continues the poem's theme of the construction of a world from bare and at first ambiguous sense data. It is, fittingly, a visual equivalent for that theme. The poem treats the faculty of sight as an evolutionary information program which somehow grows from prickling skin cells to sophistication; Egypt is a parallel, perhaps as the origin of civilisation and its first step:

> the primordial snake, Neheb-kau, 'Provider of Attributes',
> holding all subsequent creation within its folds
>
> we are here
>         gods apparently and yet
> our faces remain unformed
>
>       'in the infinity
>       the nothingness
>       the nowhere and
>       the dark'
>
> we are the uncreated
> the predistinguishable
> we are the characteristics of the Abyss.
>                         ('Cairo')

There was a third book, composed in roughly 1982. It was published in *Shearsman* magazine during 2005. I am inclined to see *Cairo* as an extension of the writer's original home in visual poetry, for example the 'Homage to Rothko'. It is as if the movement starts with pictures and the verbal accounts are secondary. Someone pursuing visual art in around 1970 was not going to be looking for beautiful landscapes but asking questions about how the visual space is organised and how the exclusion of almost every feature from it could create an acuity, a philosophical urgency, asking the spectators to look at the programmes underlying vision rather than the objects of vision.


*Conclusions on Long Poems*

With so much material (towards 4,000 pages) all kinds of pattern can be found and say nothing about a bemusing diversity. Nonetheless some emergent themes are worth discussing.

It seems to me that long poems by mainstream poets like Thwaite, Hooker, Wain, Hill, Humphreys, are similar to the alternative poetry. The opposition tends to dissolve if we look at the genre of long poems. There is a separate issue for poets like MacLean, Bowen, Turnbull, Gwyn Thomas, who obviously belong to different realms of style. These shared features include the restriction of the poem to the experience of a single individual, or privatisation; the shifting of stress from factual knowledge to intellectual method in framing and highlighting the material; the move away from narrative or drama or action; the collapse of a stable system of moral norms and imperatives, to be replaced by unquiet but essentially personal intellectual curiosity and model-making; the advance of untunable noise or dissonance within the models, and the pre-eminence of doubt as a response to it.

The form strained the capacity of a trade adjusted to magazines, anthologies, and short books. The current which swept poets away from the market, and into these uncharted waters, must have been strong. The long poem is a vote against the common stock of knowledge. It allows the poet to seize the context. It permits the construction of a whole new space, with its own rules. The long poem replaced the conventional knowledge of the Movement poem with knowledge which was constructed inside the poem. The Underground came into being because the mainstream structures failed to support the way poetry was moving. It made extra demands on space and funding, and the restrictions came to be emotive issues. The difficulties which editors and publishers put in the way of long poems demonstrate that there was a huge *creative* pressure to write in this way. This did represent a line of advance for British poetry.

The starting-point for these poems is questions which are rather older and which were often put by readers of poetry. The questions were, *what is your moral and theological vision?* And *what is your political commitment and system?* The long poems connect to the questions but don't answer them – the answers are more offers of an aesthetic pattern or an open method for reasoning about history and social processes. In fact, dealing with social narratives converges with an aesthetic stance – the way you reason is a display of sensibility. The answer is always *welcome to my world* (and that world only shows in a longer context).

These poems rarely address politics, but Kazantzis's poem 'Queen Clytemnestra' is a precious exception. It contains a narrative. The story has an authority figure behaving badly – a king, in fact. He vacates his office by murder. The murderer, Clytemnestra, ruled Sparta while he was away at war – and rules the place much better than he did. This fulfils my idea of a political poem. Admittedly the events are taking place some thirty-four centuries in the past. I cite it because it shows up almost all the other poems. I am guessing the background is counter-cultural boredom – a total lack of interest in the thoughts of anyone over thirty. More forgivably, it could be a view, linked to the *Annales* school of historians, that the powers in the land did not matter and tiny shifts in the structures of everyday life were what counted. Either way, all these left-wing poets don't show much interest in left-wing arguments.

The reason for the larger scale of poems in the 1970s is an internal exile, a rejection of the values of the news media and of what political and cultural authorities were saying.

This rejection could either be from the Right or the Left and was certainly more to do with the failure of authority than with dislike of their success. The power structure had lost its grip, basic relationships were changing, and radical groups were powerful and courageous. The Cold War conservatives were in a pessimistic mood, really anticipating shifts of power which would weaken the grip of the rich over the economy, the military build-up, the political consensus, or industrial discipline. It makes sense to talk about "the system", because an alternative was right outside the door, and really seemed about to walk in and take over.

There was an alternative *everything*. The increasing innovation, depth, and complexity of art in the 1970s have to do with a wish to develop new values. The despair at current politics also looks like a nervous breakdown.

The reasons why the values of the Labour-Conservative consensus were failing also, obviously, highlighted flaws in the new values. The motive for the long poem was probably, therefore, a state of conjecture and uncertainty, where the organisation of personal and collective behaviour was up in the air, as part of revolutionary social change. A key factor is then the reader's capacity (singular and collective) for dealing with incomplete forms.

Perhaps they define them as improperly formed, and reject them, with a businesslike snap. Perhaps waiting for a long time amounts to despair and disillusion. And perhaps the incomplete is an object of optimism and fascination. To give up completeness is also a renunciation of authority. The reader's rules for treating uncertainty certainly dictate the quality of their experience when reading these conjectural poems. The end of the bar line?

The short poem can challenge social and semantic structures by omitting them (as pop poetry did), but cannot demonstrate new ones. Poets escaped the reach of banal judgments either by *involution*, the development of radical styles, or by *extension*, giving the poem more duration, allowing more complex semantic configurations. Both of these tended to lose any reader who did not have the same level of openness.

If the geometry of a cultural matrix is truly shared, then a fragment of it implies the whole, and it is possible for poets to make statements about social relations within the stylistic plane. Reflexive poets attuned to this regard with contempt poets who are not. The question for us is whether any of the reflexive poets are working with more than a highly organised narcissism, the skill of a couturier, or whether they are addressing something outside themselves – the space within which language is spoken, or the rules by which social action is ordered.

Narrative is rare in these poems. The question of what line of sense flows from one page to another is hard to capture in what are offered as sets of juxtapositions. When does a link stop being a link? We can distinguish between a *style environment* and a *narrative environment*:

*style* (static; self-referential; one person only; cannot engage in test and conflict; self-conscious)

*narrative* (changeable; deals with a shared reality; unpredictable; not self-fulfilling; exposes characters to test and conflict, to learning experiences)

Style is differentiated and unified in the same way that a narrative is, but populated not by characters but by figures or distinctive features. It reproduces its own internal memory whenever the style re-appears; this context of interpretive rules can also flow from one author to another.

Style can become a social logic, recording a social vision of short extents as a narrative records a social vision of large-scale events. *Instamatic Poems* (by Edwin Morgan) is a transitional point between a narrative and a poem whose subject is its own point of view; the poems in it are playing a shared game but have no unity of scene or situation. This game unity could reflect a poet's temperament, but is for the ultra-sophisticated Morgan a deliberate break with the (personal and social) past in the form of a set of rules, i.e. almost a naked social structure. The shift from a serial poem to one which represents a field of which all parts are present at the start and the end points also to the idea of lifestyle – affluence makes choices about daily life central. The shift away from social radicalism to privatisation, in which ideas and poems are forms of consumption, is hard to date even if it seems to make the whole effort pointless. If the poet is offering a whole subjective world, we are interested in depth rather than in going ahead, and we don't want to leave. *Soliloquies of a Chalk Giant*, by Jeremy Hooker, is about a chalk giant. You could describe its poems as a vortex – energy moves *around* a point, you could print the poems in any order. Each one lets us sink deeper into the situation of a chalk giant, in his hillside. I am not saying that this is boring, more that it is like the dissolution of forwards and back in a two-chord song structure. Is this a private world or one in which we all belong together, divisions dissolved?

Myth appears in these poems, as part of the palette; but they form a strong contrast to Classical mythological poems. The oppositions which are significant to them are: central versus local-communal authority; the power of money versus less impersonal social bonds; tradition versus reason; Wales versus England; alienation versus fulfilment; symbolic versus sensory experience; subjective versus objective knowledge. These are not topics which mattered to Hesiod.

Four of the poems discussed mention the Anglo-Saxon invasions of Britain, generally dated to the 5th to 8th centuries AD. Perhaps there is a shared imaginary which poets go to in order to find their visions. The significance of the Invasions is that they represent a meltdown of the system of land-owning, which is basic to everything else. What is the point of taking us back to 500 AD? One answer is "showing your materials". The poem is written in the English language. The point of origin of this "material" is the 5<sup>th</sup> century AD, and its shape is due to the geography of the Settlements, the shape of Britain and of the coasts from which they departed. The poets don't seem interested in saying that the land was unequally divided. The attraction is seeing the board at move zero – the field before the game began to be played. All the poets seem interested in the "fore-time" before the rise of mediaeval civilisation; all seem interested in the origin of our customs and social structure; none shows a situation between several people, and which is altered by a series of events which it structures; all see the power order as arbitrary. All have suppressed the signposts, the "ifs" and "therefores" which lead an argument: the discourse of the poem is "before" these, and this beforeness is part of poemicity. This points to a latent theory about the ambiguity of reality, which is chopped and channelled by the social structure, which is stored in subliminal cognitive filters distributed over the whole population.

The intrication of poems with the contents of books (of radical philosophy, politics, history, etc.) depends on collective representations, expressing wishes and the need for play as much as re-arrangement of experience. These long poems show us, through an exhausting effort to seize and externalise, experience itself, as it is staged by human agents, in long or short strips.

The age of long poems came to an end. I have the impression that the logical development of long structures was checked by the budget problems of harassed editors – the Underground could not afford it all. It attracted too many writers, not enough readers.

Publishers became reluctant to risk this kind of work. If it was for aesthetic reasons – well, somehow I've never heard anyone mention or explain what these were. Possibly, interest shifted towards montage – which is really an aspect of parataxis. But also, a return to governmental authority, and majority governments, removed the basis for the long poem. The unavoidable questions of the mid-70s were resolved by a wide-spectrum surrender to the power of capital – a return to an older state of affairs, the status quo. Alternatives became less fascinating.

# Generations

The active poets of our decade run from one born in 1897 to several born in the first half of the 1950s. Generational shifts form a low-resolution pattern, if any. Yet shifts in recording emotions, in the use of heightened language, in the mapping of inner experience via grids of objective knowledge, in the belief that describing objects is a proof of feelings, that feelings can be proved or disproved, seem to occur through time. The shifts may connect to acting styles.

## LUSH AND DATED

In the 1940s, both poetry and films were going in two different directions: one of intense subjectivity and one of documentary. We have a group of pre-empirical poets, in our set of data, and they all have a strong religious bent: this is true for Jones, MacLean, Bowen, Raine, Barker, and Beeching. It is noticeable that Barker's poem (*In Memory of David Archer*, 1973) and *Deserted Shore* both have a biographical focus and include significant amounts of present-time scenes being lived by human beings. Raine and Barker were born in 1908 and 1913 respectively, and this may be part of the chronological shift which groups poets who matured before about 1950. It becomes obvious that the personality of the poet-narrator is being foregrounded, and this is a key to how Raine and Barker write. I associate this with a certain kind of film of the 1940s, where the turning of the lead actors from humans into stars is the main thrust of the design. This focus is exacting and other elements of the film have to be lightened to make it flow. It cuts down the action to a few individuals, it reduces the focus on realism, it makes music more important. The films (which were the house style of Gainsborough Films) were called melodramas at the time. Actors like Stewart Granger, Margaret Lockwood, Sally Gray, Anton Walbrook, James Mason, only appeared in this kind of film. The preoccupation of Barker and Raine with the human personality matches this genre of film rather well. It may be helpful to imagine their poems as being delivered by Margaret Lockwood or Stewart Granger, and modern acting styles certainly couldn't do very much with them. The line sweeps social analysis off screen to allow feelings to be at the centre all the time; restoring the effects of financial limits, economic calculation, etc., would weaken the central thrust. The effect of making the reader's feelings more vivid and less contingent on other factors is profound and I don't think it has gone away with the decades. The films did have plots, but the intrigue of events was secondary, instead emotional scenes involving close-ups, and the reactions of two figures to each other, are central. The other person is the most important thing in the first person's life, just as the faces are the most important thing in the film. The plots are hard to remember, and I speak as a fan of this kind of film. Both *David Archer* and *Deserted Shore* have plots which are weak to non-existent, but this may be part of fulfilling the needs of a genre. The prominence of music in the films may give us a clue to the prominence in Barker's poem of surrealist or allegorical passages which have no clear meaning but which are subjectively charged. To reiterate, most British films were not star-based cinema.

What it looks like is that the Christian religion had supplied a language in which the individual soul was central, and that poetry had absorbed the language of religion note for note. The notion of the cosmos as going through an emotional drama of love was intertwined with the idea of biography as part of a cosmic drama. The love between God and the Christian was the model for all other ideas about love. But the decline of religion meant that humanity was no longer at the centre of the cosmos. The collapse of sublime religious feelings brought, it would seem, the collapse of sublime feelings in poetry, and especially in poems about love. Life no longer involved moments laden with destiny, and liberating or imprisoning the soul, so poems could not record them. The shifts in public taste around 1947–55 involved a package in which pictorialism, grand egoism, surrealism, the sublime, religious feelings, rhetoric, were bundled up together and all became old-fashioned. The older poetry was richer in some ways, take Beeching's couplet

> An obsequy for ghosts, a firework flower,
> Since, like black seed, the young and brave are dead[.]

The newer poetry is just not so high-flown, laden with meaning, charged with internal tension. But people also saw the sublime style as theatrical and out of date. Avoiding writing about feelings is a big topic in British poetry.

The physical world obstinately remained devoid of any messages from God. While the undermining of egoistic lyric is associated with the Marxist-inspired new literary criticism of the 1960s, it is clear that this undermining was a major feature already in the 1950s.

Unwinding the text in classrooms, over decades, also meant unwinding the author. It looks as if the empirical bias of that decade deflated autobiography along with Communism and the excitements of the mass media.

It is possible to describe all these changes as the arrival of inhibitions. Artistic figures, simultaneously linguistic and psychological, had been desired and envied; each stroke disallowed some of these. They receded into costume drama. We can get at modern poetry through its bareness. I am not persuaded that the poetry audience cares for these inhibitions. I suspect that the audience would rather have passionate love poems in suitable language than something sceptical and linguistically awkward. New poetry often believes in private myths – a recurring affective pattern which involves reality; and Raine might be a model for this, with her vision which includes strata from the stars to patterns in turbulent water to human passions, which has that dense internal lattice binding it and almost no connection with reality.

In our time-bound list, *In Memory of David Archer, On a Deserted Shore*, and *Myth of Myself* are all artistically compromised. They still aspire to the sublime but they don't instantly prove that modern poetry has gone down a wrong track.

## THE SOUND OF PRESTIGE

The short version of Thwaite's "two poetries" essay is that poets persuaded by meritocracy wrote poetry with declining aesthetic appeal but upscale rigour and moral authority; then they lost the initiative to a group who *re-aestheticised the poem*. He draws a convincing connection between meritocratic educational styles and inhibited poetry. For, "Given an academic situation, the student will do what he's been trained to do, whether it makes sense to him or not. But he won't bring to the work a wholeness of response or even the full play of his intelligence, because part of him feels that he's inherited a meaningless and arid methodology. The art that really touches him will be spontaneous, easy, unambiguous, untouched by academicism and disapproved of by it." If the essay has a weakness, it is that he stays inside the education system, which most people concerned migrated out of at the age of 21 or 22. Surely alienation continues in adult life, and the conclusion is that during the working day the mode is meritocratic and conforming to directives, i.e. employed, but in leisure hours the mode is hedonistic, social, and culture-oriented. Again, this asks poetry to be enjoyable rather than results-oriented.

The new poems did not have moral density – their goal was to offer conceptual models which would be as interesting, and productive of unforeseen variations, as possible. Thus they elicited a chorus of calls saying they did not release a series of signals which would convince the audience (those over 30) that they possessed rigour and authority and so were Real Poems. The new style essentially switched off the functions of exact memory, of exposing ideology, and of recording moral truths in a declining religious tone, which emerged as being part of meritocracy and passing exams rather than of artistic creation.

The style of the 1950s has an aspect which needs careful unpacking. Most of the poets who got into print and reviewed in that decade, and in the Sixties too, had a secure educational background in Oxford or Cambridge universities, probably following time at one of the country's best schools, public or grammar. Allott's anthology of modern poetry (2nd version, 1962) included 86 poets of whom 6 were female (7%) and 34 studied at Oxford University (39.5%). Thomas Blackburn's anthology, from 1960, narrower in focus (1945–60 only), also included 40% Oxford poets. Education made people more confident as writers, but there is a consumer-pull effect too – the product captures an Oxford-lifestyle nimbus and this was a significant part of what the purchaser was paying for. (Sean O'Brien's comparable anthology of 1998, covering the whole period since 1945, only has 22% Oxford graduates.)

Most people who approach poetry from the angle of sociology ascribe to the tier of privileged individuals a kind of display attitude towards their knowledge and social position, as if they were expensive cars which had to be driven out and up and down all the time. But this is not what we see in the 1950s. The prestige style of mid-century was, obviously, something penitential and drab. It was deeply unpleasurable and sought to repress egoism. Social esteem seemed to mean a lack of self-esteem. The reader is not being offered access to the wonders of cultural expertise and elite institutions. The offer is more a cold bath.

The sociological approach generally goes on to assume that all these educated people wrote in the same way, and further that they all disliked another kind of poetry, usually the kind of poetry which the writer has a stake in. This is also hard to prove. This privileged group not displaying assets or selves is not acting like a ruling class. Yet they also seem to own the rules.

Sociology may be pushing us in the wrong direction here. There are other societies where display and high-flown language work quite differently. In traditional Welsh and Gaelic poetry, for example, the subject of the poems is families at the top of the social system, they are shown doing high-prestige expensive things, and the language of poetry is of the apex, it corresponds with the subject matter because it is audibly prestigious. This all seems to fit together very well. The poems are about display objects (or animals – horses etc.) and are themselves display objects. This gives us expectations about how poetry should work which modern English poetry is disconcertingly far from.

As it turns out, the English poems are not about important individuals. They are replaced by the poet as a domestic creature. The expensive objects and exalted language are discarded in favour of the existential, empirical, unenthusiastic, domestic, etc. This is radical but it is not obvious why the resultant poems would be worth reading. There is a counter-argument which holds that poetry is dominated by Oxford graduates and the Oxford atmosphere and that whatever style they adopt is high-prestige. This is not wholly convincing. However, the rules of the game say that a highly developed auto-critique was a mark of high educational capital – and so could become a form of competitive display.

If we go back to the society of mid-century, we can see that in many workplaces there were people at the top of a definite hierarchy who were different from the others because they were austere – harder-working, more conscientious, more qualified, more focussed on technical outcomes and less on conversation, and generally more *worried*. They were not extravagant. They had also had more years of education, and the effect of the education they had received was quite connected to their working style. So, it is plausible that people associated high incomes with austerity and seriousness. But how do you make poetry out of this?

Thwaite's portrait of successful students who don't enjoy the poetry they academically study is devastating. We rapidly "get" why that whole class of students didn't read literary poetry for pleasure – although they might dig Adrian Henri. Worse, the window opens up where we see a meritocratic system where the system wants to define an elite and this process culminates by excluding everyone else. Pupils who are going to do well in exams actually enjoy the exam process. The element of approval by authority and of testing to expose the exact level of people's talent is so compelling for students that they lack interest in anything else, such as artistic values. Poetry ends up belonging only to those with unusually high verbal intelligence. It is a test environment where they are the outright winners and a hundred other psychological talents don't win any points. This is too bad to be true, but we have to ask why so few graduates go on reading poetry after graduating.

## A CELL OF LIGHT

If we imagine a small cell lit only by a sort of gleam from the sense organs of the person inside it, we can describe aestheticism and empiricism as kindred systems for exploring the gleam. Both are privatised: they are ways of accumulating knowledge, almost as property. The cell stands in for a self; aestheticism sees the mind as an organ of pleasure, crudely.

Both principles have a core of greatness: a way of slowing down light, almost, which creates a new world drop by drop. Both have a local site, in an individual and in the moment of acquiring knowledge, which gives the acuity needed for a poem. Simplifying, we can say that the poetic point of view favoured by university graduates began with aestheticism but moved on to empiricism, and that this took place in the 1930s. Around 1970, we can still see the older model at work in Sacheverell Sitwell (b. 1897) and Adrian Stokes (b. 1902), survivors of the Twenties. Both of them were poets in between being (untrained) art historians. Stokes is in a transitional stage because his love of art has transformed into a form of knowledge via the variant of Freudian theory set out by Melanie Klein. Many people see this as not knowledge at all, but pure subjectivity. The shift out of aestheticisation towards the rather grey, unpossessive, almost managerial manner of mid-century is loaded with significance. I can think of half a dozen reasons for it. The silent rule is that you haven't identified with other people – that is why you only have a cell of lit area. You are using the sense record because you are suppressing the information gained by relating to other people – the empathy record. This empties out the intimate realm, but gives an effect of seriousness and reliability. So this effect could explain why the model Oxford poet moved away from aestheticism.

The temporal incidence of the lowly style in educated poetry suggests a link with the closedown of the consumer sector during 15 years of war and reconstruction, and the ethos of egalitarianism which took part in the war and continued at least into the Seventies. A poetic style which avoided conspicuous consumption at the expense of being flat matches the spirit of the times. It involves guilt but is also merito-cratic – the poet is visibly working hard and is visibly not narcissistic. This also implies that their privileges were not susceptible to confiscation by some new wave of commissars.

The essence of prestige poetry is the consumption of prestige objects. Once this is blocked, you have a structural problem. Mid-century academic poetry was keen to maintain a distance from the consumerist world. Part of the complex is the rejection of advertisements. This entails a rejection of overt consumption and display of objects. Ads deal with spontaneous moments because those are when (unnecessary) purchase decisions are made. At least some poetry is against spontaneous moments because it is primarily anti-advertising, and *anti*-ad-related cultural realms, of Pop. Ad-men made a lot more of Surrealism than English poets did. What the poetry didn't deliver was an elite consumption pattern – there were inhibitions about this in an age of austerity.

In a meritocratic society, what you display is not extravagant acts of expenditure. You win by putting on show private times of self-denial, study, long hours, analysis, so as to out-compete other people with a similar repressive focus. We are talking about a new middle class, not anything to do with a proletariat or democracy. Notoriously, 6 of the 9 poets in *New Lines* were Oxford graduates (the other three, daringly, had been to Cambridge). This consecrated a break where the Oxford aesthete flits away and the Movement-style meritocrat takes over. The return to an apical language – and to expressivity – was inevitable. Stokes and Sitwell were still around and writing in 1970 – bearers of the 1920s Oxford idyll of hypersensitivity and personalised cultural knowledge. Dare one suggest that they were succeeded by people with greater academic knowledge and infinitely less sensibility? a generation of scholarship boys? The organic aestheticism was to return in altered form as the new hedonism. Does it matter if knowledge is wrong? much more to academic families than to everyone else. Can we define the '60s as when the scholarship boys realised they had won and stopped feeling guilty about abstract knowledge? This is too simple, but these games about the seriousness of play do have some explanatory value for the poetry we are looking at.

I think the austere poetry of mid-century has been underrated – not about its aesthetic quality, which was grey and feeble, but its originality in pursuing anti-aesthetic means. Mid-century poetry has this tension about impulsiveness, austerity, domesticity, high educational status, knowledge of the past, narcissism. The preset positions made it difficult for people to assess the poetry they were supposed to be reading. Poverty, scholarly work, bare cold rooms – these were features of university and public school life which people didn't much covet. My guess is that the apex group have ways of exhibiting membership which other strata do not recognise. This is perverse because it doesn't ring the tills in the bookshops – no retail advantage.

It is clear, too, that it was not the whole of mainstream poetry which was attached to this greyness and saintliness. It is possible to follow certain critics (Alvarez, Raban) in distinguishing an academic and a metropolitan line within the "high end" of the mainstream. The metropolitan end would include Peter Porter, Christopher Logue, MacBeth, and Alan Ross, for example. When the Movement lost all its credibility (a process which was completing, spectacularly, during the 1980s), this more socialised kind of poetry took over the mainstream altogether, so that today everything is its descendant. Raban gives a very clear account of this metropolitan poetry, in *The Society of the Poem.*

It is only fair to add that the whole cantata of Seventies loss of restraint did not apply to poetry in any striking way. That is, when feminism came along and took on things like violent and sexually explicit films, manipulative and stereotyping advertising, military-phallic symbols, the predatory attitude of men, etc., poetry did not have to adjust very much. Poets just weren't on the list of targets. It is possible to say that the critique of male egoism began in the Forties and at the origin had no feminist component, being rather directed by Christianity, existentialism, class guilt, and a sceptical philosophical project examining individual desires and self-projections. It may not be true that feminism was absent, since wives and girlfriends were unlikely to have been silent when this critique was being developed. As so often, the story of the self-critique was not interesting as art (or anything else).

An implication of resisting impulses was not seeing the life of ideas as pleasurable. In a previous essay I discussed the arrival of the immediate present as the tense of poetry, saying this was a feature of the Sixties. Fairly obviously, hedonism and immediacy are closely related, while delayed gratification, hard work, and depression belong together. This hedonistic shift has a link to a very prominent aspect of the publishing industry which we have touched on, namely that fact was becoming interesting –

mind-expanding rather than functional. It is easy to see that poetry ran to keep up. Also, that poets like Tomlinson and Larkin were not able to get away from inhibited and puritanical writing in order to enter this new modernity. Several of the critics I looked at were convinced that Underground poetry was impulsive, unreflective, instantly giving way to facile sensations. There is an argument going on here which involves the opposition between hard work and soaring impulse. This is native to the education process and is essentially a distraction from poetry. It gives the wrong answers. But a lot of people involved with poetry had jobs in education and spent much of their time trying to make teenagers study rather than follow their impulses. There was even a dispute between education thinkers about child-centred learning, which was supposed to arouse the child's curiosity, and other kinds of learning, which were centred on something else, possibly the budget and exam results.

The colour and culture supplements have long been determined to get as close to the ads as possible. Such magazines put people in the mood to consume by including large amounts of prose about travel, or food, or cinema, which maximised the effect of the ads and so put up the rates which could be charged. This prose (actually interspersed between lavish photographs) puts stress on connoisseurship and on delicate variations of sensibility and pleasure. It draws in knowledge of history and foreign countries, as a basis. These are the qualities which *poets* bring to the market. The key is to drop people's inhibitions. Because almost anything can be sold and consumed, this material spreads over most of the topics you could write poetry about. If the realm of poetry has shrunk, it is partly because the act of "translating experience into display" has been taken over by this zone of gloss, where patronage meets erudition, where prose meets photography. Narratives of an enhanced sensibility flow at will.

If you list all the cultural assets which Oxford literati had in the 1930s, it becomes apparent that as a set they were supplying the contents for the Sunday magazines of the 1960s. One exception would be the Latin language. I suppose it was replaced by the names of exotic foodstuffs in Elizabeth David's *Mediterranean Cooking*. The question which nags at me is whether people needed *poems* once they had the whole panorama, Mediterranean to California, of luxury culture.

THE SPECTRES OF SCHEMAS

Two people can agree that prestige exists without agreeing about just where it lurks, in art, or where it parts from qualities like merit or authenticity. Does the surface of poetry hide solid structures? Evanescent moments are easy to find. They are in the printed characters of the text. Print records syllables but nowhere shows structures beneath them. The depth has to be constructed. How do we get from the evanescent surface of poems to intangibles like the Oxford manner and prestige? Suppose we take 100 books of poetry, with a typical count of 1,400 lines each. That makes 140,000 lines. If we imagine each of those lines as a dot on a scatter graph, then we can say that critical generalisations are like drawing a line, or a polygon of lines, through the dots, and saying this is a good fit and this is the conclusion which the fit leads us to. If you look at this imaginary scatter graph, you can see any number of patterns. So many swoops, swirls, crushingly dense overlays, white strips with no dots. If numbers work for counting Oxford graduates, they ought to work when we are testing generalisations. 100 volumes isn't very many compared to the literary field of the 1970s.

Lucie-Smith's 1970 anthology of *British Poetry Since 1945* replaced Allott as the standard anthology. His start point was 27 years later and he fielded only 29% Oxford graduates. This is certainly down from 40%. Mottram's 1974 presentation of 46 poets as the *British Poetry Revival* (it is 46 if we count in the second, 1977 text) included only 3 Oxford graduates – a risible 6.5%. Why the difference? Did this lack of links to the centre of values explain why the poetry establishment rejected modernity in poetry? Did really existing prestige inhibit innovation?

I do not have a proposal about the narrow radius of the successful. Once you start talking about it, you arouse all kinds of emotions in people who ask for an explanation even if they have already made their minds up one way or another. This creates a pressure which makes it hard to speak. I wonder if we can adapt this problem with finding explanations to shed light on the breakdown of language and the pining for innovation. Of course, there are hundreds of such problem areas. I can see why people wanted to get away from the problem of meaning by deciding that truth didn't matter – the post-truth phase.

Perhaps sociology will solve all the questions about how poetry works, but that is sometime in the future. The ideas of prestige and status are vague in themselves, they cannot clean up the subjectivity of poetry criticism because they themselves do not reach agreed results. It is possible for schemas to start walking and talking, leaving the data far behind. People may use simplified attitudes because they save time – specifically time of *uncertainty*, because people find this wearing. Art is marked out by high ambiguity and uncertainty, offering multiple paths which allow choice and new learning to come to the fore.

# The Little-Magazine World

As we saw, more than half the poetry objects being bought were maga-zines (*Poet's Yearbook*, 1978, p.62). They are things which are now unlikely to be looked at, having been replaced by books, so we have to pause to reconstruct the experience. People always talk about privatisation as the inexorable direction of modern poetry, but the consumers spent an amazing proportion of their time in anthologies or magazines, where the dominant message obviously *isn't* about an individual. People may go on to submerge in a book which is exclusively by one person, but the magazine stage may actually be the climax. In fact, we have to respect that where a poet is characterising the poem very strongly, injecting an insistent signature, they may be designing for a context where they need to make an impact in a short time. The excessive signature may be tedious when you see a whole stack of poems blasting it out.

While England was having the counter-culture, Wales was having a rise in nationalism. This had similar forms of students being arrested on demos, etc., but in poetry it meant neo-formalism. Alan Llwyd was editor (from 1976 up to 2011) of *Barddas*, a magazine dedicated to strict-metre poetry and which has the second highest circulation of any poetry magazine in the UK. (It is connected to the 'poetics society', Y Gymdeithas Cerdd Dafod, and both were founded in 1976.) One of the key processes happening in the 1970s was, we understand, a 'formalist renaissance' which centred on *Barddas* and involved thousands of people. This did not mean the eclipse of poetry in free verse or in more relaxed metres, rather the whole scene became more animated. There is a position in which someone 'adores the metres codified in the 16th century and abominates the modern style', but this is just one position and Alan Llwyd was always saying how valid poetry in English, or free verse, was. *Barddas* is famous for its crusty conservative columnists, but even there we can suspect that people enjoyed those sweeping, but rather clear, views without agreeing with them in detail. The -as is an abstract formative, so *barddas* is 'poetics' (and cymdeithas is 'society'). In Gaelic, you get the same formative, so from *ceann* 'lord' you get *ceannas* 'lordship'. Maybe the two languages *are* related.

In one of his small press reviews for *The Guardian,* Jeff Nuttall quotes Paul Matthews' pamphlet *The Grammar of Darkness:* "If I define the universe as meaning we must realise the paradox in this: a poetry of hints and riddles, no longer just in the sounding. The silence too is recognised. 'A frog jumps in', and we listen to the ripple of it long after the words have died away. A poetry with hollows in it, pause and hiatus, to admit the universe. Form always merging, never fixed, formed and chaotic at the same time, allowing for interventions. A language turning into music, playing between sense and nonsense, (they both limit the language). A poetry which has come to the end of itself (and so come close to its beginnings). Thrown back into the crucible." (November 1979) Peter Finch's *Second Aeon* (1966–74) was the best magazine of the Underground. Finch also says 'matthews never ceases to amaze me, this time he's done a short surreal prose piece that completely captivates. One of the best small press books this year' (*Second Aeon* 19–21 on *Belladonna*) and "paul matthews has certainly hit a new stream as of late, his poetry is still gentle, lyrical but carried by far more unconventional means than it was before. here the shape of the blots has decided the content of the poem and it works well too" (*2nd Aeon* 16/17 on *8 Inkblots & Poems*). In issue 16/17, in 1972, Finch says "during the last few years a crop of new magazines has sprung up. Dedicated to publishing real poetry and possessing that rare thing – the editorial know-how to do it. Their number grows almost daily: *earthship, skylight, grosseteste review, joe dimaggio, curtains, sixpack, strange faeces, sesheta*, eric mottram's *poetry review* & others." History wiped out almost all the lines that people were following but it is not necessarily true that this was an optimisation process. I don't think all the trajectories die at the edge of the page – the data running out where the graph stops. I don't think that all of the interesting ideas ever reached the stage of a book. Buried in the magazines, you can find dozens of lines that didn't get consecrated. Part of the rules for an editor is that you only print unpublished poems. This gives any issue of a magazine a vital limit: it is confined in time, like a race. It defines that fleeting moment – maybe with precision, certainly with panic. The editor is really strongly incentivised to pick up new writers and ideas because those are the ones which other editors haven't already grabbed. You aren't allowed to reprint the poems you like, but if you are quick with poems you don't like yet then you can win. Finch won because his sense of where he was was years ahead of anyone else; most British editors are in love with the past. In the 'English Small Press' section of *Second Aeon* 16/17, I counted 203 items. The count could be higher if you count seven (oversize) single-sheet issues from *Transgravity Advertiser* (Paul Brown) separately. Also, a few of the notices were written either by John Tripp or Barry Edgar Pilcher. But, in sum, you have Finch reading 200 new publications and forming crisp opinions on them. (In issue *19–21* I counted 276 items.) What does he say? Finch is very tough on high prices, so a book from Sinclair's Albion Village Press is sanctioned as "it's an expensive book", costing 75p. *2nd Aeon* was for young people who had no money, not for the luxury market. He records 3 Paul Brown pamphlets in a single issue.

In 16/17 he reviews Paul Gogarty saying "gogarty or 'tommy oranges' is one of the strangest poets at work in the uk today. his poetry is almost meaningless in the traditional sense, owes much to dada, to the european tradition. parts of it could be reworked found text, although just where he manages to find his outlandish images is anybody's guess. […] I enjoyed it." In 19/21 he reviews *Act*, by Tom Raworth. "typical & beautiful asa benveniste production job with nothing left to chance. this is the largest raworth book yet to come out.

I've spent a long time with it making sure that my eyes have not deceived me. all the elements are there, almost sound poems, almost concrete poems, almost haiku, almost dada, almost everything. but nothing quite absolute. raworth is elusive […] an almost there. almost. most of the poems are short, and very very cryptic. basically I don't like it. I feel I should but I don't. its tough going and going no where. perhaps its drugs and raworth's reactions. but then that's no excuse at all. back to the earlier stuff." This grates a bit, but I believe that Raworth's work is like Op Art and is genuinely immersive and without holds to cling on to. Possibly we have naturalised the trackless and shimmering surface, and agreed on a reaction almost as a mechanism of defence.

These goods are not going to be on the shelf of a local bookshop – the "underground" (u/g in *Second Aeon*-speak) may mean "postally linked". Of course you could meet u/g people face to face, and in fact the question is whether the poetry was an empty object referring back to this seething grooviness, or whether the poetry retains its charge when the humans have retired into secular life. I am not sure how to evoke several hundred little magazines.

I can see that I haven't really been describing the poetry in these magazines, although Matthews and Finch have been doing that rather well. It is hard to write about the poems in *Second Aeon* because the pattern doesn't emerge: reading 50 pages by one person reduces the ambiguity and makes prose possible, at least for me. So let's go and look at one of the key poets in *Second Aeon*, Paul Brown (b. 1949).

*Missing shadows reported to the police:* **Paul Brown**

The release (in 2012) of Paul Brown's *A Cabin in the Mountains* (work which "spans [his] poetry from the 1980s to the early 1990s", so written some 20–30 years earlier) faced us with some problems. First, why hadn't we chronicled Brown's work and placed it in a pantheon many years earlier? Secondly, what in fact was its place in that landscape and how could we describe its peculiar excellence without obvious distortions and assumptive overlays? The work includes *Meetings and Pursuits* (63 pp.), *Masker* (80 pp.), and now *Cabin* (105 pp.).

The first poem in *Meetings and Pursuits* (1978) is 'Memorandum to all field-staff' and runs:

> At the near-point painted interiors
> sometimes gardens representing
> a corner of a room
>
> sometimes the prospect of distant
> telescopic hills
> an invitation to a single glance

The incompleteness is seductive. Careful handling and objective detail do not disguise what is surely a longing for a world captured in an image – a vista of endless time. The "near-point" is I suppose the point at which a flat picture comes closest to the spectator outside it. The picture is described as if it were merely a picture, but it is surely a state of longing. The idea of a garden representing a corner of a room is genuinely original – a deft inversion of a room, perhaps in Pompeii, where the corner of a room includes a painting of a garden.

Typical of Roman domestic wall-painting, we think. The idea of plants imitating a building is intriguing, but nature is full of mimicry. The question is, still: why are some lines selected, not others.

One poem from *Masker* (1982) is called 'May 22nd' and goes:

> A tribe of ancient bridges span
> the river's source
> the estuary
> academic

This congress
interests me
two nouns in the workers control
that makes its nest in you
like a duck
on the deck of
a row-boat or
an ear between the eyes
the world screamed *when* to

No more crap about a coming or a going

the vanity of an Iron Age
links
rivetted to a land
shifting under
as verb
for its predicate

We have the impression of a postcard from a world which is stealing silently away and is only retained in a few verbal traces. The idea of a greater whole does not mean that something is missing – the poem is in fact complete.

Another way of starting is with a visual piece published in *Second Aeon*, 12, of 1970. It is constructed as a grid, like a page from a comic. The first frame is clipped from such a comic, and shows a haggard figure in a raincoat with collar turned up saying "I am the mysterious traveller! In the main, my role is that of the silent witness watching wondrous events motionlessly from the shadows! But there are times when I am empowered to *Intervene!*" The next frames are a street map of what seems to be High Barnet and Hadley Wood, on the Great North Road. In the middle, a blacked-out frame with some blood-curdling words spilling across it. The last frame has the Traveller telling us to "come closer" – a tale is about to start.

It is fairly obvious that the allover and yet depthless quality of this 'pop art' piece resembles the strange completeness and lack of documentation of the 'May 22nd' piece we have already quoted. It is as if the visual pieces represented a breach with the discursive world and the later verbal poems continued on from the visual pieces, never declining back into discursivity – or moral accountability, as the Cold War critics demanded of every writer. The groups of poems which Brown favours could be like the frames in the grid of the comic-book page. The title page of *Cabin* cites only two earlier books by Brown – the booklets of concrete and visual poetry with which he began have been dropped from the record. While I don't think the reprographic quality was very good, it is irrational to just throw out those early stages.

Information I withheld is that there is an epigraph to 'May 22ⁿᵈ': "Depend upon it, there is nothing so unnatural as the commonplace" – Arthur Conan Doyle; and, a biro note in my copy (from the author, I hope) says that the sequence 'Log of *The Rose*' which includes 'May 22ⁿᵈ' is "a week in the 1871 Paris Commune". So the bridges are ones over the Seine. Expand: 'span the river's source / or is it the estuary / an academic point'. The part about nesting may be about a mind being colonised by language – the dream of a spiral into our present economic and psychological state and a slit leading to a spiral path out. The idea that two nouns are now in the workers' control is something which would excite many Seventies poets. The "congress" is literally where the bridges come together with the river (and roads with the bridges) but may also be the congress of a political party, communists perhaps. The "vanity of an Iron Age" is the arrogance of 19th century civilisation, of the Second Empire indeed, with its pomposity, punctured by a revolutionary communist regime, Paris in the summer of 1871. The bridge is iron but it is attached (riveted) to a land which is shifting. The title 'Log of *The Rose*' implies a late 19th-century story based on a mysterious ship called *The Rose*. We are back with the Mysterious Traveller. The novel (novelette?) of that title is not present, it is just a notion on which the poem floats. The bit about "this crap about coming and going" echoes the idea that the difference between source and estuary is "academic". Brown is saying that there is a directionless flux. This leaves no place for the ego. The ego as duck on the water's back. Max's beasts were all *canards*.

The cover of that *Second Aeon* has a graphic which actually resembles Brown's 'visual poem' in significant aspects – notably in including a figure from a Marvel comic strip and in using an urban landscape as the main image. The cover has an impressively thewed super-heroine diving in man-powered flight over a vast cityscape. The branches of a giant clover-leaf interchange radiate out at the same angle as the flyer's legs, relative to her body. *Second Aeon* 12 has prices still in shillings, so it is safe to say that Brown's visual piece in this is a very early work. Yet the

same issue announces a booklet, 'The Reason for Leaving Black Daniel',
price 2/-, "prosepoem dada explosions". *Masker* picks up one of these
early pamphlets, 'It ain't no Sin to Take off Your Skin'. (Opposite the
'Work Areas' poem in *Second Aeon* 12 is a poem by Derek Telling which
runs in part "razzmatazz red hot jazz / come throw off your clothes / strip
right down to your bones, / dance 'til it hurts".) 'Skin' was published by
X-Press, one of the completely legendary small presses of the era which
was impossibly well informed and had an impossibly high strike-rate.
Brown was publisher of Transgravity Press and Actual Size.

In the early Sixties, Lee Harwood travelled to Paris to meet the
original Dadaists, who were still there at that time. He edited a magazine
called *tzarad*. He was presumably the best-known Dada-influenced poet
in around 1970. The practice of most interest for Brown is Max Ernst's
collage narratives, of the 1920s onwards, such as 'Une semaine de bonté'
(1934). By decontextualising the source material, typically prints of realist
engravings of the late Victorian era, Ernst released the most opulent and
insanely detailed aspects of the originals. Removing realism made the
visual objects incomprehensible and miraculous. Also, by superimposing
parts of different organisms, Ernst created monster beings, susceptible
of the most wondrous adventures. Ernst's collages have a preference for
composites where a bird's head sits on a human body – or an insect's.
Since humans find it obvious that different species have the same limbs,
reorganised and re-connected, anatomy provides a basis for narrative, as
a dissolute practice of substitution and connection. Why cling to those
archaic species boundaries? The narratives were there to pass the time –
the fundamental need.

Ernst was re-creating narrative rather than abolishing it. Those
collage-novels seem basic to Brown's work. He did a folder of collages
called *le donne di colore*. His visual or psychological sensibility is very
different from Harwood's.

Perhaps it is fair to quote a prose piece from *Second Aeon* 12, not
picked up in the books:

WORK AREAS

Reasons for leaving Black Daniel
"we ate each other and spat it out in a pool on the sand"

Ice Cool Warp
"the light is fading, lights will have to be turned on and missing
shadows reported to the police.
the sky only exists in the breaks between the branches
and the leaves, and it is white"

Thank you My Lady in White, East Finchley
"like a necklace of wind, the white lady in the long silver grey
tube. clutching the blueprint for an engineer he entered the
cabin"

Estsanatlehi & Ushas
"the woman who changes, and the opening of the gates of the
sky leading together the white horse of the sun; a scream torn
from the broken jaw before the guillotine"

Heritage
"later he picked up a dead newspaper from the gutter of the
last century, and began to read."

Bitter Dolls
"eating earth under the motion of the moon. can you hear me,
Tristam? Listen. Listen. the world is full of dead meat"

Miranda's Ghost
"deep, below the crystal city i looked in a mirror and was
afraid i saw the reality of dreams in every page of water turning
in upon itself and in every motion of the hand that is the
movement of fear"

"everyway I turn, the world is my shadow"

Tristam is, and is not, Tzara. Ushas (genitive Ushasas) appears in the
*Rig-Veda* and is goddess of the dawn (cognate with Aurora, for those
19th century scholars). A few words in that stanza may well be taken
from the Rig-Veda. "Estsanatlehi is a Navaho goddess from the Arizona
area" (according to Witchipedia) and is "the woman who changes". I
really like this piece and its structure is quite likely to shed light on
how the later work is made. It is the attenuation to which I would

draw attention. Speed is crucial and yet the selection of a single frame means that everything is immobilised. Recovering the technique, however, is quite different from defining what the final poems are like. The technique is a kind of "nozzle" or lens which could take anything on. Moreover, if we looked at a dozen other poets (more or less) demonstrably using montage, found materials, decontextualising, their work is extremely different from Brown's.

It looks as if Brown found *Second Aeon*, the Cardiff magazine, a sympathetic outlet. Matthew Jarvis' talk 'Visual Poetics in Wales: A Note on Previous Engagements' excitingly recovered a burst of visual poetry in Wales in five years around 1970, linked quite probably to *Second Aeon* and to Peter Finch's enthusiasm. Second Aeon Inc put out two booklets by Brown (*Reasons for Leaving Black Daniel*, 1971, and *Venus in Black Light*, 1973) and also *Midnight on the Diamond Air* by Will Parfitt, one of the visualists whom Jarvis recovered for us (at an event in Hay on Wye). Jarvis even found Parfitt, 45 years on. Quite apart from the brilliance of the visual poems (some of which I had to re-create for a Welsh retrospective), that was a moment which expressed a distrust of the taught system for recording speech and its rigidity in relation to speech (and para-speech). The split from the legacy was a moment which radically affected the way people wrote – even when they stuck to the alphabet. Brown may have redefined his work in terms of three volumes which don't include any visual work, but all the same he belongs to a whole class of "post visual" poets. The relationship between foreground and background was one of the things which shifted.

Generally, Brown seems to imagine the poem in terms of a plane, so of overall relations, rather than as a sequence of unique moments, each one present briefly, moving forward (with a 'before' and 'after'). This is more like pictorial organisation than like a passage of speech. Because the foreground had involved the speaker of the poem, a disruption of the foreground also means a shift of the ego – a different limb design, perhaps the wing of a bat. The difficulties of description arise partly because the firmest plane is the most inexplicit and the evocative quality is revealed in manipulating the undifferentiated level of dream or drug trance. These novels cannot finish and yet they freeze on movement. Finding plane edges allows the narrative to hover on a wispy surface between disappearance and revelation. A strip you only find by luck and retain by a curious predatory immobility.

The surviving words are like flakes floating on a sea. Just as the flakes are flimsy so the underlying plane must be firm – a gestalt. We could look at the deletions rather than the surviving text. The implicit is different from the deleted.

Brown's poem is a sparse surface but the underlying pattern is not necessarily sparse. The breaking down of the foreground allows the background to become more dominant even though it is not verbal. It is a fertile fragmentation, animated fragments. The plane could in fact be the source narrative from which the scraps of language emerge – the holograph log of *The Rose*, or *The 39 Steps*. The poem arrives from the destruction of the original narrative but not of the "canvas" on which it was painted. The unifying plane is not in fact the original. It is genuinely the undifferentiated, all-containing. "By the Miskatonic River", a nostalgic slice of a Lovecraft story, is closest to a straight re-enactment, but surrounded by poems which are anything but. The poems based on *The 39 Steps* ('False Denouements') are not regressing back to *39 Steps* but driving on through. The Navajo quote in 'Work Areas' has non-integrity: the wisp about a goddess is not leading back to a documentary about the Navajo, it is pointing to a gestalt that isn't there yet. This is why it was split out. This is very clear in 'Work Areas' but it may persist in the very different structures of *Meetings*.

The 'Mysterious traveller' thing is minimal. Changing the subject, at a certain point in my childhood, Marvel changed its corporate name to Marvel Pop Art productions. How do we get from "bold – immediate – pop art" to "sparse – cryptic – Underground weird"? I am not sure the poetry changed all that much – it was more the framing. Underground methods are populist because they are spontaneous and anti-authoritarian. It is only by great effort that the world pretends they aren't populist. Peter Finch actually is populist and Brown was frequently published in Finch's magazine. Just possibly the "framing" sheds light on the "context manipulation" which is basic to Brown's poems.

Brown has a quiet, even melancholic, approach. The acquisition is somehow to do with a small, vulnerable, ego rather than with a royal size one. It is as if there were a negative eye, which sheds images just as the receptive eye acquires them. His behaviour towards this found material is austere even if fascinated. Non-documentary, non-egoistic: we are in open waters.

*Masker* includes several photographs of people wearing masks, or masklike make-up, and sitting in a café alongside people who just look like rather tired people grabbing some food. Was this part of a performance piece? I don't know. Maskers is a word for mummers, in some parts of the country. The word *mask* occurs in a poem, in the sequence 'Oyster Bay' –

> The earth was young then – focus on that
> still no lightning but always hope to wake up
> hell to think the pump should ever stop
> (first it's a playground, then it's a cage-out)
> So much for so little she said and set the sparrow trap
> a chestnut bay cantered in on the wind
> lime lay on the field gently digesting
> I had thought all this but a temporary disorder
> an afternoon in early April if you like that kind of thing
> At the lake I witnessed only myself shot through
> with light and facing the new mask with the barest
> of smiles he stepped in – and in no time at all
> was up to my image – and beyond

This is a good moment to point out how unconvincing any description of a poem like this is. A good paraphrase for "At the lake I witnessed only myself shot through / with light" would be "This line actually means that at the lake I witnessed only myself shot through with light". The 'myself' is presumably reflected in the lake which the other person steps into. The last four lines contain a compressed story – about the exchange of identity. This may possibly explain why masker was a book title. It also offers a possibility that each poem is there as a mask which a reader puts on to enter a role – the phrases of the poem are minimal but robust props to enclose the imagination in its role. Or even – as a poster for a film which was never made. You can spend time gazing at the poster. This is not a universal formula – it works for some of the poems. We still wonder, why were some tags selected and others not. It is not a satirical principle – more one of aesthetic preference. Brown is not being sarcastic about Richard Hannay.

In *Meetings and Pursuits*, the fabric is utterly minimal and the implied narrative strange and unrecoverable. The melody is of profound dissociation but in terms of breaking out into dream, into the infinity of narratives which surrealism wanted to dissolve the barriers of, that dissociation may be effective.

The publishing of *Cabin* makes life better and allows a feeling of ease, on the lines of "we have now got the Seventies taped and in only another 30 years we will have the Eighties taped as well". It coincided with better information becoming available about Paul Evans and Paul Green – surely signs of progress even if, arguably, not quite the end of the Seventies project. Anyway, Paul Brown's work is evidently significant and composes a world in itself.

## Open Field in the Badlands:
## Colin Simms, *The American Poems*

In the Seventies, Simms (b. 1939) published a series of long poems about journeys in the Great Plains which are now collected in one volume as *The American Poems* (2005). They include *No North-Western Passage, A Celebration of the Stones in a Water-course, Parflèche, Carcajou, The Compression of the Bones of Crazy Horse.* It is arguable that they are not part of one artistic whole, but the likelihood is that they belong to one single impulse and that they vitally support each other. The note to *Rushmore Inhabitation* says "This is the first of a series of works begun in long walks, motorcycle rides and bus journeys in the American West and in North-east Britain in 1973 and 1975. […] *Rushmore Inhabitation* sets the theme of dishonour in an honourable land whose wildlife, spirit and native subtleties we have to honour along with the Red man who belongs to them and can interpret and coexist with them." The poem was published at Marvin, South Dakota. The subject is not the whole of the West, but really the area over which the Indian Wars were fought in the 1870s, so that the Dakotas feature heavily. But everything visible is part of the poem:

> Life in the grass is             seed heavy with its message
>     to us clear        full of bones            as we walk it
> the wire                any wire does the same
>     a country built once of feeling things
>             the telegraph?        Sand land, again
>     in bed alone, but coming to,  wind-land
>     running in cuttings like the eternal train
>                 the noise insistent again across the plain
>         its grain                lines run down about a century
>     [no-one goes by train in the Dakotas now]
>                         old pick-ups prowl
>     the rocks which are        loaded with fossil fish of all knowledge
>     no new species every half-mile even            as in the redbeds of
>                                 Scotland:
> this is a stretched out land

    […]

```
They talk of              loaded brutes
              'Only cargo acceptable is twenty loaded brutes'
by             oilpipelines miles
broken-down        to mustang
                             musty warning        Indian
[by smell, its music]        mustered
        must assemble
              red-beds like Cromarty in Scotland
full of fossils             life extinguished
is not life eroded.
The dinosaurs remain bone by bone
the plants they browsed on    stain by stain.
```

(*'Brute' is a unit of railway load.*)

So here we hear about telegraph wires (possibly barbed wire fences), railways, the fossil record. The material of the poem is what would also be used in a documentary about the West. So, if you are in North Dakota, you would want to film dinosaur bones, they just happen to be there. I don't think you can draw a structural link between the Indians and the fossils, but they both belong to the place and the poem is about the place. The material about the two dinosaur collectors, Marsh and Cope, is there because parts of Wyoming are exceptionally favourable to the preservation of very large Jurassic fossils ("with the coracoids of dinosaurs his coracle is clavicled") and to revealing them to sight, through erosion and through a climatic lack of tree cover or even of underbrush. The vast spatial extent of the poem is partly because the Indian campaigns of 1876–7 covered such a vast distance, since the Indians were on horseback and had a strategy of mobility, partly because the Great Plains region simply is vast.

Simms is a naturalist and so a professional observer who is also very perceptive. The poems are made of the observations. This fits in with the lore of the West – so if you happen to be watching *The Way West*, film, there is a scout character who is unnaturally perceptive about reading signs in the land and sky, and this was in reality a skill that was needed to live in the wilderness, and one which many individuals, living in the wilderness of North Dakota, Montana, Oregon, and so forth, actually possessed. Even going on a journey connects the poet to the past of the West, because accounts of journeys are how we know about it. That is how it was pioneered.

Simms told me that his natural father was an American of partly Amerindian descent and that he had gone over to the USA to visit his relatives. This is a strange story, so I am glad that it is confirmed in the jacket note to *American Poems* where it says that a Ghost Dance costume, shown on the front cover, was "worn by one of his ancestors". There is a poem at p.147 referring to this: "T'other grandfather half-Piegan; that's half-Bloods / with relations among Arapaho, Teton-Sioux[.]" The *Piegans* are Blackfeet.

This is a poem about big skies. The parts of the text are simultaneous. The visible world has no focus – the landscape does not really disappear as we travel through it. The syntax may not be Old English but it fits constant motion and big skies. It is travelogue, not arguments. The Great Plains are a landscape of velocity, and yield their truths to Sioux horsemen and railways. Simms uses the notorious "open field" method but his poetry is quite direct and easy to follow. There is a fake problem here, because any poetry about landscape has to deal with a field of information which is naturally static and extensive, and the poem has to refer to that even if it is itself a straight line, a series of phonemes and words. Even when the poem seems to move forward, the landscape stays where it is. An open field is one where succession does not apply and so causality is only there as one among a plural set of relationships. The line follows how the I is moving through a landscape which is hardly changing as the I moves, even if the eye tells the brain that it is, and how the verbal structures suited to documents break down to allow the voice to record movement, great tracts of land slipping away on either side. But that makes it difficult, when this is an easy text to follow. Maybe for open field we should set down "travelogue".

A key term is biogeography, the way a creature's way of life fits into a terrain, so that the animal can only live in certain regions and also its behaviour is adapted to where it lives, and to the biology of the creatures living there. The landscape is supreme and the way of the Cheyenne and the Sioux was highly adapted to it. But territoriality also gives rise to politics: the land was taken away from them. This was an era when Amerindians were inspired by the civil rights movement, which attracted FBI attention, since their land was extraterritorial land governed by Federal treaties: "Shot at Pine Ridge by the FBI / Two fall guys    like twin fallpipes / propped at the side of the house". Simms repeatedly remembers the North of England, and also the Scottish

Borders, because sights on the Great Plains remind him of home. In fact, the name Hugh MacDiarmid keeps cropping up, because Simms was visiting him in Langholm. It is a "road movie", made of things that are on the route: like that moment where Colin glances at a sign saying ALLIED EXTERMINATOR and says that animals and Indians were both subject to failed extirpation practices. He talks about the prairie dogs of an entire state being poisoned.

*Carcajou* is a word for wolverine. *Parflèche* is originally "arrow-deflector" but by extension the cured hide of which many objects were made, such as *travois*, in the technology of the Great Plains tribes. *No North-Western Passage* is about the survey voyage of James Cook along the Pacific coast of the American continent. This is a shade outside our geographical scope but the notion of James Cook, as a fellow Yorkshire-man, being part of the story of the West, and author of some of the charts that Lewis and Clark had to work with, was altogether too much to resist. Simms refers to Cook, in 1778, missing the mouth of the Columbia River and then Puget Sound as well. It seems the weather was very bad on those days. Lewis and Clark didn't know where they were, when they found the coast and its sea otters. Typically, Simms superimposes Whitby onto the coast near British Columbia and Oregon, as Cook's basic experience of seamanship guides him through a strange ocean. From Cleveland in Yorkshire, and his father came from the Scottish Borders:

> here in Cleveland and along the Border hills
> of the extended black primary-wing-feather fingering at last lightly
>     on the snow so
> the tips lift first to test by touch the strength of the hill forest
>     tumbled air that trees
> ease into, stand on or lean on there along the Olympics and Mount
>     Rainier, burst the hayhairst and the birds
> flying over, calling, cob of pen and anser, anser, Apricarius,
> the mudrun and the miles of roads, bend-swinging stairs to stars
> re-crystallising ice from snows No Old Black Crow to fly back
>     home to Ted Hughes
> with the message of no passage       This The Raven of Rainier

(*Anser* is goose. The raven bearing the message that there is no seaway is an echo of the dove which told Noah that there was land again. The

Raven is the key figure in the mythology of the Kwakiutl, who was strenuously adapted by Hughes in his *Crow* book.

Hayhairst is "hay harvest", in Borders dialect.) The frequent use of onomatopoeic runs to record birdsong is parallel to the exact recording of dialect. The poem records that the chart of Taner (Henry Tanner?) shows a Whitby Bay on the Pacific coast. A variant says "in / your syllables you stress the first of the downstroke like the primary feather / of the heron's or the raven's wing". There are three variations of this passage. The idea that the feathers of varying length along a bird's tapering wing are a "histogram", metaphor for the level of stress of syllables in a word, is fairly simple. The rush of air along a wing is also like the puff of air in a syllable, I suppose.

You have that vast scale in which the range of a species involves hundreds of thousands of individuals and a scope from Kansas to Manitoba, over a geological time, and the millimetric scale on which a single sighting of one individual supplies the observational detail, on a timescale of minutes or even seconds. The details of the planned action where behavioural programs occur with physiological powers and in the "field" opened by species who provide food or competition, show why the range ends where it does. It is simultaneously true that Simms is empirical and shows observations which are far more precise than those of most literary and non-outdoor poets, and that these poems have a scope of endless possibilities which is radically exciting and lifts the atmosphere of dullness and limitation which paralyses the average English empirical poem.

The painter George Catlin appears in one of the *American Poems,* in one of Eric Mottram's *Elegies,* and also in Roland Mathias' *Madoc.* Simms mentions the poet Eddie Flintoff (*Sarmatians*) in *Stones in a Water-Course.* Catlin was evidently part of the active knowledge within which Seventies poets found themselves. Having some local words I should say that at page 30 "as seabhag to its stac" *seabhag* is hawk and *stac* is an off-shore cliff island, good for birds, off the north of Scotland.

Simms was a naturalist from North Yorkshire who wrote very unusual poems which are also great poetry and also easy to read. High Street publishers wouldn't touch this material. The title page of *American Poems* lists 40 small press publications by the author. This may raise reflections about the composition of the small press population of poets. I don't really know the history and I don't know what Colin was doing as a poet before 1972 or so. I think the story is that all over England there had been eccentric poets, going back many years. There were strong filters at the centre, which broke down in the Sixties. This insane variety of poets could then be pressed into the category of "small press". There were, also, centres where poets clustered together and developed through interacting.

There is a poem in the annex to *American Poems* ('April in 1622, High Plains') about how the escape of a few horses from Spanish control and into Plains Indians power changed the whole geography of the Great Plains and gave a new way of life to the Sioux and the Apache. Can you write the history of the human species without also writing about the other species, plant, animal, and even yeasts and bacteria, with whom we live? No. (The annex has another 64 pages of material not in the original Seventies poems.) I thought too how the Indo-Europeans may have been a horse-hunting ethnic group, on the Upper Volga, who got lucky by discovering first wheels and harness, and then horse-riding, so that the European Bronze Age was launched by horse pastoralists intruding from the east. Distance depends on how fast you can travel. The whole way of life on the Great Plains was different before the arrival of the Horse. Social structure collapsed to make way for a battalion of geniuses, revolutionaries, or even lunatics, who made a new society. We can barely imagine the Sioux/Dakota/Oglala before they had horses. But it is *like* imagining Europe before the horse. If not for the horse, and a change in ways of exploiting horses, Indo-European might still be spoken on the Upper Volga and nowhere else.

Maybe the real America is in the Badlands rather than some bar in Florida.

# The Geothermal Turret:
## News of Warring Clans

We can hardly get away without some report on J.H. Prynne, even if there is no version that people can agree on. I will start with assumptions which are not going to be discussed at this point. First, the most direct influence in Prynne's new poetry in the Seventies is the poetry of Ed Dorn, also his best friend, in poems like *North Atlantic Turbine* (1967). This means that the focal point of the poem is shifting very quickly, and for any poem, or any long poem such as *Warring Clans*, there is no unifying theme and if we crack one passage it is not going to give us any big central idea. Secondly, the principle of the poem is spontaneity, the "site" of each line or sentence is where the poet's attention has moved to, and there is no code to be cracked, all the language is natural but the context may be moving faster than our grasp of it is. This is the feel of modern life, isn't it? It follows, thirdly, that we are not able to use consistency as an eliminator – statements may seem to disqualify our sense of context but this is not a proof. It is like the 6 o'clock news, stories follow rapidly one on another. You should not scrap interpretations because they do not match with something which comes along a page later. The consensus among readers is that the way to read it is durational, working out phrases gradually and not wishing to seize the meaning at one fell swoop. This is a meritocracy – a box in which we sit and are asked questions and are intermittently humiliated and gratified according to our answers. It is certainly nice when you *capture* a line.

The move onwards from *White Stones* (1969) to *Brass* (1971) was a break which seemed to end an era and which confused Prynne's fans in the deepest way. *Brass* therefore seems like a moment which made adhesion to the previous era, its ideas of what was Alternative, seem out of date. It was a jump, a spiralling into the sun. It may be helpful to think back to *The White Stones* as a way of explaining why the change shocked people so much. 'Frost and Snow, Falling' has that beautiful unity which would fit into a veneration by W.K. Wimsatt and be a verbal icon. Admittedly it moves from Iceland to the Ukraine or Kazakhstan, but the themes of luminosity (the sun in Iceland never quite setting) and snowfall (the return journey of John Piano de Carpini, in 1247, from his mission to the court of the Mongol Khan) fit together rather well as examples of climate – the relationship between impinging thermal energy, in the form of sunshine, and events at or near the surface of the satellite, earth. In fact *luminosity* covers the shine of the snow as well as the unfading glimmering of an Icelandic midnight. The snow on the way back from what would now be Mongolia, the moving camp of the Khan known as "the yellow tents", features in another poem in *White Stones*, which is about the cold of the tundra belt, north of the zone where trees grow, supporting rough pasture which humans can only exploit by being nomadic. Everything in that poem folds back onto everything else. This is not at all true of *Warring Clans.*

Raban has given us a brilliant characterisation of *Turbine* which is suggestive for Prynne's new style: "This deceptively throwaway style … On the one hand it is a verse of ambitiously large statement: it explores the essentially Marxian notion of the way in which particular features of the superstructure – the small details of social life, cigars, deodorants, clothes, possessions – cohere around an economic and ideological base. [*on the other*] it is all done with a marvellously quirky individuality … my feeling is that the language of *North Atlantic Turbine* comes as close as it is possible to move to the public demand for a humanizing voice which will speak clearly from the centre of what often seems to be an increasingly impersonal universe." To follow up that humanizing, there is no doubt that when Prynne says something like *Good taste was shunted into the slogan vestry and / reconstructed as billboard nostalgia: the purest / central dogma in the history of trash,* that the poet reacts to the behaviour on show with a judgement which not only captures the behaviour so that we can see it but also normalises the alien present, that is suggests that a higher order of social knowledge places it and qualifies the decisions of the social actors involved. In fact, we are at no point being presented with a breakdown of the capacity for judgement. The strain is rather in our ability to assimilate the extraordinary speed at which political events are rushing past us. The poem offers modernity and the matching collapse of our powers to keep up with the plot, but at no point suggests the irrelevance of behavioural norms, acts of social bargaining and exchange, or of the decisions which people make in the course of behaving. This is radically different from poets who start with an overload which blocks access to any pattern analysis of the too jangling and subversive data rush coming through any modern signal apparatus. The combination of high-resolution photographic data and addled and putrid brain tissue as signal concentrator was typical of an era. (Slogan vestry is a place where *verbal* vestments are hung when not in use.)

*News of Warring Clans* was published in 1977 and takes about 300 lines, presented as a continuous text without sub-titles, although the first section is printed in italics and may represent a preface. There is a quotation or motto on the title page, a Latin couplet which means "you do everything after consulting the looking-glass; the image will deceive: in the end (whatever you swear) ruin is waiting for you". This is from a 1652 poem by Edward Benlowes, which is both Puritanical and metaphysical. The couplet means that however much time you give to self-adornment, old age will in the end make you repellent.

The *sera ruina* may refer to Mao's theory of capitalism, that it would collapse of its own lack of restraint, if you wait. The West is narcissistically focused with the effect of misreading geopolitics and the longer timescale.

> At some moment in the clan's prehistory
> there was panic that the high points would not
> be completed in time. In the sense of "what
> counts is strictly under age", emotional
> negativism and fatuous serenity are states
> like a loose rein on quite the wrong horse.

The overall feel could be one of the political needs of England at a certain moment, projected into the description of a clan – which would be satirical. This is "fronted" as a guess because a number of poems in Prynne's Sixties work were about the state of the nation. In fact, the *English Intelligencer* (a magazine in the form of debate between poets) was about prehistory as a way of recognising the effect of geography and building up to a geographic interpretation of English society and politics – in poetry, naturally. Prynne was the major contributor to this correspondence debate. The bit about under age could be a reference to the youth element of the Counter Culture – with attendant flaws. The fourth to sixth lines are an unusually clear statement about the failings of members of a political project – which Prynne may also be part of. The panic passage has a strange sense of time: the persons concerned know what the clan's history is going to be even though they are still in prehistory. There is reflexivity involved: the persons have a text available and are trying to live their lives through it. Who on earth drew up the schedule by which high points could be completed *on time*? Also, this involves intimacy: they are side by side with us, as if we were all in the same room watching it all on TV. As a repeat, I suppose.

Terms we may find useful are *vividness of phrase.* Every moment is vivid. The phrases echo in the memory even if you don't understand them. *Asymmetrical yoking* – a single sentence structure binds elements that do not bind. For example "The limit / of combat between spools lies at the capstan / north & west of Kalat, two miles out of Kendal. / The pitch is first sung over a drone, then laid out / in expensive copper." Kendal, Kalat – Cumberland and Baluchistan – they just don't belong together. (Wire reels were a medium for recording sound.) *Rigorous presentness* – a belief in the elusive and pure Now which guides the whole style of the poems. *Anthropology of the present* – treating the society we actually live in as something to be understood and described like any other human society. *Detourned science* – the scenery we are passing through derives from scientific knowledge even if the way it is used is as "thought models" or metaphors for something quite different from literal, truth-owning, statement.

The title might be a reference to the intellectual Left in England. That might imply that the whole poem clusters around a political line of thought. I don't find any point in the poem, though, which refers to internal strife and dissent. The title can be left in suspension and the translation of it can also be left suspended. Any version would have to be compatible with the motto, I suppose. Kalat is in Baluchistan, which would be a likely place to find warring clans. The poem is not, though, a documentary about trouble in the Baluchi-speaking tribes in the arid region spanning the Iran-Pakistan frontier. In 1977, there was some kind of war going on between some Baluchis and the government of Pakistan. What is roughly stanza eleven runs:

> Musing again at the geothermal turret,
> a stray engineer looks for a tap. The sun strikes
> a stone in its patient station, between rock
> and more of it. A broader scan picks up
> the mute with the mouth-organ, pulse coding
> his own resentful spike. You take me for
> Valoroso, what kind of haemophiliac variant
> is that, in the bravado now doggo, what kind
> in the residue of upland grasses, holding fire.

I am not going to produce a commentary on the whole poem. Geo-thermal energy production relies on the heat in rocks far beneath the surface – which you have to tap. The shaft to the surface would be long and thin – a turret shape, you could say. If the sun is striking stones, we are somewhere rocky – perhaps upland, very likely infertile. The word "clan" implies "Highland" by collocation. The "resentful spike" is a riposte to the geothermal "tap". Pulse code modulation (PCM) is the basis of digital signalling and is the name used in the original patents. The code is the means by which the signal is sent as a series of numbers, capturing samples of the signal at intervals. These would occasionally include spikes in amplitude. The Dir Scouts (who appear later) are a unit of Pakistani light infantry set up to operate in tribal areas not subject to governmental law and order in the full sense. They might operate in the vicinity of Kalat. Valoroso means "brave" – the back-definition of the term as one of the names for variants of a genetic disease is sarcastic and scornful. (It is also a name for a kind of Chianti.) A haemophiliac could literally be someone who loves blood. The "doggo" seems to be a physical situation, someone is lying prone, so hard to see, in some withered upland grasses, so perhaps in hills in Baluchistan, among the clans.

*A broader scan picks up / the mute with the mouth-organ…* could be a description of the character played by Charles Bronson in *Once Upon a Time in the West,* one of the leading Marxist Westerns of 1968. He is mute and plays the harmonica. He is resentful – of Henry Fonda. The harmonica part in the Ennio Morricone soundtrack is a pulse, barely modulated to form an elementary melody, and reaching occasional spikes. The film is all about the development of the railway – sleepers held down by *spikes,* indeed. This raises a question about context. Context, we normally declare, defines some poetic feelings as possible and others as not. This allows us to read a poem without dissolving into multiple possibilities, like sugar into a coffee cup. But it is possible that Prynne is trying to take on the whole content of a panorama of, say, a shopping street in Cambridge. Hyper after reading Henri Lefebvre, he is willing to capture the structures of everyday life. This would permit the entry of Charles Bronson into a poem. It would show, in fact, that the convergence which allows other poets to be unambiguous connects to a funnel effect in which the diversity of a street or a town is reduced to the monoculture of their personal perceptual habits – poetry thus reduced to the propagation of a personality. This leaves us with the problem of false positives. There is a heretical view that Prynne imposes uncertainty in order to expose people to speculation as autonomous as anxiety. This is totally different to wanting close reading.

In stanza two, we hear about "The clan, *très primitif* in variable kinship with / notes on anomaly", language which slips right out of some anthropological treatise. We stick with the clan, so maybe the poem is coherent and ethnographic, but again we seem to be in a book about the kindred rather than watching people in live action. The word clan appears four times in the poem. The fifth stanza is the most satisfactory to analyse as a description of people's behaviour, with fascinating details about war-paint, ceremonial facial scarring, and teeth-filing. Stanza 6 has a key statement about progress: "Each étage bespeaks the cost / of the one preceding" – *étage* is the same word as stage although literally it means a storey of a building. The clause may draw on stage the theories of social development in which one society stands for the past of another one, and in such a narrative a clan society based on pastoralism would stand for a past stage of our society. The clause depicts Evolution as a building in which storey 7 carries the weight of storey eight – so that any stage is paying the cost of development. Then "spiral cladding / is tonic to those who see what they can't eat" – the outside of the building shows a spiral ascent, in which people can see the future – although it offers wealth which they can't have. The stage concept links the behaviour of the warring clans to satire on Britain in the 1970s.

The poet warns us about the problems of the futures market.

> Option trading has become
> the hottest game in town.
>                     And does the option
> wag the stock, with peace and gentle visitation?
>                     They rivet the stick
> close to strike, shorting the stock
>                     against call;

The *option* is presumably an option on a *stock*. *Shorting* means buying an option to sell at less than the price obtaining when the option deal is struck. *Wagging* is a sign of option trading affecting the trading price of the stock itself. The *call* is the summons to carry out the trade hypothesised in the option contract. Enemies of the futures market or its players would say this also threatens the jobs of people employed in the haplessly productive firm which the holders of stock own. The *strike* price means more than one thing but could be the price above which options traders would collect a profit. *Stick* is likely to be the sticking point, where a price movement comes to a halt. It was shorting the pound sterling which attracted most attention in 1976 or so.

> the water forays
> see to that, and thus each slat of the "cultural
> horizon" is geared up according to form.
> Axes are ground back and fluxed. The diodes
> are tuned by costly milk splashing, or by spot-
> welded hints from all advanced outfits.

The welding words collocate because flux is what you use when welding to make sure that the joint is sealed. The stuff is solid until heated but then flows, hence the name. I think the *flux* may actually be to fill holes in the forging, perhaps on the helve, and the *grinding* would be to sharpen the blade. A *diode* is a simple electronic component, a tube that can have two states. *Slat* is part of a blind, closing light off at a window; *horizon* is a line where visibility stops so might be composed of slats. Their angles could then be like the *axes*. The whole is saying something about the influence of aridity on social organisation – the *"cultural horizon"* is an even area of shared culture, even where groups have different languages. It is a notch less specific than the term "culture" (as in "Andronovo culture"), which would imply an ethnic (and, probably, linguistic) unity.

A moment which discredits the idea of a documentary ethno-graphical poem is the one about credit cards:

> We munch and munch
> along planned parenthood, getting and spending
> on the same credit card. False tedium
> bids up each braggart by his plea bargain,
> to set the motif as if vicious, viz., *takes
> the getting out of wanting*, but in fact
> the *Kung* out of *Fu*; the final arts are martial.

Hong Kong kung fu movies were big at the time. The slogan for the first bank credit card was *takes the waiting out of wanting*, which Prynne reverses to a comic summary of frustration as the motif of consumer society. Obviously, this is Britain in the 1970s and not Baluchistan or some pasture near the Altai Mountains. *Plea bargain* means an admission of guilt in exchange for reduced penalty.

> the possessed lady
> denounces cuts with jabs about standing
> shoulder to shoulder
> with the rock-like boulders of
> the zen tea-room;

This is almost at the end of the poem and connects with the withdrawal of public services due to inflation, overspend, and retreating revenues. As so often, the most abstruse poetry connects more directly with events in the workplace, or as recorded in the newspapers: none of the other poems I looked at actually got the government deficit crisis of the mid-'70s on stage. The phrase "standing shoulder to shoulder with rock-like solidarity" is wriggling beneath the surface. Prynne is actually mocking this sentiment, a cold bath for eager students. The metaphor acquires an independent existence as the bluntly rock-like rocks evolve into motifs in a tea-room set out in a Japanese style, with rocks and miniature plants depicting nature.

Paraphrasing roughly 300 lines is just too much. To rush to the conclusion, at the end we come back to the clan, so that it is possible to think of the whole poem as a story about an ethnic culture, a real historical object. But then, it was almost all excursus. The balance between coherent story of a clan and excursus which touches down with a notional "ethnic group" from time to time is firmly on the side of the latter. The poem ends with a passage:

> The old melisma in the frame
> set by a new battle jittered like spring-water,
> a painted stone in a painted picnic. Nerve
> and verve broke for lunch and were gone.

This is a high-point of Prynne's Seventies style, perfectly clear, unique, and yet shimmering just out of reach. There is an echo, naturally, of Coleridge's painted ship upon a painted ocean – and we are back inside a legend about an upland clan, rather than with live action. Just before this, a note "lay stunned by drab hints from the sandy empires / of the plain" – this hints at geographical determinism, a feature of the previous phase of his poetry. The final sentence could almost be a lament about history going wrong – something disappears. If we pick up the word "drab" (and "stunned") as an opposite to this, the story could be that peasant existence lends itself to immense and homogeneous authority structures, whereas mobile pastoral societies lack the overburden (as well as the accumulation of possessions). In European terms, this points to pastoral zones where feudalism never took grip – for example Ireland and Northern Scotland. Empires do not thrive in hilly terrain.

It's not organised the way art before the 1960s was organised – the conservatoire standards. None of the effects is familiar. They just start from the point where every line is original. Conversely – there are no explanations because that would break the thread. You have to go with the flow. This is impossible unless you relax. This is Sixties art and the approach is of radical spontaneity. It is extremely like other artists who got into radical improvisation – for example painters, actors and musicians. To complete the set, it's hedonistic – with ideas as the source of gratification. We can see the style as a convenience product – the poet switches from theme to theme without artisanal effort – as if by hitting a button on a console without leaving the sofa. The next idea is always there waiting. Think also of the motorway. The car zipping perspectives on landscape together and apart, without slowing down, leads the poem onward past contexts that have no relationship with each other. Mobility is central – we are at cruising speed. It doesn't matter if you don't get it.

Looking at other Sixties spontaneists tells us something about Prynne's path of development but not about the specifics of any of his poems. Something else that comes from media saturation is a certain blasé attitude – the compère is joking with us rather than trying to fade into the scenery. So the "pentecostal peneplain" (stanza 4) is a joke rather than anything else.

It crosses from country to country and setting to setting – like TV – it is the speed of modern life or even of modern boredom. Suppose you had a tape of 8 hours of TV from a day in 1969. How do you summarise it? This could be a key to how hard it is to thematise Prynne, and yet maybe it gets us closer. He is a man with a camera, like Dziga Vertov. He goes around capturing textures. If you count the transitions, you have a way of describing the flow – avoiding a list of all the scenes which the camera is pointed at. It's like someone is watching TV and writing a poem which jumps every time the camera moves its point of view. You know, first it's *Star Trek* and then it's five minutes of ads and then it's the news. You sit by the TV and it takes you everywhere, so we have poetry which is always the total present, like a camera eye, and which makes transitions all the time. Maybe the idea is to seduce a generation of TV viewers. So the pace and variety of old-style, 50s style poetry were inadequate – they were stilted when put up against television. The coherence of viewpoint basic to a Movement poet had become paralysingly boring. Maybe it was knocking on that door when it started. A poet who aimed to play along with advertisements, to jump to a new scene every time the camera setup on screen changed – this would be radical. Are ads set to fit our fickle attention spans? Absolutely, that is the whole point of making them that way.

Themes that don't thematise. A mosaic. So actually you don't explain the content of the poem but still declare victory? Isn't that what all critics want to do? Yes, my most delirious wishes fulfilled.

Prynne was the librarian of Caius College and so responsible for buying all the new books. Obviously, the students were doing a range of different degrees, so the job involved studying catalogues and rapid summaries of books of many different specialisms. In 1977, this sort of job as information worker was less common than it is now. It wasn't a marginal place to be, unless you regard the forefront as marginal. So Prynne was daily absorbing specialised knowledge in tiny snatches and moving rapidly through hundreds or thousands of these, to buy books. This is possibly what we are seeing in the poems – a zipper pulling together a million zones of language. The poems could be a treatise on specialisation in negative – they ignore the subdivision of knowledge and chain everything together. Readers of Prynne commonly talk about the importance of difficulty, reacting I guess to a 1962 essay by the poet, 'Resistance and Difficulty'. The search for pattern is a duel and its end is fatal to attentiveness. The poetry offers a search for pattern that does not end with a self-consecration. It is a serial that does not reach a climax and *dénouement* at the end of every episode but simply moves on without slowing down.

We have to address matters of tempo. Let us consider the total dock of stage sets available to a poet in, say 1652 (for Benlowes). It is limited – the readers will only recognise a certain range of scenes – other scenes will not be written. The poet re-uses Biblical stories, Classical myth, other things. The modern world has a much larger range of information – a thousand times as much. This does not roll with poems being a thousand times as long – your slim volume of verse now clocking in at 80,000 pages. So it is that velocity surfaces as the key value. It is played in a bebop time signature, as opposed to Ben Webster. A theme which Prynnophiles keep circling back to is the idea of undoing the effects of velocity – finding something wiped into a streak around the horizon and decelerating it to show an articulated shape. We accelerate in order to draw level with a rapid signal and find it becoming clear. The blur at the horizon contains all colours and they can be split back into information by a lens of the appropriate silicate.

I don't know of any statements by Prynne on this, so we can only reach motives by an attempt at reconstruction. Ideas of purity and authenticity can find a station in the time dimension. That traces a tempo frontier where everything is decaying rapidly, but retains a pristine quality for long enough to be recorded – so long as we do not pause to bend it back into literary figures. We are thinking of something transient but controlling enormous power. Each stanza has its moment – but withers when that moment has passed. The fading process might be neurological as much as musical. Everything is recuperated but there is a prime time before the recuperation trucks arrive. The question is, why would someone decide that the folding back on itself of 'Frost and Snow' is undesirable – tired. Much depends on this. 'Frost' is at least partly about nomadism, the regime of total mobility. It is about leaving tracks in clean snow which are effaced by new snowfall. There is a mismatch in writing about nomadism inside a form where everything folds back on itself, where every A is followed by a B and there is no depatterned residue. If we think about a line of argument which holds that a sedentary form of civilisation makes for accumulative wealth, for a facility of social control which favours authority, and for a circularity of habit which is the basis for knowledge as the depot of what is predictable – we may be close to this unsettled purity through nomadic tempo. So that a book, as we have them, is a sedentary feature, and a product of accumulation based on stability – staticity, in fact. Nomad cultures are normally illiterate (although the Mongols knew symbols called *tamgas* as property marks). There is some link between not leaving distinct tracks and not having the written word. The Sixties had a very wide range of people using improvisation as an artistic principle. The common currency was that the merit of art was its originality – thus injecting the idea of decay as the basis of art-historical values. This presupposition could be criticised at great length, but there was some consensus in the post-war settlement that things withered as they were repeated and recycled. It was as if everything followed a time curve and the peak of that curve was right at its beginning – with the planetary surface littered with half-consumed and not quite burnt out wreck anatomies, the horizontal features.

An accepted definition of artistic form is as repetition with variation. Looking at *Warring Clans* does not show any repetition – nothing recurs. In this sense it is not a pattern – following only an arrow moving out through space without any falling back or regression. Or – we could define the speed, the blink rate, as the founding structure. It wraps everything in the same cellophane.

Whereas archaeology and antiquarianism uncovered the history of the village as the classic form of a civilisation dedicated to controlling crops, a later development of the myth-geography movement discovered that modern man lives mainly in cities and that this asks for an exit into finance as an autonomous technology of value and so into velocity as the enhancement of habitable space. The mid-century literati dwelt in the Imagined Village, the Communist Party asking its members to listen to folk music as a bath in authenticity. Prynne was suspicious enough to move on to the dematerialised economy of finance and information. He is streamlining poetry to reach the speed of abstract thought.

The social field around Prynne's work is outside the poems themselves, but was after all a key feature of the decade. The sense of breakthrough as one grasps a moment from the quicksilver stream is thrilling but led unavoidably to a sense of a cluster of initiates close to the man himself who owned innumerable breakthroughs and formed a clique which gave *everyone* else the sense of being less close to the poems, which was a less thrilling feeling. This secondary and rather vile effect is not within the poems at all. There is no short cut to understanding them, and the test of time has shown that many people who were certainly big Prynne fans, and lived in Cambridge, did not hear what the poems were actually saying. The need to believe that you are Prynne fan number one was exciting to an alarming and corrupting extent. Commentators on this work need to eschew denouncing all the other commentators. There is also the phenomenon of Prynne imitators – a cultural translation which could only occur within the limits of what the secondary poet understood of the primary one's work. The logic "my poetry is completely incomprinnsible – therefore I am like Prynne – therefore I partake of the living godhead – therefore you are not worthy to understand my work" made sense to altogether too many people.

We all agree that one gets further with Prynne by reading the texts than by floating analogies. However, we may think of Eric Mottram in connection with the project of taking on the whole troposphere of modern knowledge within poetry, in terms of speeding up the pulse rate and making transitions so swift that they fling most readers off at the curves, and not least in terms of owning the Olson franchise. Both bring us up to the problem of obscurity – another pungent flavour of the time. It doesn't exist on its own – it is just a by-product of powerful drives towards speed, towards the unknown and unused, and towards the intimacy of in-groups. If you switch those drives off, you can end up with some mighty banal product.

# Still Life With Pears:
# Conceptual Art

The first step in composing conceptual poetry is to stop all the steps which are used for composing non-conceptual, or organic, poetry. But, what is it that non-processual poets do to compose a poem? We could spend thirty years thinking about this. Everyone feels a sort of panic on encountering conceptual poetry, at the loss of security and gratification involved in reading habits attuned to poetry the way it used to be. A large part of the conceptual programme is denaturalising, and unspooling what is thus denaturalised. It is like taking the back off a radio and looking at the circuit board. It is illogical to discuss the programme without talking about the findings, the exposé of the components of the organic. Organic poets have so far proved very reluctant to examine what composing a poem might include. That is, if we except bluster, intimidation, self-sanctification, elaborate claims to territory. Early results would include *I do it because it feels right* (retort: you don't know what you are doing and you may have been infiltrated by all kinds of ideologies, vested interests, etc.); *it is an irresistible impulse* (retort: you make your personal impulses into the centre of the universe); *it's an expression of me and so authentic* (retort: you are making possessive individualism into the source of what is right in the world whereas it seems more like the source of what's wrong); *it's what poets have always done* (retort: you just said it came from inside and now you're claiming it's a package of legacy legislation). Why do you repeat yourself? Claim, *because that is authenticity and it reflects the eternal me*; retort: because you are reflecting a preset ideology and your ego sounds like an ideology. Why is your work always varied? Claim: *because of my sensitivity*; retort: you're just being inconsistent. The legitimation from intuition gives power to something that only exists inside your head and the argument from tradition gives it to rules that were set down thousands of years ago. How can these principles both apply? Your intuitions weren't around before you were. And so on.

Conceptual poets used explicit, preset, rules and part of the plan for this was to generate outcomes which were unforeseen and not a reflection of the self.

Poetry manipulates implicit knowledge by means of intuition. Some people who wrote process-based poetry would be Edwin Morgan, John Powell Ward, Allen Fisher, George MacBeth, Peter Finch, Andrew

Crozier, Paul Brown. Something very important to British poetry from about 1965 to 1975, and with abiding consequences ever since that date, was a critical project, a putting into question of the means by which society reproduces itself, of which *conceptual art* was one phase. Of the various views of 'how much do political arrangements affect poetry?', this group took the view that their influence was total. They replaced the reproduction of social experience with the interrogation of it. It seems likely that conceptual art comes out of close reading – the rejection of identification in order to examine how a text works as a piece of logic and rhetoric. This process of disenchantment is basic to the idea of what one learns at university and so to the demarcation of the graduate middle class from other population groups. How related was this to the French Marxist line of new criticism? This is one of the waves that was splashing around in the 1960s. It does not necessarily overlap with what people were doing in Paris, and its start was distinctly before that line reached the English-speaking world. Yet, there may be some resemblances.

The Conceptuals did not like legacy art. Left alone in the National Gallery, they felt confused and untouched. This raises an interesting problem – the ability to enjoy art is partly a habit, and a childhood in a cultured family equipped someone to enjoy the legacy culture of the museums and libraries. The confusion of a group of (would-be) artists in the face of these ornate and partly arbitrary sign-complexes had a class aspect – the confused came from families where culture was not being transmitted. This sheds light on another confusion – where people stroll through an exhibition of conceptual art and feel nothing and are unsure how they are supposed to react.

I thought to collect position statements by English conceptual artists. There is a convenient source in the volume of documentation collected by Richard Cork for a 1976 British Council exhibition in Milan. Is this the best way of doing it? English poets may have plugged into American conceptual art (and possibly the European variety). Also, looking at the artworks themselves could be better – but this poses problems of reproduction which words don't.

"Looking at art [...] it seems to me that the most widespread manifestation of a socially divisive class ideology transformed into terms of art is the practice of abstract painting and sculpture." – Victor Burgin, who said:

We are not a socialist society and the dissident artist is thus caught in an essential contradiction [...] Our society is rife in such contradictions. [...] So, we might say, a job for the socialist artist in our sort of society is to foreground these contradictions, and in so doing help society through its transition to socialism. [...] By Formalism here I mean not simply Modernism but Formalism in the widest sense of the term: an immanent mode of analysis which concentrates on the autonomous structure of the artwork, upon its interiority, its intrinsicality.

Certainly, there is strong opposition to one of the central thrusts of Structuralist thought in general, that which has sought to decentre the subject; in our present terms, to undermine the status of [...] 'outmoded concepts such as creativity and genius, eternal value and mystery'.

David Dye describes his work *Western Reversal*:

(*The*) still version (1974) consists of sixteen shots from a performance piece (1973), in which a typical cowboy film is projected via a framework of sixteen movable mirrors. One by one the mirrors are moved so that sixteen fragmented parts of the image overlap at the centre of the screen; the image is, as it were, imploded, leaving a rectangle of shimmering light. "The Western" is both archetypical film genre and archetypal myth of Western Capitalism. Here violence and territoriality are turned against themselves. By fragmentation and superimposition, the parts are made to cancel out the whole. In this still version of the work sixteen shots from various stages in the performance are arranged in a grid that duplicated the division of each image into sixteen sections.

John Hilliard:

You could say that since 1969 I've been investigating the reliability of photographs as representatives of their objects [...] But my attitude to the use of photographs is ambivalent. [...] I value the peculiar properties of photographs, where space and time are frozen in an unreal stasis which invites an abnormally objective scrutiny, and I like their discrete form.

The film-maker Annabel Nicolson says

> The realization that nothing has a finite meaning, that nothing
> escapes the mercy of circumstance, has emerged as condition of
> all my work. […] My early work with film was mainly on the
> level of fascination at its materiality, emulsion, particles, fugitive
> layers of colour, the effect of time and delay on the chemical
> process, the brittle celluloid. Similarly, the projector was an
> instrument to be played.

The film-maker Malcolm Le Grice says he insists on the materiality of
the film medium, and attacks "illusionism" and "narrative", which he
considers reactionary.

Mike Dunford: "All perception of phenomena is unified by
ideology and therefore political. 'Still Life' [*Still Life with Pears*, his
film] is not non-political, it accepts the bourgeois class ideology of
aesthetics, and the bourgeois idealist philosophy of empiricism, and
necessitates participation in them. […] It was a product of my colonised
consciousness and continues the process of colonisation. I hope that
nowadays you will criticise the film and ask the question 'who does it
serve and how?' I no longer make such films."

Miller and Cameron state that their performance work is not seen
in theatres but in "streets, beaches, forests, parks, ferry-boats, shops,
railway lines."

John Stezaker, showing montages of images from advertising and
popular art (e.g. 'Liberty Misleading the People'), says "But ideology is
not communicated in the well-systematised cultural directives which
we call 'ordinary language' but in the outer periphery of unsystematised
cultural directives, in connotation. Language is a system of our ordinary
shared beliefs and those which are not shared are not systematised into
the form of a particular culture-use, but exist in the transient zone
outside syntax. Thus no academic argument can articulate ideology
against an opponent."

The idea of presenting this material is to teach novice readers the
procedures of an art style which deeply influenced a line of conceptual
and documentary poetry. I want to emphasise that I am not evaluating
the work and not browbeating anyone into liking it. I do want to add
that writing off an entire genre of art strikes me as ridiculous. I just feel

that people need to understand something before rejecting it.

Conceptual art is better documented than modern British poetry. The point of departure for conceptual art was the rejection of the object: this was a no to commercialism and the gallery system. The object was felt as distracting from a project already taking place, of thinking and coming to understand. The object of understanding was Eisenhower's America, evolving into Nixon's America. Conceptual Art began with a group of half a dozen people in New York, it was based on intimacy; the British project has had the same qualities of intimacy and developed a shared language. The more it belongs to a few dozen people, and to particular venues in a particular part of London (Camden), the less it is universal and the less it seems like a philosophical project. Part of a game is that you know the other participants. The more an art style is based on what the players of the game already know, the less it actually says in any move in the game. Some of the features of conceptual art were:

new data intakes;
new informalism
dematerialisation
catachresis (parody, denunciation)
montage
foregrounding technique
games with restricted rule sets; automatons
artist intervenes in the classification process
serials (permitting fine comparisons)
attack on narcissism and on the subject
stress on editing as opposed to 'inspiration'
prose as dominant mode
spontaneity (no set programme, cool, heroism)… avoidance of choice
casualness
stress on relations between the material and the illusory

These are an over-fulfilment of various middle-class traits: impersonality, criticism, the wish for authority, the urge to measure things, love of serial repetition, prizing of the act of recording and of storing results. We have also to mention the bringing on stage of already existing art works, as the objects of critique; this was art about art, although of course that really means art about behaviour.

Conceptualists liked to produce serial pictures of the same object or scene, leading to awareness of slight distinctions. This imitates the accounts which record daily events in a shop, or the serial observations which are the basis of science. The hyper-bureaucratisation of art fitted in very well with the growth of higher education, a mass intake into the middle class. The mood was didactic because childhood norms are being abandoned; the work is forever answering questions like "what is the world like" and "what shall we do with our lives".

The conceptual movement was very well equipped to recover the process by which individuals are directed to their position in the social structure, by breaking through the narratives which naturalise that process and make its outcome certain from the first. The idea was, you could say, to move the government of this process from the impersonal and 'authoritative' to the hands of the individual. These artists wanted to make the rules of the game visible rather than to play it.

The Scottish anthropologist Victor Turner has described an *anti-structure* as an inversion of values, occurring in a defined space (which is outside the functional and hierarchical world) created at specific phases of a ritual process, also often a conflict process. In the anti-structure, having the old knowledge is ignorance, the powerful are not the most virtuous but the most malign, breaking rules is virtuous, spontaneity takes over from formalism, etc. He recorded anti-structures, along with liminal places and anti-languages, in a wide range of countries, but he was definitely thinking of the British counter-culture in the early formulation of the pattern.

Not all conceptual artists were Marxists, and the political affiliation of the initiators was at the time (*circa* 1966) something which intellectuals in the USA carefully hid, due to legal persecution; however, the background of the style is sufficiently pervasive that we can say that even non-Marxists were drawing on a Marxist culture when they used it, and that the bareness of means was a way of sidestepping accusations of bias by reducing the argument to "common sense". The evidence was to be transparent and not enriched by artifice. Much conceptual art only acquires a meaning if you accept that there is only one, favourite, alternative social structure, and dissolves into nebulousness if you decide that society is adjacent to a million other social systems, all equally likely. Early conceptual art was allusive because it was referring to a syllabus, known to the in-group, and was not at all a research project in which the unknown had any role to play.

The rational vestment of Marxist argument means that it is an antistructure which is not possessed of an anti-language; its apparel is just that of system-loyal lawyers, economists, and so on, which is why it possesses legitimacy but not emotional appeal. The relationship of any linguistically radical poetry to this official Marxist prose, and the mental procedures backing it, is problematic; the avant-garde legitimises Marxism, for the cultivated public, but is de-legitimated by thousands of public statements of vested Marxist leaders.

Marxism represents the greatest possible degree of delegitimation, and in this way too concretises middle-class procedures in a more extreme way than any other group. An Oxford academic may delegitimate any academic not trained at Oxford, or by someone trained at Oxford, but a Marxist delegitimates any academic who is not a Marxist. The new critique stands in a tense functional relationship to the procedures of any social group caught up in the increase in the social power of graduates and professionals, and simultaneously in the social downgrading of anyone outside those groups; it supplies such an over-fulfilment of the basic acts of delegitimation (of one's rivals and of theories and credentials), validation (by appeal to a monster authority raised above mere earthly standards), and network building (the Party as conspiracy). All aspirant professionals carry out such acts; the Marxist carries them out repetitively, and without nuance.

The project of reorganising society, on paper at first, and telling everyone where to go and what to do, was an enactment in fantasy of what managers and employers do daily in real life: a distribution of power, in phantom form, which was one of the central pleasures of Marxism and of its art. As if in a film, we are taken into the boardrooms and the control towers. Without renouncing the project of reshaping the histogram of ownership, the revolutionaries unconsciously adopted a wide range of the ideas and values actually held by the managerial class; concrete and authentic details whose genuine nature props up the fantasy and gives it staying power. The fantasy could not unroll without officiousness and fetishisation. So, the methods adopted by artists also imitated the daily practice of managers and administrators – along with, fortunately, Dionysiac gaiety, vision, and fraternal warmth.

Western Marxism has never ceased to be contestatory, as most of its tenets have been accepted by very few of the people who might be reading it or voting for it. The arguments always tended to pull the zone of thought out of daily experience and into a realm of speculation about possibilities and origins; the act of rejection created an empty space which we will recognise as the white space of print and as the original void of critical poetry. Dealing with conjecture and opposition trained up formidable intellects – still more productive if they stayed the course and then abandoned the prejudices of Marxism itself for a truly curious approach to the world.

Conceptual art came out of Marxism. The conceptual artist was theoretically for the flattening of the class pyramid, and practically created art which corresponded with unerring precision to the anti-sensuous prejudices of the most educated group, and ignored the artistic taste of the proletariat. This stance was suited, in fact, to a much more definite group: people of lower-class origin who were coming up through the State education system, and who, while they were licensed to use elite ideas about objectivity and scrupulousness, and were eager consumers of culture, were uncertain about the manners of the middle class, and inclined to write off its assets in the suspicion that the old middle class was going to write off theirs, and toss them back onto the housing estate. Microscopic examination of the lifestyle of the bourgeoisie was bound to appeal to them – after all, they were about to assimilate to that lifestyle, and notes could be taken. This match explains how conceptual art came to be so thoroughly taken on by public museums and galleries, by academics, and by the State's art training establishments; the progress of the group through the stages of life explains why conceptual art shed so much of its original impetus, and why its audience constantly vanished, seduced, as they became more secure and less competitive, by more sensuous forms of artistic pleasure. The failure of radical poetry to reach a similar degree of legitimation and sponsorship by the State is one of the keys to modern British poetry.

Historically, it would seem that the great wave of teenagers who were offered higher education (and access to the higher income groups) in the 1960s or late 1950s were consumed by guilt at this anointment as the future managers. A typical response was to be against the middle class even while acquiring their behaviour patterns, of which the cognitive ones were the most significant. They built a critique of the whole of bourgeois civilisation.

They did not wish simply to become the new middle class. As time went on, and the 'new class' of graduates came to regard its privileged condition as normal rather than as unequal or as an experiment by the State, the sense of guilt faded away. Solidarity with the rest of the generation, everyone who had to pay taxes to support higher education but was not going to receive it, disappeared. The process of becoming the new middle class completed and the idea of any other outcome faded from the horizon, even as a vision. This left a gap which was filled by intense competition between individuals, often won by proving that a rival had not successfully internalised the norms of the new class. Challenging those norms became less and less possible.

The artists, too, abandoned the original rigorism of Conceptual Art as time went on: coming back to expressivity from the other side, in a reflexive way which could be either original or shallow and ineffective. The passage through conceptual art is held to institute and coat in prestige the subjectivity of its ex-pupils. Much of what I see tries to lash together the didactic and the slackly self-indulgent.

Much of its appeal was extrinsic: it evoked a fantasy of investigation which was quite intoxicating; but if you didn't have the fantasy, or lost it, or had access to good-quality "discursive" history and sociology, it began to look alarmingly subjective, heroic, and self-referential – just a Romantic art movement, in fact. The refusal to sell objects led to selling lifestyle; a puppet theatre of hero tales, or, dime novels about liberation.

Because scale is something that emerges from a very wide range of exact comparative observations, the "emptying out" produced work with persistent problems of scale; either encyclopaedism or barrenness. It was either derivative (using a network to permit a conventional knowledge system, awkwardly partial) or gigantic, or irritatingly incomplete and gnomic. The project of questioning everything leaves you over-exposed to the social influences closest to you; the lack of reassurance yields projective anxiety and the elimination of other people's voices yields a heroism of the wilderness. The lack of proportion gave rise to anxiety and the sublime: we are thrown up in the artist's hands and are forever falling. All of this will remind us of the initial link between sensory deprivation and suggestibility.

If we posit everyday life as 0, zero, middle class practices can be seen as 1, that is zero plus one; and the practices of conceptual art can generally be interpreted as 2, that is zero plus one plus one. Conceptual art pursued the whole middle-class project along its own axis, a complete over-fulfilment of the techniques. To reject conceptualism – as so many people have so often done, reacting to its unpleasant procedures and conclusions – is to reject the principles of academic study and of business administration and of modern government. Even this rejection is of great value. But it is hard to argue, since (for one thing) the laws of argument are obviously part of this rationalist machine, and to apply them successfully you need to believe in reason. If you apply temperament, passion, intuition, desire, etc., as principles, you earn contempt from everybody, because the social norm is that we try to control those affects, and only give way to them when we are at their mercy.

For this reason, conceptual art has been, since some point in the 1970s, the prestige norm in State-funded institutions, but only in visual arts, (for example in art schools and in "modern" exhibition spaces such as the ICA and the Serpentine Gallery), not in poetry. Art students who want to create images or make something sensuous are regarded as unintelligent. Your voice is tied up with social self-presentation, with prestige, with class, and is expected to be "natural" and transparent; experimenting in poetry generated huge resistance, which painting, recognised to produce made objects, did not suffer. The resistance still takes the form of denying that the experiments ever happened. British painters are far better at theorising than poets, because they learn how to do it at art school. To reiterate, the links between this wave in art and 'theory' in the universities are very hard to measure, and may not be there at all.

The proposal here is that 'question everything' is a crossroads: that a great deal of poetry has not reached that crossroads, and that conversely very much poetry has passed through it and benefited from it, seems obvious. We can propose further that this is a watershed, it explains a great deal of the visible landscape of poetry at the present time. But conventional poets would very often insist that they had 'questioned everything' and that their work was precisely the proof of that. Questioning what syntax does does not mean that you have to throw syntax away. Using syntax, or even rhyme, does not prove that you have never thought about them. We would need a different category for 'art that throws every device away', and in fact a lot depends on just which structures you throw out.

Conceptual art was 'art without objects', rejecting the act of making paintings. Poetry was already conceptual: a poem is made out of concepts, not objects. The idea of 'conceptual poetry' is questionable. The equivalent of rejecting the art object is, I think, the rejection of the secure autobiographical voice as the binding element of poetry. At one remove, this means the abandonment of the autobiographical project. Further, this is a necessary accompaniment of the project of criticising experience rather than reproducing it – so this probably comes first. The personality of the artist is the thing dislodged by modernism. It is the stake that one side hopes to win and that the other side throws away.

It may seem like a clever trick if I point out that the erasure of individual consciousness (as promulgated by Burgin) is the diametrical opposite of the poem as monologue which Jonathan Raban described for us earlier on. Structuralism was diverted to show that what really mattered was something no individual was aware of. It is really difficult to see how poetry aiming to be read by individuals can uphold the idea that the individual does not exist. This only appealed to a fraction of the Left – it involved the jettison of a securely heroic left-wing speaking voice. To clarify, the line of Left poetry which goes back to the Chartists or to Shelley had a secure voice and integrated itself around an autobiographical awareness, in fact that of the person speaking in the poem. 'Critical' poetry got rid of that. It was not interested in characters from socialist states or in dialect poetry from the Northern English working class. Overwhelming reliance on personalisation and the attack on personalisation were happening in the same time-frame.

Because the speaking voice of the poet, as vehicle for a self, was so central to the agreed manner of poetry (then as now), poetry in which the self had been evaporated, to show an entire environment, unlabelled but full of openings, could seem to be incomprehensible and in fact unfinished. The proposal was partly that a cold, depersonalised, and ambiguous verbal environment mirrored a social landscape which had those qualities. The audience might not enjoy this, even if figuring it out helped you to understand where you were.

Another parting of the ways would be where you say that 'art based on identity politics cannot use any of the style modules based on a critique of the personality as central to art'. It follows that people who have invested in identity politics may not be willing to admit that modern art even exists. Also, I suggest it is not true that 'egocentric art reflects identity politics and is therefore modern and progressive'. Surely it is true that 'egocentric art reflects a consumer society' and that 'egocentricity holds art back and is an old principle in itself'.

When we see Allen Fisher coming to written poetry after a long career in the Conceptual movement, if we look at Andrew Crozier, whose brother was a conceptual artist at times, it becomes perverse not to see links between poetry and 'conceptualism'. Crozier composed a poem of 24 parts (*High Zero*) in which one part is made up of a line from most of the other parts. The use of a grid structure and of found material which is processed following arbitrary rules must remind us of conceptual art. (Actually there are 24 poems in the main body of *High Zero* and the derived poem is only 20 lines long, but you see my point.) It would be wrong to think that conceptualism is the key to the whole of the poetic Underground. The Underground was a vast terrain which had space for a dozen different aesthetic approaches, which may have common elements only at the level of shared infrastructure.

Another question we could ask is 'how far does the Underground own the title deeds to radicalism', since after all feminism would propose itself as socially radical and yet very few feminist poets write in an innovative style. They wanted the stories to be clear and to sound true. They wanted to Get the Message Across. Obviously, radical feminists would claim to have questioned everything even if their poetry is conventional and ignores most modern poetic innovations. Someone could follow a principle of 'question everything' without being an artist at all, certainly without being enrolled in Conceptual Art. This is probably more generative, but does not give rise to many works of art in any specific way.

We can define this impact of conceptualism as an area of anxiety, where poets simultaneously fear to be unconventional and lose the tolerant but easily bored audience, and fear to be thought of as not having questioned the rules of art and society (implying that they were simply egocentric in motivation and mimetic in content). This brings us back to the question of 'homeopathic modernism' and how a small dose of structural innovation may be a desirable asset for the young and conventional. If something is the object of envy, then you may well grab a dangerously large dose of it once you get unhampered access to a supply. Prestige and competition are very much to the fore in this game. The radical art of the 1970s was plugged into misery, poverty, distress, injustice. One of its limits was how ineffective it seemed in the face of all that. It was a way of avoiding guilt. The "spaghetti Western moment" where the radical art took on the dominant representations in a duel and subverted them was all too rare. Mostly conceptual art seemed very thin and unconvincing put up against illusionist art.

The idea that conceptual art is basic to contemporary critical art may be over-optimistic. Is there a simple structure that we can recover by looking underneath so many phenomena? Maybe there is a 'shared language' of literature which wasn't there in the 1950s but which was visible in the 1960s, and which people are still living inside. Or maybe poetry can be written on a dozen different bases.

The 'conceptual project' in Britain was mainly to do with self-education. It throve in a situation where official education was remote and a bit boring, but yet it seemed attractive to spend most of one's waking hours in the pursuit of knowledge. The students who were bored by the universities of 1965 came, in time, to run those universities and, on a massive scale, redesigned the idea of knowledge in the humanities to make them interesting to study. Forty years of satirical jeering at the word 'relevance' do not disguise the fact that academic study has become more relevant and that students have been allowed to pursue what interested them. Students have ceased to be an elite and it is now very difficult to think that the knowledge you have is unique to you. A separation of the poetic project from the knowledge project in general is not credible, but the economics of information have changed and the value of the individual, or of individualism, has been changed by the total market context, the sounds of thousands of other people also acquiring knowledge. Students, by being co-opted, have ceased to be an autonomous and radical group. As their frustrations have been released, the energy which drove notably autodidactic and research-based projects in art has waned. We could advance a thesis that the decline of the Underground has to do with the increased formalisation and bureaucratisation of the knowledge relevant to poetry. The eccentrics have been sucked in and made Productive, and the people who remain eccentric genuinely have socialisation and cognitive difficulties.

RECOLLECTIONS OF THE FRINGE

There was a big scale survey of the (British) avant-garde in 1973 at a place called the Gallery House, which was run by Sigi Krauss. The building was basically given free but also belonged to a cultural institute which was owned by the (West) German Federal government and so supervised (indirectly) by the German Embassy. There was a gap between the sponsorship plans of the cultural institute and the desires of the Embassy. Krauss remembered the high old times in an interview *circa* August 2014.

SK: He was so energetic and so full of ideas… I mean John was he was full of tricks too you know… and so he would come and read one of his poems and I'm looking at him and say well … and he had glasses on and there were no lenses on them so he is reading and he is reading

like um 'yes yes yes yes yes yes yes yes yes no yes yes yes yes yes yes yes
yes' and then ended up with 'no no no no no no yes no no no no no'
and on for an hour. Yeah that's John Latham… And then we had Stuart
[Brisley] an artist in residence … upstairs in the room … we had people
using the kitchen … basically a musician and composer so the whole
house was used, the basement, the garden … the elevator … Painting
… the ballroom … everything the ceiling, the floor and that was after
Stuart Brisley did a meat sculpture there he was in a wheelchair for 14
days and a microphone on his heart … and everything black … very
quickly drips and … black paint you know … art … you know …
screaming in Gallery House.

*[Sigi explains that the German Embassy had paid for a special souvenir
programme of the Munich Olympics in a British magazine which also
featured David Medalla protesting the Vietnam War and other political
issues. The Embassy felt embarrassed by this and tried to close the House.]*

Finally, we had to protect the exhibits, [placing] somebody at the door,
securing [it so] that nobody came in to destroy the pieces…
　　…Hundreds of artists were shown … these were exhibitions
without the big exhibitions. [For example,] The Big Breather in the
stairwell [Latham] had that structure going on between the space of the
staircase all the way up to the ceiling with a bulge on top with a flute in
it, a bilge, so he was demonstrating the tide of the ocean especially in the
Irish sea which is the high[est] … and then [Latham] said well we can
have an iron and the ocean will lift the iron and that would be power
and he wanted to lift it up and then the water goes down like the ocean
and then you have the sheer weight of itself again turns over… and there
was a plumbing problem and we tried it out and he said, Sigi you have
to go down there and fix it, and then he put a rope around my ankles
and put my head upside down all the way from the top, all the way into
this 2x2 construction of plexiglass and wood and aluminium and I did
some plumbing at the very bottom and [had to] catch a hose and get the
water in there and it would push up a plate and the water would try to
go up and it would make a sound and as it went up it went *[Later in the
conversation Sigi indicates that the sound was like that of a foghorn.]*

**SK**: It was more like a, maybe like from a boat, it was a dark sound
whoooooooooooooo not just for a while you know whoooooooooooooooo

and once the air was in and the tides would go down and you know the air would go out and the whistle was... it might have been two whistle... and once it was up there and the water goes down then it would make the sound again... Eventually, just the day before the opening of the Düsseldorf show I heard [Sigmar] Polke laughing and talking and coming down to the office with Rosetta and saying that water was coming down and everything was flooded. It made a crack in the plexiglass so the entire floor, [and on] the street ...there was water everywhere we had buckets, we had to do that and keep quiet about it...

**LRN**: There was an opening [*leak*], the carpet was squishy.

**SK**: Oh Dr Schultz, the carpet is squishy. What we did we couldn't hide it... it was late at night and [we had to] be back at 9 am to be open in the morning... So then we were told to leave this kind of political stuff out.

Also on the Net, the Mexican, Felipe Ehrenberg, working in England, recalls working with Krauss on an earlier occasion. The show was called 'The Seventh Day Chicken' and was at Krauss's original place in Neale Street. Ehrenberg lived in Cullompton and worked with Allen Fisher and Peter Finch on a number of occasions; I can't recall the details.

> It was the so-called "Winter of Discontent" and dustmen all over went on strike and rubbish started piling up in many of London's open spaces, including Clapham Common. Richard and I decided that the best way of understanding aesthetics was by studying what was happening with the dustmen, and it's a pretty long and nice story. The city gave out plastic bags, different coloured ones for each borough, and, of course, people used them for their rubbish. Orange boroughs would throw all their orange rubbish nearby, yellow boroughs would throw their yellow bags a few blocks away, but then you began seeing black bags in red boroughs and orange bags in green boroughs... Makes you think, eh? Who on earth will take the trouble to throw their rubbish in their neighbouring borough's rubbish? But it actually looked nice! All that yellow and a couple of black bags and several red ones peppering the yellow piles... So naturally we started talking aesthetics, and the breakdown of social relationships [...] So Richard and I began recording how

rubbish grew, like ideas grow, like concepts grow, like people grow… […] We traced a walk downtown London and adopted a few piles along the way, photographing them every two days. […] we would stop at Sigi Krauss' frame shop gallery, next to Covent Garden and have our tea with him […] so we decided to show everything we'd processed at Sigi's gallery. We actually produced an "unlimited edition" of miniature rubbish bags which we sold to help us recoup our expenses. We had a table full of rubbish bags and performed an "official transference and sale act"… lots of people bought the little rubbish bags (*laughs*).
VF: Different colours?
FE: No they were all black. We were faithful to our borough.
MA: Empty or…?
FE: No no, full of rubbish. Limited edition miniatures.

Actually this wasn't the winter of discontent, which was six years later. Felipe Ehrenberg, interviewed on 2 December 2009. The artists may have been on their best behaviour when writing statements that were going to be enshrined in print, but on a daily basis they were crazed Bohemians very much like the poets I find interesting. Ehrenberg anticipated the habit, three years later, among Punk girls, of wearing bin-liners as dresses – revitalising sheer monochrome PVC. John Latham, asked to revitalise an area of huge shale bings (slag heaps) in Midlothian, decided against any landscaping or adornment but re-framed some of the bings as 'The Five Sisters' with their dramatic contours as curving parts of an earth goddess depicted on a monumental scale.

There is a conceptual style in poetry but there is also a pictorial style, which is older. In our set, if we look at the poems by Wain, Turnbull and Thwaite, we find dense arrays of sensory data (primarily visual) recording real scenes and objects. These poems evidently correspond to pictures. They are pictorial. As you read them, you visualise the pictures. That is the right thing to do. They are an older style. Conceptual poems are more modern. If you look at poetry of 2017, people are still writing pictorial poems. The newer grammar has not erased and replaced the older grammar. There is an issue of quality. If I look at Thwaite's poem 'Monologue In the Valley of the Kings', or at *Residues: Down the Sluice of Time*, I don't think that they needed replacing, or that what came next was better. But it is arguable that Thwaite was unfashionable and that this was a kind of appeal which he did not have.

# Two Visual Poets

## WHITE CUBE, WHITE RECTANGLE: MICHAEL GIBBS

Michael Gibbs was involved with Fluxshoe West and Ehrenberg around 1971, in Exeter, as a post-grad student of Mike Weaver. Gibbs (1949–2009) studied at Warwick University and his artistic conversion came in 1966, with going to London to attend a series of exhibitions, called *The Destruction in Art Symposium*, organised by Gustav Metzger and involving a number of people from what was about to become the conceptual/performance avant-garde in England. He was a student during the key year of 1968. He assimilated the history of visual poetry with incredible speed, started the magazine *Kontexts* in 1969, and did a research thesis on 'Chance operations in Modern Art'. He released a book with Beau Geste, *Lifeline* (1972) and a pamphlet, *Connotations* (1973) with Second Aeon, the most vital centre for concrete and "visual" poetry at the time. In 1970 he wrote "the concrete poets [...] have abolished the linear structure of conventional poetry that is also the linear framework of authority." He was in Amsterdam organising an exhibition, in 1974, when his job came to an end. He decided to stay on in the Netherlands (initially in Maastricht) and lived there for the rest of his life. The *kon* of Kontexts is short for konkret, the German word for concrete (poetry) as developed by Max Bill and Eugen Gomringer. He began with visual poetry made on a typewriter, and always stayed with words even though his business and exhibition links were primarily with the art world in the Netherlands. A position in between Dutch and English was favoured by linguistic formalism – he was focusing on individual words rather than creating dense texts affected by the spoken language and by the complexity of daily verbal life.

One of the books cited in *SomeVolumesfromtheLibraryofBabel* (1982) is an Antwerp publication of 1617 by the Jesuit Bernard Bauhus, *Unius versi Librum*. This text consists of a single line of Latin which is varied (not infinitely but over a very long series) to generate a series of different but still meaningful Latin lines. Tiny serials in 1617? There is a point, which is that the very long continuous series, or multiples, of the Conceptual Art movement, were already present in 1617, and so that the impulse was very old in 1982 and so likely to persist for a long time.

Bauhus was not the founder of the Bauhaus (also Bauhusius, van Bauhuysen, etc.). Probing a bit reveals that van Bauhuysen wrote the original line but someone called Eerrick van de Put produced the 1,022 variations on it. One is *Tot Virgo dotes, quot sidera, sunt tibi caelo*. The short poem was 'Proteum parthenium', and was about the Virgin Mary, and the work of 1,022 variations was called *Pietatis Thaumata* (wonders of piety). *Quot sidera* means 'as many stars'. According to Ian MacFarlane, Ptolemy's catalogue identifies exactly 1022 stars – the number of variant lines may have been rigged to match this count. The concept of continuous tiny variations is like calculus, which hadn't been invented in 1617. The title means "the infinitely variable Virgin thing" and the variations refer to this meaning, i.e. that the Virgin has many divine attributes. Van De Put is not saying that Catholic poetry had been saying the same thing with tiny variations for 14 centuries. That was not the go in 1617. This citation turns me on, it connects with things which systematically turn me on, not to say that I really know about them, and is a showing of what a conceptual artist does: he or she just points to something, carefully arranged so that you can see it clearly and conveniently, and as you look you are subdued by fascination and break through a narrow yet bright passage into a new universe. It was already there but your relationship to it was not the same. I don't have all of Gibbs' books of poetry but I do have some of his publications. What gives the work its quality is his untiring enthusiasm, he has unexhausted creativity and never gets tired of the formal world he lives in. I suppose that visual thinkers have that finer perception of visual distances whereby they can see the millimetric scale and its resolutions. The lift of contact with their awareness is that you temporarily also see things more accurately. This is the impact of Gibbs' creations – they are not exactly pictures, he is often just re-aligning something that was already there, but he permits a breakthrough for the spectator. Key values in modern art generally are the ideas of the infinite and of chance. These are mathematical concepts of immense power which are universally present, that is possible, in nature. Normally we cannot perceive them, partly because they would make daily functional behaviour impossible. Gibbs gives access to them, and of course what follows is a condition of Utopian speculation: you perceive that anything is possible in social arrangements and psychological experience, and this condition is one we wish to stay in. Rain falls on the mountain-top; as soon as a drop forms it wishes to fall, it wants to go down the mountain-side to where things are more corrupt and forms are more rigid and your view is more obstructed. But you need a guide, to hold you there at the summit, where an entire world is visible and nothing is hard and there are no objects. Because the idea of the infinite emerges from the setting up of formal systems where small increments are allowed, without a ban at any stage, that idea is related to the tiny variations which we saw in the *Pietatis Thaumata*. Gibbs had as if an ability to slow time down: every visual moment he offers is ideally clear and this clarity takes us where we want to go. Space is a name we give to the all-capacious, and Gibbs never loses sight of the overriding power of the white space to yield to everything that is here and everything that may come here. He is hardly ever documentary but always attuned to potentiality.

One of the advantages of Gibbs is that unlike some fringe artists he wasn't crazy and not given to megalomaniac utterances about the invalidity of any art except that produced by him and his business associates. Only I know the truth, etc. Not manufactured with this florid aggressivity and lack of proportion, he is an attractive mind and someone pleasant to spend time with. Is it true that poetry arranged in lines promotes authority? This strikes me as Spenglerian. (Spengler declared that the imagination and organisation of space distinguished different civilisations. This was the original cultural criticism in the 1920s, and Gibbs was using it in 1970.) It alerts us to the meaning-bearing structures which the artist perceived in their own art. The dismissal of poetry which has a serial flow is authoritarian enough on its own. *I declare your assets valueless*, etc. I don't buy it because all speech is sequential and follows an imaginary *line*. If you recorded everything I said over the course of a week, you would find that I am never pronouncing two syllables simultaneously. Speech occurs in an order or row, and the value of phonemes depends on which order they come in just as the value of syllables depends on which order they come in. So it would seem that linearity and a rule of successiveness are inherent in speech rather than in the embezzling of social power by one person or another. This heretical idea about linearity has value in forcing us to work out what the rules of design of texts or social interactions are. Indeed, it would seem that semantic context is a field which is static (partly) rather than rapid and serial like the flow of coded sound. Gibbs was being simplistic (aged 21!) but such dense utterances (hundreds of them) had an impact on me, as a novice, because I hated them and had to work out why I couldn't accept them. The idea of being able to depict authoritarian conduct without words, simply through geometry, is intoxicating. What follows, that every measurement of the text yields information about the nation/state which originated the signification, and can be distorted to express cultural critique, has been endlessly productive. That dispute between static fields and dynamic processes was important in the period. If power is resident in geometry, you can apply the geometry of transforms to alter its nature.

There is a 1976 book which the author has described. "One can however easily imagine a book whose every page is taken from another book; page one (and the verso) from book A, pages three and four from book B, and so on. My book *Pages* (Kontexts Publications, Amsterdam, 1976) was assembled in this manner. After obtaining a supply of more than a hundred second-hand books, including volumes in French, English, Spanish, Dutch and German, I first removed all the covers and cut off the spines. The task of collating one hundred sequential leaves from different books, plus new title and colophon pages, was akin to playing a monstrous game of 'Patience'. Each one of the hundred resulting copies of *Pages* is unique."

(I have a copy of the later *Certain Pages*.) Gibbs remarks that this assembly foregrounds features, such as typescript, paper texture, etc. which are normally not consciously noticed. "All books are rectangular, have covers and title pages, and contain sequentially ordered (and usually numbered) pages which are printed with horizontal lines of letters and punctuation marks which combine to form words, sentences and paragraphs." *Some Volumes* was a collection of, or on, thirteen books which did not obey these rules.

Formalist work of this kind bypasses the communicative aspects of language. Natural language involves two individuals and is instrumental to what is happening between or inside those two people. Treating language as something visual, which can be altered by altering the object or fabric it is inscribed on, is radical. Gibbs was a very social man, he spent so much of his time editing magazines, and that model of collecting what a number of other people have been doing and linking them as a collective display is not only sympathetic to him but quite similar to his creative work.

Robin Fox's theory of language is that it developed to replace grooming when the size of a pre-human band grew too large for grooming to work as a social binding in the way it does for baboons. If we spend several hours a day talking, that is also like baboons grooming. The elements of language which Gibbs retained have nothing to do with the grooming stratum of flattery, soothing, intimate attention, reflection of mood, and so on. This has been cut away as if with a razor. Somehow this is one of the moments of disconcerted self-awareness which conceptual art brings, and somehow it sheds light on the group feeling of the faction which produced work for *Kontexts* or *Artzien*. They enjoyed lots of mutual identification, friendship, kindness, etc., like any human group.

Gibbs was involved, almost from the first, in this world, which provided a context for him but which made his work baffling for a larger poetry audience. So maybe the visit by the teenage Gibbs to those DIAS events in London in 1966, seductive and saturated in tomorrow's world as it was, was a fatal moment and left him on the outside of a stable retail world which simply didn't understand.

The retrospective volume quotes a 1975 statement by Gibbs in which he says "19$^{th}$ century concepts of linear order, of time and space, have been superseded in 20th century literature by strategies of *silence* and *synthesis* (including a return to source). External reality proving too chaotic and indefinite has resulted in withdrawal into the self. Into the solipsism of Beckett where the self is the last remaining sign of life / or into the private realm of art." He goes on to recommend language as a game where each move conditions the following ones.

It was not surprising, looking back, that Gibbs found a home in the Netherlands, because that is the home of creating space, and the abiding impression of Gibbs' work is his creation of empty and pristine space: not the objects he distributes through it, but the clean space which takes us right back to the beginning of time and where the history of objects also starts from fresh. The tiny shifts in the 1,022 variations of Bauhusius' line are thematic for what Gibbs does: the shifting of sensitivity to the millimetre scale which renews space itself. Better lenses bring advances of knowledge.

I am trying to disguise the fact that I haven't seen most of Gibbs' books of poetry. There was undoubtedly an avant-garde in the 17th century, even if it only included Eerrick van de Put and Jacob Balde. The Latin language and the Jesuit Order are good places to look for it. I know almost nothing about it. Has British poetry of the Seventies already achieved this level of invisibility?

FROM ALPHABET TO LOGOS

John Powell Ward published *From Alphabet to Logos* in 1973. It is a loose leaf folder of 15 poems, each produced on a typewriter and in the

visual poetry mode, and in A4 format. (Three more poems are on the
cover.) The poems are made of words but these are spread over coherent
visual shapes which dominate the page. A foreword says "the alphabet is
the lowest common factor of the written language […] the logos is the
highest achievement that arrangements of those twenty-six letter forms
can produce. A society's logos is usually imperfect; a society may not
have this logos at all." The one which struck me most was 'The words
of John 1: 1-14 re-arranged', which takes the account of creation and of
Grace, at the start of the Gospel, breaking them down into component
words, and grouping them in blocks. Logos means word, so what an
alphabet naturally forms, but it also means the power of reason, and in
the context of the creation narrative of the first verse of John it means
the creative mind of God. *En arkhe en ho logos*, in the beginning was the
word. Ward said, in 1972, "The typewriter […] is a grid system, with
each space of equivalent size. It goes across and down, one space at a time
and is best used that way. […] So the typewriter lends itself to geometry,
abstraction, and therefore, perhaps, to the infinite, the deep truth that
'number holds sway above the flux'." I like the way the disposition of the
words points to a depth behind which they are suspended, and which is
like the sky which God created on the first day. The sky gives shelter to
the star which was the sign leading the three Magi to Bethlehem (in the
Gospel of Matthew). The object-page is allover and simultaneous. This
loss of elapsing time suits a state of trance: Ward's poems are pitched at
the frequency of the sublime, and this separates them from the other
concrete poetry published by 2nd Aeon. The words in the poem literally
are the words which created the world and the space in which they
expand is outside the Earth. Even the lack of staples reinforces the allover
quality of the pictorial space. A staple would allow the page to revert to
something where the left is the beginning and we move through it to
the end. In that case the wholeness would disappear. The point is that
there is no before and after. Because we re-arrange the scattered words
(where 11 copies of the word "was" are grouped together, for instance),
our memory re-enacts the unscattering of chaos into order which is the
specific function of the Logos.

In three other poems, he decomposes words of a sacred text by
progressively removing their elements as letters, re-enacting in reverse
the miraculous process by which isolated sounds combine into articulate
language, and analogously particles of matter cluster together to form
a material universe, obeying the shaping order of the Logos. The whole

Gospel of John is a single frozen shape, not passing away in time, and linked by multiple internal matches – like the ones reflecting each other in the visual poem. The compelling quality of the space is partly mimesis of the emotion of the poet setting the fragments with such care. The microscopic precision evokes this care – not realism, since the space does not reproduce any measurable space. It is non-dimensional but carries a charge of piety in the way that an embroidered cope, with its thousands of stitches, would. The fine scale of scruples is present alongside the non-finite – the cosmos in the process of being patterned by the Logos. It is possible that the poem (from John) recalls the infantile state, or oral phase– because it is repetitive, because it has no syntax but a boundless flow. The cosmos is apparently passing through an oral phase. The text is full of references to birth – the first moment when we see the light (physical).

I am hesitant about reproducing one of the poems, because, when I did that, in digital form, the poet was unhappy with the result.

# Twelve Vortices for Twelve Brothers:
## Iain Sinclair: *Suicide Bridge*

Just to get the time-lines straight: *Suicide Bridge* was originally published in 1979 and the new edition includes a new title page reading PUNK VORTEX / X-FILE, and "At the end of the book, as it now stands, I will introduce some new material… (found in magazines, or typescript). Three new books. Westering. Brerton, The Darkness. Bowen, His Journey." This material dates from the original time of the rest of *Suicide Bridge* but has never been published in a book before. (Some more extra material has been added in the 'Hand and Hyle' book, describing the mother of the gangster twins Hand and Hyle watching 'High Sierra', a film by Raoul Walsh, on TV, and flashing back to seeing Walsh as a bit actor in *Birth of a Nation*, the first film she ever saw, sixty years before.) The new material represents the monumental end of the Seventies: it means the material is finally there.

The title page shows Sinclair's own label for his work, of punk vorticism; and refers to the status of this work, at its point of origin, as underground, self-published, ground to dust in the margins of malign generalisations, as an X-file. It resurfaces as great writing. Intimate as the text might be, thematically, with other work of the time, Olsonian and mythologising, it transcends what was flowing all around it. A problem which is simply one of book-keeping has limited discussion and anthologising, since *Suicide Bridge* (henceforward SB) is written, at least half, in prose. All the same the scale and intensity and originality of the work simply defy description; this is a modern classic and Sinclair probably now commands a wider spectrum of admiration than any other poet from that time.

*SB* was originally published with the sub-title 'a mythology of the South and East' (mainly London and Cambridge), but the new books add myths of the South-west and North. It starts with what is almost an essay:

Myth is breech: faces backwards. The Siamese twin is place. They are sown together & cannot be separated, dependent systems. Man is the messenger substance between them. He is a raised tube, opened at crown of head & base of feet – so that it flows through him, conscious or unconscious, the power, the surge, the tachyonic voltage. He is erect. That is his vanity, to lift skull to the shafting sun. The wiser animal, the ally, travels with the ground in a relation of mutual benefit, low over the force-lines, guided in his essential journeying. But man is like plant. He is utterly possessed by what place is. He stands where a precisely defined exchange is consummated between star & ground. He is the saline medium. He marks place with a stone. But he is not rooted. He moves away, inflamed, into myth.

Myth is the living breath of place; is life. Place, in travesty, ordains & invests man. He gleams & glistens like the new born, he is […] mythic hero. The lives & virtues of many men, many cycles, are compressed into the one: Demi-God, Sword Bearer, Astronaut, or Suiciding Martyr. Place requires […] that man become myth. A blood bond is contracted. A known place must hold within its definition, edge, the mythology of a known man. Blake tells it: 'PEACHEY HAD NORTH WALES.' It is a sex, a hunger. Man recognises his place by a lust in the skin, wants to go into the side of the mountain, come gold.

So Charles Olson is one point where Sinclair starts from, and this essay ('Myth & Place') could be a commentary on *The Maximus Poems*. 'Tachyons' are particles moving faster than light which have never been observed. Their virtue is to move backwards in time, for some observers; thus 'myth is breech', facing backwards. They do not interact with ordinary matter.

Imagine this New Apocalyptic poem, published in 1943 in the pages of *White Crow* along with Vic Turner, Anthony Souvestre, and J.F. Keery:

Winds out of time's entrails, weaves,
hand, winding tongue-twist myths.
Burst out of the tendrils' dim
the first sights of first light,
the drama of the myth by mouth

at onset and outbreach: where all else was drops,
dank dew is rigoured to ice on the corpse,
the land is scaped and casts
star-sperm into the sky's belly.

Winds a living water, under heel of dust
writhes out the shape of the creature
who must grow into his own shadow,
male, containing, flesh of dew-light, female.
Rears, rod, to ray the length of what remains.

*SB* starts with this paragraph by Sinclair:

Hands out of the entrails of time. Myths are lies. Out of the
bucket. Retain those primary, first light, dramas of aboriginal
creation: *getting*, how here, dew freezing on the corpse, the
erected land hurling star-sperm into the sky's belly, a moisture
snaking among the dust to make the shape of the creature who
must grow into his own shadow, male, containing female, put
flesh into the morning. It is the length of what remains.

The poem is obviously enough a fake, retro-engineered in Area 51. The
demonstration, that Sinclair had not forgotten the Neo-Apocalyptic
tunes and could knock one out when the occasion called for it, perhaps
holds some water. Sinclair has said that early on he was besotted with
Dylan Thomas and wrote poems full of imagery of skulls and so forth. If
we found a Sinclair text before 1960, perhaps even before 1962, it would
sound like Dylan Thomas. Thomas' apprehension of Blake was especially
profound, and Sinclair may even have 'received' Blake via Thomas. (The
*getting* is like 'begetting' but probably pronounced *jetting*.)

*SB* is a series of narratives about mythical characters, living in
contemporary London or Cambridge. According to Wikipedia, "The
Sons of Albion feature in the poem *Jerusalem*. They are 12, and are
named as Hand, Hyle, Coban, Guantok, Peachey, Brereton, Slayd,
Hutton, Scofield, Kox, Kotope, Bowen. These names are mostly drawn
from figures from Blake's 1803 sedition trial." These are the twelve
heroes of the book (and the new material restitutes this pattern).
(Names modified to Slade, Skofeld.) Blake's trial was a nightmare
experience for him, and they are malign figures. Start, in 1937 perhaps,
by deciding that Blake is the flagship of poetry, you have to write like
Blake. How can you do this? After scrapping all the kit of existing
'literary' poetry, you probably go on to scrap the idea of writing sequels
to Blake's existing poems, with that mixture of the Bible and the poets
of Antiquity, all received in translation. No, you don't imitate Blake,

you go back to where Blake started: an available wilderness where you begin to create an original mythology. The history of modern British poetry about this could also be called 'failing by imitating Blake, 1938–1980'. We don't have documents of Sinclair doing Blake sequels, but *SB* is the full-blown plunge into mythological creativity.

We have to get, this early on, into the idea of coherence. *SB* presented itself in 1979 as five books, now become eight. In the book 'Victims' there is a section of seventeen pages on Howard Hughes. What, you may ask, does Hughes, owner of much of Las Vegas, have to do with eastern England? If the 'myth=place' topos is not in fact the core on which the book is wound, then we have to ask what grips the book. Because *SB* has another subtitle, a Book of the Furies, there is another candidate for the overall theme of the work. If we push 'Myth and Place' out of the focal area, we can unify the other material: it is all about characters, human if only barely so, seized by demonic energies, Furies. The rich people are seized by the demon of wealth. The 'tyrannicides' story has an internal coherence as a story about arrogance, abuse of power, and failure, linking three doomed figures and their fall: they were Bladud, Harold Godwinsson, and Chatterton. This presumably gives us the 'suicide bridge' label: a metal bridge spanning a ravine between two hills, in Archway, North London, which several people jumped from (none of whom appears in *Suicide Bridge*). It was part of the folklore, in the Seventies, and linked with a generational theme of people who reached freedom and hedonistic release, partly via drugs, but found that part of their story was the release of sadness, despair, desolation, and died in this phase of the cycle.

Bladud was a character in Geoffrey of Monmouth's twelfth-century historical novel who flew on man-made wings but plunged to his death at the 'temple Apolyne', which stood where St Paul's now stands. This connects to Chatterton and 'the Nine will be mine', meaning the nine muses led by Apollo. Chatterton had written a poem about Hastings, describing the death of Harold. Bladud was dropped by his feathers, Chatterton was poisoned by the contents of a quill, Godwinsson was slain by a feathered arrow. Hand and Hyle may actually be The Furies, as opposed to their victims.

To answer the Hughes question, let me quote one bit of the 'Book of Howard':

There are forgotten men in small town temperance hotels &
mining shacks, mid-continental inertia, who have literally
been waiting in their rooms, sitting by the bed, looking
out on meridian main street traffic, bills paid by computer,
for over thirty years – for the phone-call from Hughes that
will activate them: & meanwhile they write, on type-writers,
science fictions & horror god inventions, squeeze nature into
aborted surgeries, work for WEIRD TALES, John Campbell's
ASTOUNDING, or Roger Corman; they invent (or are made
aware of) impossible literatures in languages that were never
spoken, the Necronomicon, or Ludvig Prinn's 'Mysteries of the
Worm'. […] The invented horrors are literal. They alone see
the shape-shifting of the windows.

They alone stare, night after night, at the planets. They
become part of the machinery. The flying saucers & Cayce-
inspirations spiral from their apparent boredom.

Visibly this is so great that it had to be in the book. The *Necronomicon*,
the 'art of dealing with the dead', written by 'the mad Arab', was a
how-to book for necromancers. The fact that both these books exist
only in the stories of H.P. Lovecraft does not detract from Sinclair's
obvious delight in a covert reference to J.H. Prynne. (Edgar Cayce was
a medium from Kentucky who published the results of several thousand
prophetic trances. An "unofficial" branch of Egyptology exists to bear
out the truth of his visions of ancient Egypt.)

Let's look at a passage from the work: "The Tyrannicides arrive.
Inside the enclosed tropic car heat, fans blowing out essence of jackal,
chicken feathers, red mud, Olduvai bone fragment, is the oracular head
of Alfredo Garcia: a whisper in fly swarm, in Muscat sand, in the swift
tongues of decomposition. Excess of wisdom has made them mad; has
dyed the skin, tanned them the colour of saddle leather. Dead meat
is changed into sound, dense insect squabble, speaking in tongues.
Their blood is malarial fast, Livingstone pallor, shivering, brandy & salt
tablets: Hand & Hyle, brass knuckled Tyrannicides."

We are in Mersea, Essex, "Overhead is the well-documented UFO
track." The spirals, implying a link between celestial and terrestrial
complexes of events, may be part of a Vortex. "The thin shaft in his
eye-socket is the periscope we use; root tendrils & fine hairs feather
the wood, lift towards the informing sun. The ash-scalded tip presses

on his brain nerve: the feather has flowered. Autopsy of linked metals, corrosion, treachery, forsworn impulses of wrist, water hand, error of history enters the chronicle…"

The arrow is a dowser's wand. Scythians fired arrows whose fall was a means of divination, this one is still prophetic even after coming to rest. Earlier we heard that Mersea is "Myrrh Sea, initiatory Magi gift, resin." "Autopsy of linked metals, corrosion, treachery, forsworn impulses of wrist, water hand": this run of five parallels shows the writer's typical vortical repetition which is not static but concentric. As the camera lingers on the image you extract more and more information. This steadiness takes us deeper, it follows a rhythm of optical reaction. It is virtuosic.

Since the 'tyrannicides' are Hand and Hyle, in person, their victims cannot also be suicides. They may have been suicided, know what I mean. Hand and Hyle may actually be The Furies, as opposed to their victims. (The book almost certainly is not named after the bridge at Archway, as we will see.)

So everyone in the book is ridden by Furies? This works better than the 'place' schema. Narratives that slide into each other show a series of Egyptian gods, East End gangsters, physicists, Cambridge poets, oracular heads, aircraft designers, occult scholars, having adventures in a universe whose geometry is not ours. Their deranged energy is related to being one dimension simpler than real people; we see the lines of fearful damage but there are no *limits*. The protagonists are like the heroes of fictions of the time, foci of energy who acquire attributes and possessions and experience to go with their super-powers. Their nature was to be re-enacted; appearances on TV enabling them to show up as toys, in comics, as picture cards. They lent themselves to serials where there was a different guest star each week. Sinclair is drawing on this popular mythology while imitating Blake's narratives of Albion. Hyle, Hand, Kotope, Peachey, Skofeld, Brerton, Bowen: each one has legends strung around their names. None of them is free of Furies. But why these people in particular? We are still thinking of *seriality*, the rhapsodic seizing of stray elements and generators, wonderful transitions to new themes, successive, unexpected, endlessly surprising, never losing forward impetus.

The climactic section of Book One, 'The Older Hidden Powers, the Secret Minds' is about black holes and re-enacts Blake's announcements on cosmology; it is led by Skofeld, a 'secret mind' who combines the myth of J.H. Prynne with Caius College's other star writer, Stephen

Hawking. ("Of course the Devil does not actually live in Cambridge. And who can blame him?") Are Hawking and Prynne ridden by Furies? In this case the Furies are creative, though they abrogate the personality of the human bearer.

A black hole spins, is surrounded by a vortex, and has some quantities approaching infinity. It is possible that this account of bending space is the basis for taking up Hawking (on time and black holes) in a book about the Sons of Albion. So 'Myth … faces backward' would repeat 'perceives… roll backward behind'. In that case, the mind-bending cosmology of the 'Older Hidden Powers' is a counterpart to the essay on 'myth and space' at the beginning. There is in fact a "bridge" spoken of in this context. The conjecture is that every black hole is accompanied by a "white hole", at a different point in space-time, where matter gushes out and its state of density is released. The link between the two holes, totally hypothetical of course, is called an "Einstein-Rosen bridge". The longest book of *SB* is called 'Punk Vortex X-file' and the most obvious deduction, that the shape is key to the book, and that that shape is a vortex, may actually be correct. The work is full of references to black holes (which have spin and so are vortices), and the theme of the book may be an exit from time sequence in which the black hole acts as a bridge, into the past, at the cost of disintegration – the suicide. We could imagine the poem as being written on a circular building, a torus. This is how Sinclair is a 'punk vorticist'. At the climax, 'The head of Slade still looks like a head, rings hollow, an elegant lattice of numbers in treaty, in alliance, re-entering the ionised dust cloud, mating with silica, iron, false carbon. The cloud thickens, all voices, all numbers, radial velocities, become the galactic motive, into the arms of the nebula[.]' This sounds like the formation of a gravity well as the forerunner of a 'black hole'. This section is largely about Coban, an elder god who (like Atum) is known only to himself.

Lovecraft's higher-dimensional monsters come into the theories Skofeld is testing.

If Slade becomes a black hole at the end, the outlaw at the very start of the book, Billy the Kid, may be the re-appearance of Slade. Tachyons are supposed to originate in (theoretical) white holes. But these are not suicides. The stories had a gravity forbidding other trajectories.

> The nature of infinity is this: That every thing has its
> own vortex; and when once a traveller thro' Eternity

Has pass'd that Vortex, he perceives it roll backward behind
His path [.]
                    (from 'Milton')

So we have Blake describing vortices and talking about a reversal of the
flow of Time. This is where you get the bridge between the Sons of Albion
and the theory of black holes as developed by theoretical physicists. In
fact, however luxurious the range of vivid sensations swooping around
in the poem, this is the pivot. (Does rolling backwards mean a reversal
of time flow? Must try and read the manual sometime.) Of course,
Wyndham Lewis was a Vorticist and he features here and there in the
narrative. The whirling around of the *punk vortex* means that any point
moves, but moves back towards its original position. When Sinclair
refers to "orbit of the Killing vector", the vector in question is a branch
of geometry formulated by Wilhelm Killing which is used to model the
rotation of black holes. Can we link this to a two-chord song in which
movement forward and back is suspended?

I have a feeling that the transformation of Slade into a heavenly body
may be the re-enactment of a process in Egyptian mythology which is
known as a catasterism. The text refers to time as a serpent, a creature
which naturally coils itself up. There is an image of a serpent swallowing
its own tail, the ouroboros, which is not mentioned in the text. Serpents
would not naturally do this. The serpent image may refer to time as a
coil, and may be an organic copy of the coil of a vortex. "Time is what we
cut from the belly of the serpent." Slade is observed by one of twin East
End gangsters breaching gang discipline. This is simply snogging in the
park with someone's wife. When the punishers cut his body into parts,
for secure disposal, this is the start of the black hole disintegrating him: as
his head feeds into the vortex a tiny amount of time before the start of his
body, his body must fly apart, travelling around the vortex on different
paths. The question is not resolved and it is something happening off-
screen, a deduction we could make about the plot of a film after it is
over. When Sinclair cites *De vermis mysteriis* (or, on the mysteries of the
worm), by Ludvig Prinn, this is a joke about Prynne's apparent eminence
in the stories of H.P. Lovecraft but also a covert reference to the serpent
coil *Ursymbol* of the book – worm as serpent.

So much of *Suicide Bridge* is a description of geometric figures. It
is as if Sinclair were watching a film and the text is notes on what he
is watching. Sinclair went to film school and his books can be seen as

descriptions of films he didn't make. The vital school of film criticism, in the Sixties, was *auteur* theory, the grand production of intense argument among the writers of *Cahiers du Cinéma*. This isolated artistic patterns of directors, typically through camera movement and editing patterns. Alexandre Astruc spoke of *caméra stylo*, the camera as biro, something which was guided by the hand of the director and which allowed the handwriting of the film. Given a length of film, you could work out who had directed it by the visual style. Sinclair certainly planned his narratives in terms of the angle from which they would be filmed and the way the shots were edited together, but for me he was interested in geometry as a way of characterising the figures of the narrative. Start with the space, deduce the character from how it moves through the space. A passage about Montague Druitt illustrates this:

> prisoner of the sharpened future cone
> [...]
> 'orbit of the Killing vector'
> old question: is there death before life
>
> MD cut it into the accident elbow
> of his glass, his black keyhole
> refined into inertia
>         it was found
> among the grinding mills, the cones
>         a pattern
> presented to him, trace elements
> of the dying molecular equation
> fuel'd his insight, brought his own decay
>        the magnitude
> of what he could not see

Oddly, he seems to be describing the geometry of the scene and leaving the psychological experiences of the characters out. Hitchcock said that a film should still be fascinating if the words cut out and you just had a sequence of images. Why a cone? *Grinder* and *cone* sounds like making coffee from beans, but that is not what is going on. The path of a body into a black hole can be seen as a cone: the body has many possibilities at the start, but its possibilities get fewer and fewer as it falls down the gravity well which was the outcome of the initial super-density. The narrowing of movement in perspective is a cone shape, wide at the top but narrow at the bottom. The volume too of the body would decrease as the gravity presses it more and more. Because this body is getting smaller and disintegrating into smaller grains, as its tip is ripped apart from its rear, at different parts of the gravity well, it is like something being ground. The vortex is indeed going round like a mill, although it is not friction which tears the infalling bodies or beans apart. The "molecular equation" is dying because it too will be ripped apart, losing structure at sub-particle level. MD is facing destruction but also has a line of sight; while light can still escape the gravity trap he can still see: a keyhole, a narrow view because it is looking down a cone and he is going towards the tip of that cone. (The vector would describe the movement of one point in the black hole, of which the whole is described by a vector field. This kind of rotation is not normally described as an orbit, but *orbit* fits the eye which is being described as part of the line of sight.) MD is Montague Druitt. This goes back to a stage, in the publication of the genuine 'MacNaghten notes' on suspects for 'Jolly Jack' listed by the police in 1894, after the murders had stopped. When the list was published by Dan Farson in 1959, only initials were used. Druitt (gifted cricketer, growing madness, Ripper suspect, suicide by drowning) returns, in altered form, as a character in *Radon Daughters*. The vortex is the waters of the Thames drawing him down. Elbow means a bend in a river: perhaps his plotline goes through a sharp bend because its proper momentum is sharply interrupted by the tyrannical attraction of the gravity well: a detour, as in a film by Edgar G. Ulmer. The *magnitude of what he could not see* may be a reference to the black hole, from which no light can escape. This is why it is black. The description of how MD's time-line crushes into the tip of a cone illustrates the consistent use of *alien* geometry where the characters are defined by the way they move. As in this Cambridge scene, each one moves through a particular space as if a character in a ballet who has a distinctive metre for all their music:

> King's College Chapel is heavily coded,
> in numerical bondage (see Pennick: *The Mysteries of…*)
> so that James D Watson
>      'staring up at the gothic pinnacles'
> is speeded, fed back, shoved into light;
> who earlier had fetched the horse's steaming heart
> from fen plain abattoir

to submit to x-ray crystallography
to find the facet'd clue, the irreducible:
the key is the shadow of the door, a template
from which the work is done, the dark unlocked

because of the shape the thought moves faster
crushed & remade to form the TETRAHEDRON;
the eye is not needed, the body
put out to pasture

So much of the text is a description of these characterising geometries. It is like the optical plan of a never-made film. Nigel Pennick is a neo-pagan writing on symbolic shapes in the landscape, the book is *The Mysteries of King's College Chapel*. The operative landscape is not without limits but bound by the rules of imaginary geometries. James Watson discovered the double helical form of the DNA molecule, here merged with the sacred geometry of the Gothic King's College Chapel (next door to Caius). Somehow the chapel is based on the ribonucleic acid molecule and the double helix is based on sacred geometry. The Crick/Watson research literally did use horses' hearts as a source of tissue to prepare for X-ray crystallography. Another sacred site is in Somerset –

we have circumnavigated the profile
of the Sleeper, the snake path
worn into his cheek, though it is
not as simple as that, more radical, stronger

– this passage refers to a theory that the terrace winding around the side of Glastonbury Tor is a spiral maze, in fact a three-dimensional maze. This is an invention of Geoffrey Russell. The maze was there for a pilgrimage. It was picked up by Geoffrey Ashe, in print. Ashe also connects the winding path to a "world-mountain" on which significant rituals take place and of which the Tor is an example – a local version of a cosmic archetype. John Michell believed that the path was the track of the coils of a dragon, associated by him with flying saucers and with a spiral energy.

Beside underground poets, celebrities are prominent in the work. This is one of the features of the lowest and least imaginative of popular prints. (*Tachyon*, a kind of particle that carries the information to make bad films.) This is where Sinclair grabs a large slice of Pop culture

– also where he overlaps with the 'Howard Hughes' figure in James Ellroy's fictions. I am not urged to connect the tales of celebrity with 'postmodernism', however we write out the warrant for that, when the whole of Gaelic and Welsh poetry, just about, is about the lives of the local aristocracy. It is natural to tell tales about the wealthy and powerful. If this is 'postmodernism' we have to apply that bedraggled label to the Gaelic 'Book of the Dean of Lismore', around 1515. More cogently, if we consider Sinclair's career, after film school, as someone vaguely employed by the producer/director Michael Reeves, we see him close up to celebrity: Reeves hired Boris Karloff for his 'The Sorcerers' (a great minor film, tagline 'Boris Karloff He Turns Them On… He Turns Them Off… to live… love… die or KILL!'). In film, the characters are ordinary people played by celebrities, that is the rule.

Devising expensive films (and Sinclair devised a few low-budget ones, as we will see), hinges on using celebrity stars as the actors. (The movie database, IMDB, shows him as director of four films to date.) By 1979, Sinclair's close friend Tom Baker (who also wrote the script for Reeves' film *Witchfinder General*), was a celebrity as the star of 'Dr Who'. The celebrity thing is part of writing myth: modern mythology rotates around celebrities. Woven into the description of Bladud's feather suit is a reference to the black feathers adorning Delphine Seyrig's dress in *L'année dernière à Marienbad*: *SB* uses celebrity scandal and megalomania, horror stories, and gangster stories. These are the pulp of the rainy streets, the staples of TV and paperbacks. It's not amazing that a poet could handle this material flawlessly and with great confidence, but it is surprising how few poets did. Sinclair simply had to write well about Howard Hughes and he could release the strength and produce something masterful (like the 17 pages about HH in *Suicide Bridge*). This releases a more basic point, that Sinclair hoovered up a huge range of themes and styles, something like *SB* shows him being successful in using all of them. And – we have *Suicide Bridge* because Sinclair wasn't at Pinewood making those films. Directing Roger Moore, Alexandra Bastedo, and Patrick Wymark, no doubt.

The verse organisation is loose, reminiscent of thiasic pagan incant-ations rather than of the remorseless organisation of Latin verse and its renaissance successors. It is impulsive, perhaps more to do with visual experience than with a rhythmic and verbal one.

Yet it alternates with highly ordered prose. Strangely, versification is the one area where Sinclair does not out-distance everyone around him.

Even if *Rear Window* is a myth about the inevitability of the married state (*à la* Raymond Bellour), which is hardly factual, *Suicide Bridge* is not a myth about trades and institutions, or the origin of table manners. This idea of efficiency, that 'myth' displays the code in which social rules are written, implies also tautology and predictability. Sinclair's work is motivated by a process of seizing and repeating vivid sensations and patterns, at every step. The Atum article I looked up says that offerings to him included 'Numerous small bronze boxes containing mummified eels'. As Sinclair equates Ely (eel-island) with Heliopolis (site of a great shrine to Atum), drawing the link is effortless for him. Assumptions of logic and efficiency can only be applied to myth by a reckless and high-handed approach to the uncut material. Do we see modern scholars whose work gained legitimation by being rational and without ornamental excess, constructing mythologies which were like filing-systems, and where everything fitted together? Real myth reaches arbitrary complexity by applying modes of analogy which are really fantasy, and infantile processes of repetition, attachment and acquisition. *Suicide Bridge* reaches that arbitrary complexity because that devises an emotional space able to contain the reader – a satisfying artistic gestalt. I am wondering about Coban. I couldn't figure out who he is, although I guessed he was the Dream Time figure who ground the sand for the Copacabana beach.

A whole hymn to Atum is included, quoted from Mircea Eliade's anthology of religious texts, ultimately from the Chicago *Coffin Texts*. One aspect of Sinclair's Seventies work is the leap from reading these archaic and anthropological texts to writing passages like them. *SB* has less material on Egypt than *Lud Heat*, the earlier book, but it still keeps cropping up. The source may be diffusionism, if anything has a beginning. In *Lud Heat* the built layout of London re-creates shapes from Egypt and channels Egyptian narratives, acting as a set of invocation shrines. In *SB* the names 'Hyle and Hand' refer to an Egyptian creation myth:

> Atum is considered to be the primeval, self-made god of the Heliopolitan cosmogony; he then created, by masturbating, the first couplet of gods, Shu and Tefut. (Karol Mysliwiec).

The hand "was worshipped as the goddess Iusaas, to whom a shrine was devoted in Heliopolis". The text determinedly attributes the creation to Coban, so perhaps Hand is simply the hand he used to do the deed. The two are thus the faces of the fallen material world (the eyes of the abyss) as well as East End gangsters (and the avengers from Don Siegel's 'The Killers' who kill Ronald Reagan). The equation of Hand with this elder god may, it is suggested, be an error of a character named Peachey, outnumbered by the texts he is reading. The creative aspect of Pennick's work is that the patterns he discusses are not there. This is why he owns them. The concept of shape as lens is ultimately the Neoplatonist idea of shapes as magically bringing events about, as expounded by Frances A. Yates. This is the belief underlying sympathetic magic, which is why the Neoplatonists are at the basis of Western magic. (Ultimately is a word that often means "this isn't true but it's fun to think about", at least in this genre of fringe literature.)

It is no secret that the plunge into a long form, with the extra load this places on all members of the poem's fabric, was not joyful and triumphant for every poet who took it. Like most ideas that hundreds of people take on, the idea is strong and the scale of *SB*'s composition is integral to its greatness, to its superiority over simpler forms of poetry. This is presumably where a background in the film industry made the difference. Composing 30-line poems to fill a hole in a magazine does not train you in the techniques that nourish a long poem – the infrastructure, so to speak. The point is not about films Sinclair actually worked on, in 1965, 1968 or later, but the intellectual endeavour of devising films, accepting simple ideas and developing them out into 'feature' length, the unpaid creativity of someone who is going to be a great director – or, to be a director on the X-list who makes films out of words. This someone is composing in larger forms and has practiced that scale of composition and developed powers for bringing it to a head. More simply, they have practiced the art of foreknowing which ideas are not going to come to a conclusion. So in fact *SB* contains a dozen long-form poems (or prose poems) and they are all successful. It may be helpful to think of the separate parts of *SB* as films which Sinclair has devised and of which we have only a written description.

Sinclair had apparently limitless stamina. As for imitating Blake, everyone was doing that; I suggest, and this has to be speculative, that someone who can take such insane risks has resources of calm and stability which allow them not to crash. Sinclair's whole lifestyle was geared to the creativity which these monumental works would demand. It is still astounding that one person can 'learn from Las Vegas' to write about Howard Hughes, and also assume the mantle of Blake.

Let me express regret that the "suicide bridge" is not the one crossing Archway, (and the "suicide bridge" phrase is used twice in *Lud Heat* about some canal bridge in Hackney).

# Who Owns the Future?
## Ideas about time

The shared memory, solidifying in, say, 1981, did not remember everything wonderful and innovative which had happened in the decade. If you turn up, 45 years later, to look at a moment when people were claiming to know what the future was, you are bound to say, The future was not where you were looking for it. This obliges us to talk about how Time dealt with the era – how the Seventies ceased to be possible. But to start with, we have to deal with a particular version of the time curve. It is the line kited by Bloodaxe Books saying that Ken Smith "inspired a whole generation" and is "the godfather of the new poetry", and by Donald Davie claiming that the whole period 1960–88 was dominated by Basil Bunting and sub-let "under Briggflatts". Mottram listed 46 poets in his momentous statements, of whom one was Ken Smith.

### Outlaws in the Outlands: *Fox Running*

The classic telling of the liminal idea, in Western Europe, is the Celtic wilderness/outlaw myth. Confusingly, this exists in variant forms around the Irish Sea: Tristan, Lailoken (Merlinus Silvestris), the Children of Lir, Sweeny Geilt.

The first publication of Bloodaxe Books was *Tristan Crazy,* (1978) a group of poems by Ken Smith. The Tristan story involves an exit into the uncoded which has many echoes in modern times. Smith incorporated a few brief elements from Beroul's *la Folie Tristan* into a story about a love affair in the 1970s; the concept was a bit simpler in the Middle Ages. The land of the built-up and the cultivated, with its dense boundaries and its outright ownership, is surrounded by a wilderness typically of forest, which has no boundaries. When Tristan lives in the forest, as an outlaw, he also becomes uncoded, leaving behind the rules which govern behaviour. This is madness, the *folie* of the title (although in fact he is faking it). Who else is roaming the forest? It was the dwelling, not only of Lailoken and Tristan, but also of hermits, outlaws, hunters, and the deranged. Collectively, they do not take part in the economic life of society or its rigid and compelling role structures, and are psychological models for life as an Underground poet. The Dark Age forests contained, not only drop-outs, but also creatures intermediate between humans and animals; these are a feature which the Underground is missing. Smith went on from Tristan to a similar story, *Fox Running* (1980), which is about this uncoded space. This takes the form of a nervous breakdown. It is a breach and exit. We see Fox running through a city (London); just running. He is a wild creature misplaced, treating the city as if it were a wild place. He lives by scavenging and is hunted by dogs. He remembers "mountain ash and the wide sky". The fox is not the poet (who says "I've seen him"), but (apparently) a man-animal creature called Fox. Many biographical details of Fox may coincide with biographical details of Ken Smith in circa 1978. Thus a reference to the river Isca (now the Exe) takes us back to Exeter, Iscanceaster, where Smith lived in the early 1970s. The motif does not involve defiance, but bleakness – no-one thinks urban foxes are really happy eating leavings from discarded fast-food containers, in the chill of 4 a.m., by the glow of sodium light.

Fox writes in the margins of the one book he has left. He shows us a film show of someone long dead (Muybridge's experimental studies of motion?), bouncing a ball. Beginning and beginning over again; he recalls a marriage which broke up. The language is sparse:

Aloof distant alert
holed up between running
in his red slash of fox body
running from the emptied distance

Crowded with townspill
of building sites' muddy footings
where will be flyover
industrial estate new bungalows

He is perhaps out of bourgeois society because of grief; he makes a living but only from hand to mouth. He gets work as a barman. He remembers the days of love, repetitively thinks of suicide. He and his wife fought; he got a single ticket to the city. He is afraid of living lonely and dying alone; he doesn't want to die naturally, wants to die dramatically. He wants to keep running. In a borrowed room in Camden, he starts again from nothing. He is 40. He travels, in circles, drinks, signs on the dole and argues it out with the social security department. He sees his double on the underground. At midnight, high up in someone's house, he recovers from his wish to die (ambiguously); he listens on shortwave radio to American Forces Network, the English-language Radio Moscow, the police frequencies; until daylight. He imagines a nuclear war, set off by misinterpreting radar signals, and the end of society. He remembers his wife and says, he was born to write but she made him what he is, a fox. He recalls being a dog, i.e. a good citizen with a home. He drifts again through the city, reading graffiti and playground rhymes. He becomes a crow for a stanza, possibly a reference to another Yorkshire poet. He chases his double and sees him killed by skinheads. The next ten pages, centring on the theme of Word but very loosely organised, seem to be about the search for a meaning to life to hold onto while imagining a lonely and seedy death, and experiencing it day by day. The focus spreads out from a particular day to a lifetime, from the concrete figure of Fox to anyone anywhere. He wanders around far-flung parts of London; applies for a variety of low-paid jobs, imagines a series of impoverished and rootless lives. A parodic flashback to a year zero, to (Neolithic?) "stonecutters" in moorland villages. He recalls men he knew of an older working-class generation, living in squalor. The death of Fox. (There are several fantasies about dying. These episodes establish the emptiness of his daily life, which fails to keep fantasy at bay; and the emptiness of his future, as he really has no concrete plans to cling to.)

Despite the objective details, the drama is taking place in the head of the hero; there is no dialogue. The action is irrelevant, and certainly no resolution. It is both true that re-readings produce quite different impressions, and that the situation on page 40 is the same as it was on page 1. We can speculate that indeterminacy at the level of the individual line is a compensatory move to replace the uncertainty once delivered by having several characters interacting, what is now lost in monologue dramas. We get the sense record, all the time; the language has a kinetic quality, which may be a symptom of frustration. Some moments take us past the sense record. Muybridge's instantaneous and discontinuous exposures added up to a continuous narrative; but photography can only show the present. Ken Smith uses the phrase *persistence of vision* in talking about the Muybridge motion studies. This is why, outside the poem, we see rapidly replaced still frames as movement. Inside it Fox is remembering his past life, no longer there to see. Cinema relies on static images being interpreted through an illusion to seem like a moving image; Muybridge did not invent cinema, he made series of stills. Fox can see the images of his past life but the connection between them is broken. He can see the city he now lives in but he can't connect the merely sensory images to form a story. The Muybridge pictures broke down what was connected. Fox is broken down because of trauma – an event in the past, affecting him at a level which photography cannot show. *Fox Running* is in reality a dizzying series of montages of frustration; there is a swerve of avoidance between the eye and what it sees.

We see a, probably imaginary, scene of a bloody murder by skinheads; then "spring festival / urban version / late century twenty", so that the death is recoded as the maiden sacrifice in *Le Sacre du Printemps*. This passage is a crux. First, it is the admission of knowledge. It is where culture could supply an articulate symbolic pattern by means of which the subject could recognise what is happening to them and go into the depths of their being and bring the truth out of darkness. Secondly, it is a transition to another mode of writing, similar to Mottram in his poems of the time, such as *Local Movement*. It probably shows the influence of Mottram. Thirdly, the description of the Stravinsky link is vestigial. It barely seems worth including if eight words are all we get. Smith does not want self-awareness. The link to a ballet is obscured by the phrasing and instantly discarded. It is not given a chance to contribute to the story. Smith really does not want to come over as a ballet fan.

The poem starts with an exit from society and ends with an exit from personal identity and a localised body as well. When Fox is listening to shortwave radio, he is a disembodied listener to floods of messages not meant for him, from which he is absent; the room is full of clocks showing different times; and it is midnight, outside the normal time of activity and sociality. (Urban foxes are nocturnal.) It is difficult, in terms of conventional narrative or drama, to explain why Smith wants to reach this no-place, with its negation of oppositions. The key is the theory of liminality, and this explains why we might perhaps want to reach this no-place, and enjoy non-local information. The scene of someone listening to the radio in the middle of the night while thinking about the atomic bomb exactly repeats a scene in David Gascoyne's 1956 verse radio play, *Night Thoughts*. Smith's special variation is to see the timeless as a zone of depression – the place you go during a nervous breakdown. In fact, the whole situation of *Fox Running* is someone on the edge of a new life – like *Change*. Dissociation opens a psychologically empty area which the mind naturally wants to populate with new associations. This energy aroused by negation is the vital force of the poem, the experience we enjoy while reading it.

Smith's feeling is that any straight-ahead account of the breakdown of a marriage is going to arouse hostility and partisan identification which could wreck the poem as much as they wrecked the marriage. One of the great themes, probably, of Western art in this period, say 1960–90, was the end of relationships – most intensely, the breakup of marriages. A fox relates to a dog as an unmarried man relates to a married (and civilised) man – this is the core image of the poem. Of course, the notion that the civilisation process could be reversed, and a marriage could break up, is revelatory and tragic. Another theme is the internalisation of guilt, often identified as a great English trait; Fox doesn't seem to be able to find anyone to blame; logically, his wife is to blame, but the other rule of the time is that women aren't to blame for anything, so we don't get that either, and he internalises that failure too. The lack of interest in any kind of politics is an example of privatisation, there are no events except personal ones.

The statements in the poem seem pointless and disconnected. There may be a linking structure: we can suppose that some of the lines follow a search for meaning and record a negative result. We can *imagine* searches to achieve dignity, to demonstrate strength (to wipe away shame), for social esteem, from their frustration. This is a way of reading the poem but raises the issue that our search for a pattern in it may be frustrating in the same way that Fox's search for a role is. The disconnected still photographs in the opening section offer a bracketing concept for this: the whole poem, perhaps, is snatches of perception that fail to add up to anything. The whole poem is limited by Smith's paratactic sentence structure, keeping us in a continuous present but not giving us explanations or judgments. The images lack definition. Smith does not record the search, only external details. It is like a film with no soundtrack: some of the images point back to the state of mind of the character observing them. You can make the link back. But, over 40 pages, there are long stretches where this isn't true. Following a suggestion by John Goodby, I looked at *The Poet Reclining* (the 1989 *Selected*) and came up with 100 uses of the word "stone" (or variants, e.g. "stony") in the first 120 pages. This does seem like a serious problem, and we have to address it. At the end of *The Poet Reclining* is an additional poem about the character Fox – 'Fox in October'. It is about 80 lines long and includes the phrase "He forgave" 20 times. The problem isn't just about re-using the same image, it is about uninflected verbal repetition – and this is a consequence of a neglect of the power of syntax, a shunning of the devices of language that relate things to each other, qualify them, find a pattern in them, and conduct an argument. What is he forgiving? The main poem does not describe Fox as being resentful or say why he was angry with these 20 people or groups of people. Smith's grip on language wasn't enough to let him establish that information. So the forgiveness is puzzling and underdefined. The repetition is a sign that the poet's verbal powers are inadequate. Some poetry uses complex language and is obscure, but this is obscure because it uses very simple language. Smith is so keen to reduce psychological processes to images that much of the plot is unclear. The main character cannot articulate his feelings. The lack of definition makes it hard to say anything conclusive about the poetry but also makes it hard to find bottom when you are in the middle of the poem. In fact, that is one of the core sensations when reading *Fox Running*: under-definition. The only source of information on the situation was a not very communicative person. Even at the end, you haven't got very much. Why doesn't Smith describe feelings? There definitely was a faction in the Sixties which believed that any description of feelings or other abstractions weakened the poem. When there was a line which wasn't about dumb physical details, they sat up and said "Aha!". When they wrote a poem, they took all that stuff out. This is related to the Fifties purge of ideology.

There are several ways of considering the outlaw situation, but one very helpful description of it is through the idea of liminality. Turner was an anthropologist of law. His idea sees dissidents withdraw from society, to a space outside fixed ownership and property boundaries, but also stresses the rite of aggregation, whereby the breach comes to an end and the conflicting parties are reconciled. My idea is that the Underground process was constructed to enact a ceremony of re-aggregation and enter a re-unified literary world. But also, that the appeal of these legends of exile and dissidence was as a mirror of the radical Left's expectations about declining capitalist society and migration to a new social order. The central myth of the time was dropping out. Poets used inherited liminal structures to express this. This deprogramming could look like an acid trip, but also like a nervous breakdown. It also often took penitential form. The movement is from myth to law. Poets found it easier to record myth than the movement of opposing arguments and interests in a legal dispute. Where they did not overcome this inhibition, the movement is incomplete.

## A NEGATIVE VERDICT

The new publishers which emerged in the decade and grew to have a major presence in the shops did not take on any of the post-'68 ideals: Carcanet and Bloodaxe each represented a literary myth, but an older one. Their flagship anthologies displaying "the new poetry" were *Some Contemporary Poets*, 1983, and *Poetry With an Edge*, 1988. *Some Contemporary Poets* takes on none of the 46 poets listed by Eric Mottram as the New Thing; *Edge* takes on only two. The verdict of key cultural players was thus that nothing worthwhile had happened in the Seventies. We need to pay attention to these versions of collective memory. Some significant players lived through the Seventies without ever finding the good poetry. But the omission of almost every good poet on the scene at the time looks like *rollback*, a big topic in the 1980s.

Why did Basil Bunting and Ken Smith become cherished by affection and evade the *erasure of memory*? The end of the age of ideology left reviewers clamouring for poetry about objects and physical work. This privileging of the sense record was front and centre in the late Fifties and early Sixties: what I am doubting is that this was also the most important style in the 1970s. My feeling is that this stress on objects was a hangover from the 1950s, out of date by 1970. A point of climax might be a moment in *Briggflatts* (1966), where the poet says, rather sententiously, that his message must be carved in stone because anything else is too soft. This equates poetic significance with stoniness. Descriptions of objects are admired, and either introspection or abstraction are seen as anti-poetic: language has to stay with the concrete even if human beings flourish in feelings and ideas. This formation includes an admiration for the working class, seen as authentic because its members deal with objects. (This version has a male-only working class and they work only in demanding physical jobs.) Their distaste for abstraction correlates with a lack of abstract values like wealth, and of cultural capital. Bloodaxe took their name from a character in *Briggflatts*, and Carcanet issued what looks like an ideologically purged version of modern history – *Under Briggflatts* (by Donald Davie).

Carcanet Press (beginning in 1969) seized a literary wish-world in which there would never be any dumbing down, there would never be any breach between new poetry and the internalised love objects of classical English literature, where every text would have been made to withstand Close Reading, where there was no trace of invading Pop culture, where the poets stood up to moral examination and could defend their work as acting out a set of moral values. It would not invite mediagenic poets. The poetry would be free of the narcissistic greed-spirituality of Beat. It would be free of drugged/guru explanations of the cosmos. It would contain precise observations. All these values enacted inhibitions and the cumulative effect blocked off most poetic impulses. The aggregate was profoundly attractive and by being stable created an emotional place which created a following, a company to be found in that place. The word neo-conservative was whispered.

Bloodaxe also offered a wish-world. Once you have piled up assets like {gruff, authentic, Northern, hills, Anglo-Saxon, hard, rugged, physical, working class} a significant fraction of the audience have already surrendered. It was an emotional place which they wanted to spend time in. This line flourished in *Stand*, from Leeds, which Ken Smith co-edited in the Sixties, and in the North. It flourished, from 1978, in Bloodaxe Books. It took on Bunting as an anti-abstract poet, and took on Smith and Pickard, but rejected anything more innovative. The phrase *dumbing down* hung around like a personal assistant. It was puzzling how a style which in Smith was an expression of poverty and alienation, even nervous breakdown, could be presented in many younger poets as normal and even desirable.

Perhaps it was asserting regional identity by discarding all the innovations of the past 20 years – the metropolitan sacrifice. There was a period in Chinese history (AD 304 to 439) known as the Sixteen Kingdoms. As a glance at my list of significant works published during the time will show, my version of the Seventies is completely different from the articulated memory recorded in *Some Contemporary Poets* and *Poetry with an Edge*. This raises a problem about historical objectivity – how can you reconstruct the history of poetry in the 1970s while disqualifying and silencing the memory of most of the witnesses who lived through it? If there were sixteen kingdoms conducting affairs at the time, the question is how you make the story narratable. Attentiveness requires focus.

The idea that 5,000 interested people could have 5,000 varying memories of what happened is a convenient door into the idea that the future was unforeseeable. The future is the realm of the 256 kingdoms. No other geography will suffice. One consequence of this is that the emotionally attractive belief that *I am the future of poetry* was going to be proved wrong, even if it took twenty years for this belief to collapse in its collective form. The future of poetry in 1975 was quite multiple and uncontrollable.

The empirical faction had made a virtue of only dealing with one person's line of sight and only accepting the sense record. The new poets gathered that and resolved to do the exact opposite. The indeterminacy of the new poetry is an attempt to resolve in stylistic terms the unresolved possibilities of social experience. Language can be used to exclude all possibilities except one, but can also be used to dissolve its own power and expose a thousand trajectories – the field within which narrow, exact paths elapse. This is really one of the big things happening in Seventies poetry.

Both publishers claimed Bunting, in the Eighties, as the founder of modern poetry – incredibly. Neither of them had any space for the British Poetry Revival, for radical lifestyles or for the poetic Left. It is hard to avoid the conclusion that Bunting (and Smith) were being selectively interpreted and used to justify a roll-back. The physical poetry is too much like retiring to a shed and doing DIY because modern life is too complicated. We saw earlier how Smith was unwilling to describe the emotions of his character – surely this was a technical failing, however much you admire stones for not having feelings. The idea that you can just write about the sense record and this will amount to Virtue is unbelievable. In the end you have to have feelings and you have to write about feelings. The period 1960-88 was not lived out "under Briggflatts". This is just silly and a cover for suppressing almost everything else. However, the achievement of those two new firms, with their rapid growth, in dealing with the retail world and giving a market what it wanted, was not less than great. Astley's immersion in the work of Ken Smith is impressive; when he makes that claim about Smith, the subtext is really that Neil Astley is "the godfather of the new poetry". It is interesting that someone from Mottram's playlist, who completely went over to parataxis and showed traces of being "open field", could be used, later, as a cudgel to beat the Underground with.

Conceptual art eliminates the sense record. Fifties-style empirical poetry removes anything except the sense record. But both were a reaction against ideology, the seepage of the Cold War. You discredit other people in the expectation that the reader will trust *you*.

FAILURES OF THE UNDERGROUND

Originally, I had a long chapter on the failings of the new style of the '70s. Obviously, I had a lot to say, after spending forty years reading the bad stuff as well as the good. But I decided that this ambivalence is not consonant with enjoying the idea of poetry. Rather than explain the failures of the time, I will just say that if there were 905 books published in a twelve-month period, as catalogued by *Poet's Yearbook*, surely 90% of them were no good, and even that is a generous figure. Naturally, it is true to say that the story should also involve people who didn't enjoy the new thing, who didn't have a taste for social radicalism and cultural criticism, and couldn't follow the freer association patterns on request. The artistic history of the time includes authors who were part of the "long 1950s" and writing excellent poetry (Peter Porter, Anthony Thwaite and George Mackay Brown spring to mind), and the social history of poetry includes also people who were conservative but untalented, and the wide sectors of the book-buying public who just didn't get the new poetry and possibly didn't realise it was there. Equally, the Underground thing was so attractive that it brought in hundreds of people who wanted to imitate it but had no idea how to do that – the new thing misunderstood and existing in dozens of different versions, only one of which made any sense. I would concede that the attempt to get outside the whole Western way of life and simultaneously critique it as if from high above it produced varieties of bad poetry which didn't even exist before 1968. I want a memory of the period in which the good stuff dominates everything else, and we identify with the good stuff.

# The Sphere of Intimacy

## I. Whatever Happened to the Three-minute Single?

One of the decisive things which the new Pop Culture brought to its people, and which they missed every time it wasn't there, was intimacy. Pop music reached people despite losing many of the structures of more formal music – possibly because of losing them. One thing guiding '70s poetry was the wish to lose structures. So far as these had captured empathy, the less formal sound-palette allowed intuition more scope. Intuition in fact replaced empiricism as a principle. Sadly, as many people are weak at intuition as are weak in verbal intelligence. We are going to address the development of Sixties immediacy. We will start with the poet Paul Evans, and my review of his 2009 selected poems, and then go on to a wider story.

**The history of spontaneity:**
**Paul Evans, *The Door of Taldir: Selected Poems***

Paul Evans, a Welsh poet, was born in 1945 and died in 1991 in a mountaineering accident. Taldir is a house which belonged to his father-in-law, sited near a mountain in Merionethshire. Evans was the son of a vicar and did post-graduate research in English, on the American poet Robert Duncan. Much of his life was spent in Wales and much in England. Evans' poems appeared in 1967 in *Love Love Love. The New Love Poetry*, edited by Pete Roche, a pop work with a jacket by Hapshash and the Coloured Coat using paisley patterns and pasted images of Hindu Gods.

Simultaneously he was a student of Eric Mottram and part of the 'poetic underground' which became known, later, as the School of London. This duality is the key to positioning Evans in the history of these things, a border zone that once existed. His key book is the first, *February*, and was strong and flimsy at the same time:

> Your hair a nest of colours a tree
> the sky hung from you constantly
> amaze me new dialects and everything
> the white clouds drifting in your eyes
> ('1st Imaginary Love Poem')

In one of the poems we hear of Plotinus:

> I will be reborn
> as a bird,
> Plotinus says
> because I love music
> too much
>
> maybe I'm
> already one
> eye winking
> from a black disk
> feathers
> ruffled by the wind
> I've launched myself on
> (from 'Extempore')

The meaning here vanishes into something as small as a bird, then into its song, which is even smaller, then into the meaning of the song – which we don't understand. The idea is utterly beautiful and flimsy. Please don't tell me that you have to read Plotinus' *Enneads* in order to get with this poem. I think it's more like, the poems know even less than a bird. This is their purity. *February* came out in 1971 from Fulcrum and evokes, for many people, a frail and beautiful mood, a lost time. 'Extempore' quotes Debussy and goes on to evoke 'three spears / of hyacinth', their 'slow bursts of blue / timed, I swear it/ by the pulse / of Eric Dolphy.' Evans had a fabulous control of passivity, the negative quality which allows a whole mood to seep into the poem. Almost negligently, his poems opened on a whole world of feeling high. This time faded away.

I mentioned *Love Love Love*, in which Evans had two poems. We need to emphasise that these neat poems he had written when he was 21, or even younger, were in a national anthology, actually a paperback one aimed for the mass market. The classic retrospective anthology by Edward Lucie-Smith which came out in 1970 included four poems by Evans. This is even more significant – at the age of 24 he is in a survey anthology, not of new poets but of everything important. In 1971, Fulcrum put out his first volume – an extraordinarily mature achievement, drifting and yet poised, poignant and with multiple foci. You can say that to start so early already implied that there might be problems in the future; and his later career seems like an anti-climax compared to where he was in 1971.

When the Underground of the Seventies formed, it emerged that he was part of it – and that the print runs were a fraction of what Fulcrum sold (which itself was probably a fraction of what Corgi sold with *Love Love Love*). So one version of the shared history of those 10 years is that there was the youth market, in 1967, for youth-identified poetry, and this poetry was visibly different from literary poetry, which came to appear middle-aged and academic, and yet it was of high artistic quality. The individuals in this youth culture stopped being so young, after a while, and with the usual "vertical splits" the new youth market did not have the same favoured culture commodities. The poetry which Roche had anthologised was left high and dry – and Roche moved into the music business. Some part of the cultural mass connected with an audience which was recognisably like the avant-garde of the past, which was much older in years, and which was able to take on technically difficult poetry. In a complete mutation, the Underground came to mean this intellectual poetry. Poets on the scene adapted to write it – in excited competition with each other. The Underground audience swept them along – but, having gone down that route, they were unavailable to a wider audience, and were in fact captives of their minority audience. Because this scene was unrestrained by external commitments, it evolved far and fast. When Lucie-Smith did a second edition of his Penguin survey anthology, he threw out the section which had included Evans. It was as if the recognition process were going backwards.

I just want to recall one of Evans' poems from his first book, 'A Sequence'. The sensations in the poem are transient and we are not being told that the poem is important because it is full of important sensations. Each new statement arriving undercuts the previous one. There is no forward movement – yet each moment is stranded in time and so never replaced. It hangs around, permitting the composite whole, which has no real focus but is a lazy array of sensations. The feeling is of calm and detachment, not indifference, actually curiosity, but of being safe and lifted above events, not compelled by anything. The condition is one of deep sensitisation to people and things. The tone is sophisticated: the person in the poem is cool about everything but always willing to move on to the next thing. This is what the youth of the time called "spacy", and it is deeply attractive. There is no argument and so in a way this is not intellectual poetry, nor political, as it does not embody a protest. It is about life being lived. Whatever else is happening, a small group of people have found a space where they can be happy and sensitised and together. The space is still visible 45 years later. We want to be there.

The overall feel is more important than the individual themes. 'Out of Unrest' is based on a quote from Kierkegaard which claims that animals do not know about time and we only know about it because of 'unrest'. I don't think Kierkegaard has any relevance to this poetry, but the attraction is really the idea of being completely free of time and free of unrest – a purely cyclic existence of benevolence, calm, and gratified appetites. It breathes out a certain sense of time, of the pace at which the world moves and at which one processes the world. A sense of ease and slowness belongs to a moment of the early Seventies or late Sixties. You could call it a "hippy" thing. It is one of the things which it is hardest to imitate in later times, when people were just more bothered about how the world was going, or how the poem was going. Early Ralph Hawkins poems seem to have the same feel.

Pop music itself evolved from perfect 3-minute singles to writing "rock operas", hour-long jams, and a deep inability to write 3 minute songs of any quality. This was a process with huge energies behind it, it involved a great swathe of rock musicians, and the increasing complexity and length of Underground poetry are clearly a parallel shift. The wish to become "heavy" and significant was animating popular culture after 1967 and poetry was caught up in it, not marching perversely away from the masses. Poetry is tied to song, and the idea that poetry could, after 1975, have untied and gone on writing the equivalent of "perfect 3-minute singles" is a fantasy.

Mottram's epoch-making definition of the "British Poetry Revival", at a 1974 conference, followed by one in 1977, can be seen as an assault on the map which cut the "pop" element out of the blossoming Underground and redefined it in terms of heavy politics, heavy-duty ideas, cultural critique, vast poem projects taking decades. But Paul Evans was the arranger of those conferences, at the old Polytechnic of Central London. Mottram just wrote the catalogues. Evans made the events happen. Something else Evans likes is discussion of stars and physics:

> Our bodies form the harp
> on which celestial music's made,
> sounds of pure pleasure
> rising from the strings

where light hands are laid.
Responding to a touch,
we move to the radiations
of it    out of time
in the time of the music.

\*


Have you felt the great wind
that blows steadily out of the sun?
You won't feel it on the skin
of your cheek, or bare arms in summer.
The earth is a small stone in its path
breaking the stream and dividing it.

"Exquisitely sensitive" the wind blows

and the universe a living creature
breathing storms of dust, its body
aching as the new children
of the stars come to birth.

\*


I wanted to abolish Time,
writing a poem in which
only scale mattered
                    (from 'We are the Instruments of the Adoration')

Could we call this cosmic? That would be a link between Evans and the
pop culture of the late Sixties. Is it a rewrite of Marc Bolan's line "My
people were fair and had sky in their hair"? It sounds a lot like Kathleen
Raine. He shows an idyllic view of lovers locked into their own reality
where nothing disturbs them, and that insulated quality means nothing is
between them and the stars which shine on them with unusual vividness.
That use of the stars is the beatific egoism of lovers and it is part of the
lyric condition, what we enjoy in these poems. The detachment applies
also to the state of love: there is nothing compulsive about it, no sense of
threat. No greed, no fear. This is the quality people liked, that sense that

a man and a woman were able to attract each other but not lapse into need, anxiety, dependency. Evans' poems of that time give the feeling of life being lived, of unimportant things happening, of freedom to move in any direction and to find fascination in each one. I suppose this means the expectation of being loved and also that this is the feeling of a moment of pop culture: not that everyone alive in 1969 was free from anxiety, jealousy, fear of rejection, but that there was a bubble including pop music and poetry and some photographs and some real people in which you could be spontaneous and there were no hang-ups. This is just the most attractive thing. The other poems in that Roche anthology have the same quality, but Evans writes in a more complex and even more seductive way. 'Launch the Mind into Space' is a completely "mind-expanded" "cosmic rock" "spaced-out" poem, a real classic of the time.

Fairly obviously, that poem about a "solar wind" is based on a much older text, presumably an example of Renaissance Neo-Platonism. Because the return of the sun in Spring causes beasts and plants to mate or flower, it is held that the Sun broadcasts love. The poem is a concealed hymn form. Yet, it is still saying "we are like the birds and the bees". It is part of the lyric poem about love which occupies the whole of *February*. It is not philosophically intense.

It is surprising how the poets who were writing poems compatible with pop music, in those halcyon days, have been forgotten and unrecovered. Paul Evans, Lee Harwood, Pete Brown, Pete Roche – the scene went on to marginalise them. A second generation updating their insights and powers never turned up to work.

Sixties-style immediacy waned considerably but also reached new heights in the work of poets like Evans, John James and David Chaloner. Suppose we describe the difference between poetry and prose. We would be likely to describe poetry as representing the childish and spontaneous elements of cognitive powers and reactions. Lyric poetry, especially, would be hedonistic, dealing with states of mind which are goals in themselves, and recording evanescent moments, and preoccupied with the emotions of people very close to the writer rather than with factual knowledge. It would overlap a great deal with songs and with advertisements, and very little with prose. Young people would be ideally positioned to reach this state of mind and because they are unmarried, not tied up by jobs, and without mortgages, they can shift in feelings very quickly and are able to follow where they lead, and are more likely to fall in love. They idealise other people including the ones they fall in love with. In this way they would be equipped to write lyric poetry, and also to be idealised by the reader in a way like falling in love.

This was an incessant line in the avant-garde, often tinted with Dada and Surrealism. The lack of premeditation basic to Abstract Expressionism abidingly meant infantility was a quality likely to feature in radical art. It was also abidingly likely to fail – for the same reasons that you give up acting like a child. Hilton Kramer made infantilism a key to his critique of the development of American art during the Sixties and Seventies. He had summed up a classic reason for failure. Nonetheless – art is play. Irresponsibility is part of the lyric quality.


## 2. New Magical Earth

Lucie-Smith said about Paul Evans, "His work seems to have something in common with Lee Harwood's – a curiously dreamy tone, a feeling for surrealist images which loom up and then melt away again before the reader can fully grasp them. Poetry such as this often implies a kind of collaboration between the poet and the person who hears or reads. The loose texture, the intermittency, allow this to happen: the poem has no definite meaning, but alters each time it is looked at." We find that this issue of low resolution keeps cropping up. There is a specific style which was there in the late Sixties and which flourished in the Seventies. I think a key to this style is in the anti-capitalist line. The social system which was being rejected, in the halcyon years after '68, was noticeably meritocratic. It measured the ability of people, on the way to segregating people by income and access to information, and repeatedly used mental activities as a way of testing these abilities. A second aspect of being a corporate human being was a sense of time. Norms for completing tasks represented themselves psychologically as a new organ of anxiety, which generated anxiety every time a deadline grew close – which was permanently, in a work context of permanent self-measurement. Capitalism needed to isolate people from a sense of community, so that they would be wholly obedient to the owners of wealth. Capitalism fostered greed – to keep people consuming. Finally, capitalism was associated with a project of acquiring rational knowledge – a mechanised universe of predictable causal chains, which became the content of knowledge and which was full of repeated effects, both in itself and in the stock knowledge of humans.

After '68, poets were bound to protest at all this, ejecting their own organs in a path of mutation and migration. They could express their attitudes by purging their language, moving towards something naïve and intuitive. Because memorising facts and making accurate observations are part of meritocracy, you could express disloyalty by writing a body of poetry in which there were no facts and no direct representations of, say, flowers, building types, other people. In the poetry, we find surrealism, intuition, direct statements of feeling replacing concrete details, the private replacing the public. The mid-century academic world had asked children to compete and be measured all the time. They had to demonstrate themselves. It had also asked poets to express a world-view through stylistic means, searching poems for evidence of ethical restraint and anticommunism. The classroom had taught students how to locate these world-views, and they concluded that, the more subjective grammar is, the more it embodies a world-view. An altered surface showed the deeper intent. So you could write a body of poetry in which there were no tests and no objective representations of the self. The geography of Magic Realism was a lesson in the historical spread of rationalism, as an aspect of the West and capitalism, which had not been there in the Middle Ages and which (apparently) was still not there in Latin America or even eastern Europe. Naïve art was an indicator of how geometry had transformed subjective space into a grid partaking of exact knowledge – and perhaps alienation. If you believe in the inner flow, the effort of externalising it and reducing it to a standard grid of grammar and vocabulary came to seem like a process of self-alienation. Poems became full of non-serial knowledge, and the grid lines became an index of compromise. How would new poets express feelings of resistance to all this? A hippie poet might start by withdrawing themselves as an object of knowledge, writing about the self in the soft energy of naive painting. Surrealism, intuition, direct statements of feeling replace concrete details, as the private replaces the public. The ideal is to reach collective being via a loss of ego.

The improvement in popular song made lyrics more intelligent and also drew poetry closer to the realm of song – to subjective patterns and mimetic reactions to waves of feeling. As poetry moved further away from prose, the feeling was that prose was totally signposted and that poetry which removed the verbal labels was more poetic. An explanation is not a poem. The belief was that emotional lucidity is an explanation of itself, and that the archaic gifts of intuition and empathy are paralysed by the explicit.

The idealists of the time wanted to lead passages of a life in which the problems of the West had been resolved or reduced. The poetry of the time is partly a record of such passages in a language proper to them. It is perverse to write an account of this wave of feeling which is itself a reproducible result, aiming at objectivity and accuracy. At another level, it is doubtful that the perceived definition of the West was completely accurate. The difficulty of finding an observer who is genuinely outside the phenomenon he is observing is obvious. There is no ground from which we could observe the thing we want to make an object of knowledge. Wishful Third Worldness is not a genuine way out – it continues a part of the inside.

There is an 1898 pre-Western named *Cripple Creek* which has a still featuring in prominent position a sign on a jug reading Red Eye. It was a kind of whisky which affected the veins of the eyes. (It appears in William Everson's *Silent American Cinema*.) This has nothing to do with Iain Sinclair's *Red Eye*, a long poem from 1973, which actually pre-dates both *Lud Heat* and *Suicide Bridge* and had never been published before the Test Centre edition in 2013. Sinclair had finalised a text for publication via Albion Village Press in around 1974, diverted the funds towards publishing Chris Torrance and B. Catling, and forgot to publish the book. (A few pages surfaced in Sinclair's 1989 selected poems.) *Red Eye* is completely different in mood from Sinclair's extended works of the Seventies. It is as if the 'furies' of *SB* are here finding their opposite, in the feelings of someone non-compulsive, tranquil, and unwilling to go anywhere away from his domestic base except on foot. We could imagine a world where Sinclair had never published any of those long books and all we had was the highly personal poems collected in *The Firewall* and in *Red Eye*. The 'red eye' in question is the moon. The phrase 'red eye' appears twice in *SB* but with a different impact, closer to the whisky, (which Bob Hope swallowed in 'Paleface').

Issue of *Red Eye* 40 years after it was written seems to illustrate the values of 'acid folk' on its own – the focus on clarity and contemplative piety which creates something beautiful and is left with no unused impulses that could exert themselves to push the beautiful thing out into the world. Indeed, the feeling is not far away that artistic truth comes out of a kind of integrity of impulse which commercial grasping and yearning damage. The documentation around the book says that the themes of the poem *come out of* previously existing films, shot I suppose on silent 8mm stock, which were about the poet's family and home, about domestic feelings raised to a kind of piety. The guiding light for the poem, as I imagine for the films, is Stan Brakhage, seen by those outside the narrative commercial film world as one of the great film-makers. Brakhage achieved an intensity hard to describe, by focusing on moments of shared attention. He was in fact very articulate about his intentions, but the words could easily have gone along with films that did not possess the spirituality and primal beauty that his do. His film 'Dog Star Man' is about a dog, the sun, and a man. There is no sound and no plot. There is light, and the light shows the grounds of our being, glints of truth from which something grand and inauthentic could be worked up, by a decline of energy. The anti-capitalist thing is not primary; we need to recognise an original set of feelings about authentic being which capitalism obstructed, and which are the foundation of any anti-capitalism, rather than dependent on it. So, with *Red Eye* we can quite easily say 'lack of precise verbal organisation has to do with a weak ego which has to do with openness to the reality of other people's feelings which has to do with a distaste for possession and power which is a version of anti-capitalism', but we want to be inside the feelings of the poem, much more than arguing about ownership of wealth and so sinking back into analytical thought. *Red Eye* says everything about The Furies by never mentioning them. A long stretch of *Lud Heat* is an evocation of watching a Brakhage film, or an evening of them. This material resurfaces in *Red Eye*:

> We should be content to work with the privilege of rejection. To ignore the calculations, histrionics, hesitations, and do-I-dares, of the reality principle, the materialist safety anchor. As Brakhage, so abundantly, demonstrates: his *Songs* elevating the human and the domestic, shared warmth within the tribe, the circle of fire. The oldest movements, light to dark.
>
> 8mm celluloid visions of childbirth, animal death, love-making, are valid extensions of the home movie. LIGHT! A prismatic shimmer encourages the emulsion to burn and bleach. Image is layered over image to finesse glittering horizons, distant oceans and star-fields within a bead of sweat on the loved one's back. This is a true beginning and sets us off down the root and tube of Brakhage's ancestor fears, into the curled slumber of the cosmos. Not childbirth but starbirth, planetary parasites floating like pollen on the slow breath of wood-stained memory: *Dog*

*Star Man*. The most basic mammal enterprise. A man climbs a hill to cut down a tree – and, in so doing, enters the corridor of archetypes, the maze of ice energies.

The Brakhage material at least is something we can share. The phrase 'the act of seeing with one's own eyes' (a line in *Red Eye*, a section title in *Lud Heat*, and the name of a Brakhage film) translates *autopsy* but also means 'seeing in first person' dreams sent by the gods. This was a practice in Hellenistic Egypt, at temples (Dendera, Om Kombu) with special rooms where pilgrims slept. It seems likely that Sinclair sees watching films as having the status of seeing theophanic dreams and that he identifies the 'visitant rooms' with the clubrooms of the Underground. It seems that his 8mm films in part re-created dreams.

This writing reminds me of the Christian theosophy which pre-ceded Blake:

> *[the soul seeks but cannot break]* through the wall separating it from the heavenly principle. And because it thereupon finds that through ascending out it had been constantly misled and had missed its goal, […] It realises that the Wisdom of God […] can be attained [only] through descending and sinking into one's own inward ground, and no longer seeking to rise out of oneself. Whereupon it now thus sinks into itself and before it the gate of Wisdom's depths is opened directly and in the blink of an eye, and it is led into the holy eternal principium of the lightworld […] in the new magical Earth[.]
>
> (from John Pordage, *Sophia*, 1675)

The focus on weakening the sound of the self as a way of heightening sensitivity is found in other poets of the period, for example Ulli Freer. There is another poem from the time which has the same unusual sense of time, free from compulsions:

> the people of annexed kingdoms
> from Odessa to Moscow    thin by money
>            talk
>      & those without
>
>        in a cell cold calm & alone

insane        on fire            rain
        are laughed at without love
likely to all nonsense
                maim of souls by wires coils water
we must call their names


I am changing direction to his birthplace
        in wonder
                        there he saw grievances
        laid hard against a people      later
his signature as he rode in a train of steel
                        against the
                speak out
of & into
                        the machine
        how do you think people make profit
lavish in hours
                        pass the
                                & years
                out of fine stock like horses
lithe leathery loose with stuffed in the blood
                        to secure ends

long ditch
        it is never safe to presume history
                its inevitable contradiction

out now in it with my snout mind
        in compost knowledge of grub & leaf
                tinsel & bark


This is from Ralph Hawkins' *soft in the brains*, which was published in 1981 but which I associate firmly with the time-sense of the Seventies, with something which we have lost. For me this represents the hippy time, before people got into anger or self-seeking and developed that assertive attitude towards other people and towards their own experience. It also represents life being led, the present tense of a transformed life, which is not competitive and possessive. *Soft in the brains* does not try to win any arguments, but shows what the goal is. (Ralph published Sinclair's poems in the late Seventies, and Allen Fisher published *soft in the brains*.)

There had for a long time been poetry which was pale, pastoral, and in good taste. What we are talking about here is something idealistic and highly wrought, as well as being unpolarised and unpossessive. It is not a secret, I suppose, that the verbal means used in poetry also have the status of possessions, of technological objects which assign status as they are deployed. To write poems which consciously lacked these devices was symbolically to dismiss the value of car ownership and of the nuclear arsenal, the planes and missiles, which were the panoply of states. This sheds light on Sinclair's preoccupation, over a dozen books, with walking. The pilgrim reaches an authentic grasp of space by giving way to it in an authentic way, without artificial aids. The poverty of means of acid folk music, and of certain Seventies poems, also maximises personal contact by minimising technology. Empty space is created to show more of human beings. The organization of *Red Eye* is complicated and the material cannot simply be described as this domestic record. Some of it is almost abstract:

GRASP A ROSE OF PALE FIRE
NETTLE TONGUES SING
THE ROOF OF HIS MOUTH

FORCE OPEN THE STAR LATTICE
 SO THAT LIGHT CAN BEND
OUR STEPPED VERTEBRAL TOWER

PLUNGE THISTLE IN HOT OIL
A FRAMED EXHIBIT
TO CONJUGATE OR COOK

This reminds me of *The Cut Pages*. The idea of eating nettles and thistles, plants willing to grow abundantly in urban environments, is part of a local aesthetic. There is a song about strikers, in about 1820, "we ate nettles while nettles was good", exit from the circuits of exchange, straight vitamin C. They are more tender in the Spring. Ulli Freer's work is a good fit for this category. I feel that Ulli represents the authenticity of the Seventies, untouched by all the other impulses, depersonalisation, territorialisation, investment in fake institutions, which have flowed over us all since.

no single stars night bowl of cakemix
     silent dusk stirs bones
       soft gold click
down from the billboards
    rattle metal flesh
jagged strata beat in tune
    rough on the ranges
stripped to stone heels
        spread to sun's scratch
the street
   hair falls   to hang
     run   down skull   blowing
darkness winged

(Poem 9 from *Sonnet Brushes*, 1976; published as Ulli McCarthy)

What about the *ice energies*? I believe that the collocation is with emotional drives of the Ice Age, and that in several parts of *Red Eye* the time before the de-glaciation is evoked. This is what we would think of as the Mesolithic. It appears as the grounds of truth, the level which possesses cyclical stability and is not an overreach due to the excesses of the ruling western ethos. In fact, it sinks through the West to become non-western. THAT WE ARE / PIECES OF GLACIER / STILL WALKING. There was a lot of fuss, prior to 1973, about some nicks on bones, of ancient working, which Alexander Marshack (*The Roots of Civilization*, 1972) interpreted as recording cycles of the moon, the "red eye"; so it could be that the moon links us to the Mesolithic wanderers. This is all successive to the *English Intelligencer* project, of 1966-8, which delved into European archaeology as a way of getting to myth. Prynne's 'The Glacial Question, Unsolved', one of the finest products of the TEI period, may be the direct source for this "ice energies" riff.

We are going to move on to *The House That Manda Built*, by Nicki Jackowska (b. 1942). *House* is dated 1981 (but copyright 1980) so it may seem like cheating if I include it. However, the poem I am going to quote is in a 1977 pamphlet. It may also seem like cheating if I fold it under the mantle of neo-folk, but there is no doubt that it strongly resembles folk songs.

> Twelve roses haunt me. twelve bruises on the tree's
> bark will denounce my intention. the tree splits,
> bearing our rose-berries, born of a double helix. a
> twin-rose message creasing the air, the room penetrated
> by dark futures. we make our way through the day
> carefully, preserving hymns and peacock monstrosities
> to read by. we are illuminated by a penumbra, a
> violence of shadow.
> you said goodbye like the interior of a candle. your
> bite was a chip of the old altar. your roses blow
> hieroglyphs into my torn face and the road that creeps
> in from the east stops short at my living-room.
> I am waiting in this matrix of silence for the wound to
> remember. your name is a patchwork of instruction.
> I can speak silences easily. I can make new beds under
> the rib of the tree. I am a woman haunted by jasmine
> and a crying skull. this day I am washed by tears, my
> new face hums for its birth.
> > (from 'Rose House', in *House of Twelve Names*)

This is one house of twelve in the sequence. The idea of light coming out of objects is like the colour printing in old popular prints, like the *images d'Epinal*, where a patch of colour spilled over the edges of the object. The peacock spills light, presumably in several colours, by which we can read.

The poem quoted shows each image appearing twice, in a sort of residual AB structure, though decalated from the line ends, which are normally the terminators for themes. The parallels run roughly (*haunt: denounce, split; double, message: future, make our way: illuminated, candle: altar, hieroglyphs: road, remember: instruction, I can... I can, crying skull: new face*). The lingering on each theme allows a serenity which allows the poem to progress continually. The images flash up but there is enough context to let us assimilate them. (The *roses blow hieroglyphs* to *road that creeps* is a very weak match, and is arguably where the scheme is not fulfilled.) The statements flow antiphonally, and could almost be a conversation, two people living in the house and echoing each other.

Although the echoing is of a bold nature, and the level of repetition is very subtle, it takes us back to the rhymes of folk-songs, the oral symmetries. The exclusive use of organic and concrete images also recalls pre-modern songs as they were being performed in the 1970s, as a simple and yet alien and puzzling element in popular music. Pop music came out of folk music. Poetry too, with its home values of symbolism and charged objects, came out of this world of primal and dreamlike images which flow so intoxicatingly in Jackowska's poetry. But, something has changed radically during that emergence. Her poetry is too abundant in its image-choice, too far from anything to do with stanza and metrical line, to sound like folk-songs. The distinctive erasure of logic and realism produces all the same something spontaneous, constantly exciting, and truly poetic in its flow of creativity.

Mid-century poetry was compromised with abstraction, documentary, the pulpy reality of newspapers, social values, and other things. Jackowska's work seems more intact, more vigorous, more pictorial – and also closer to folk art.

Examining the passage quoted shows almost everything happening in the present tense. But, that isn't quite true – there are traces of a past tense. The autonomy of parts shows a central rational project dissolving but a new landscape is being constructed by the arbitrary acts. The poems have over 100 pages an amazing rigour of composition, of what is excluded from their precincts, which almost certainly embodies an idea of authentic being. This is what could draw us close to Sinclair or Freer. The endless shifting of the metaphors gives us the signs of an inner life which transcends facts but is too unsteady to be egoistic, which engulfs the land but is vulnerable everywhere. This is a kind of waking dream and with the eternal present not dulled by social calculation or repetition.

I want to present at its true value the originality of these poems, unprotected by regressions to authorised and canonised public treasures such as the fairy-tales of the Grimms. Their autonomy is at a deeper level and the rewards to be won from them are more intact. Their creativity proves the existence of a new life, hidden only behind worn perceptual and emotional habits. The erasure of reference to law, reason, measurement, transaction, etc., brings us back to the theme of exit from the West and its strangely arbitrary and repetitive patterns. The poems enact the kinetics of a new tribe in a new and undamaged landscape. More exactly, the features of the landscape spring out of the movements of the principal actors. Folk art offered to its fans an exit from Western achievements – a periphery discovered by falling or lapsing, *beneath* the level of enlightenment. Its bright colours and uncentred patternedness welled up from what progress had rejected and retarded. Its vigour came as it were from an inability to anticipate, which forced a creature to rush into every corner to find things out – this is the eternal present. The whole of the 1970s is buried under what came after. This is one emotional flavour which just disappeared. There is nothing else like it.

## *blue with the reflected coldness of strangeness:*
## The Bloodshed, the Shaking House

In the folklore, Martin Thom and Brian Marley are remembered as the supreme moments of the Seventies, the excelling goals for journeys to bring the decade back to life. This is partly because their publication record comes to an end before the decade closes, mainly because their work is at such a high level. The greatness of *The Bloodshed* and *Springtime in the Rockies* supplies a clinching argument against the enemies of modern poetry in the Seventies but also reproaches the modern faction – because these works were not reviewed at the time and they withdrew, as if the idea they had seen, which shone back out of their eyes, had already been ruined. There is some horror in the fact that they stopped.

Thom's poem is organic, impulsive, enchanting, pictorial, narrative, even wide-eyed. It is full of transformations. It explores individual freedom rather than including the figure of malign power which would, essentially, mean the frustration of the poem and whatever impulses it is pushed by. When we hear

> 'mon front est rouge encore
> du baiser de la reine'
>     at 2 a.m.
>     3 a.m.
>     pleasure, joy
>     completely alone to
>     roar head and limbs
>     there are loud percussions
>     snappings of the will, love simply in blood
>     There is cause enough
>     Know!

– it is like a romantic ballet, with an ornamental queen and her lover. The line about the kiss comes from a sonnet by Nerval which is a subjective collage of themes of different origin, and which was also used in *The Waste Land,* which itself is a subjective collage. The linking both echoes Nerval and is romantic and enchanted in itself. In *The Waste Land*, we have the fortune-teller, Mme de Sosostris, at the beginning, and at the end the "Prince d'Aquitaine", with his "abolished tower", which is a tarot card. Sosostris was the name of a Pharaoh, and the tarot pack was known as the "Book of Thoth", after the Egyptian god of writing, from the 18th century on. Thom was born around 1950 and was a student during the fateful years of the late 60s. He did the Archaeology and Anthropology tripos at Cambridge, reading for which supplied much of the imagery in the poem. The poem was published in 1977 but dated 1974 in the text. It is some 46 A4 pages long and divided into sections: 'The Bloodshed the Shaking House'; 'Sea Creatures That are the Visible Tide of the World'; 'Door Music'; 'Iron Work'; 'Frightening Happy Glow'.

We can start with four proposals about the design of the text:

One, *it does not just field material from anthropology or linguistics but is carrying out an argument about the subjects and has a thesis which you could connect to arguments among scholars.* By inspection, this is not so. The material is all taking place in a present tense and is faithful to primary texts rather than to scholarly essays dealing with concepts.

Two, *it deals with some mythological character and is the story of that character, like the primary texts we just mentioned.* By inspection this is not so. No more is it a story about some particular tribe, because the imagery comes from all kinds of places.

Three, *it is "projected autobiography", the story of a figure alive in the 1970s, who studied Arch and Anth and is named Martin Thom.* This is not so for most of the material but is evidently so for some of it. Thus, the dreams are almost certainly Thom's dreams.

Four, *the story is about a series of memories or dreams which some narrating subject had, which involve meaning-bearing structures taken from works on Indo-European linguistics and culture, about anthropology, about psychoanalysis, and so forth, each of which arrives because it is beautiful and we all want to see it, and which inserts itself in a series following the impetus of the material itself.* This seems to explain the text as we see it. The opening passage, about a person who is simultaneously a figure on a chess board and the player who moves the figure, may illustrate how someone intensely involved in mythographical material can both read about it as a 20th century European and find themselves inside it as a kind of lyric spirit which is carried along by texts and goes wherever they go.

Something of this kind is true of the Cambridge School often, at least at their best moments: that when a true intellectual is reading about Russia in 1917 the gap between them and the subject dissolves and the poem is simultaneously about events in Petrograd or some area controlled by peasant collectives and about the personal life of the poet, in 1975 or 2015 or whenever it is. There is a moment of being swept off your feet – where the poet loses footing in the world of domestic anecdote and starts to move with the flow of the ideas. The history of this sector is marked by the double event, that the scene taken from Deleuze and Guattari, Mike Rowlands, Ian Hodder, or whoever, is much more shared by the audience than something personal would be, but that the ability to recognise these shared scenes sharply divides the intellectual audience from the rest of the poetry world.

Thom wrote:

> and have no shy
> nervous origin. Mirrors none
>         the map streaked
> with present joy. Jet, Iron
> Amber / from the North in
> long trade across Mesopotamia
> delirious in no-home, days and
> weeks, a manic loop of assimilation
> writing these journals to hold time
> against all loss of shadow. A true
> night of pale registrations
> spread out coldly above
>         the nomadic line spilt through sand
> sinking in the impossible
> and no relief
>
> Blankets burnt at the Indus source
> far from any German sky-pole of the world
> raw with all change in nerve and loss
> of known quality

Until the moment breaks
rain to earth, valley to range of hills
rich off the dead structures they
build terraces, splint earth with kindness
and gather quiet and dark
the quiet and the dark flower
Persephone was
    Not in cruelty. I do not live
to rise from sleep to strike
these birds of impossible design
held by no poem to sing in ears
sharpened to receive
below the threshold, as in that unity
spoken of in trance
    The bird-dancers
all crazed in head and holy
sick with images since thirteen years old, now rich
in poetry and hidden chants
whirling their iron dress, taking blood from the ear
and waxy gold
    Now we are blue with the reflected coldness
of strangeness affecting us.
    In night
the glass of the world does not speak
washed out to the image of the
disappearing axe
to every sign on these hills, and no call to


and all tired herds sink in rain
to ashen valleys, lie there
    to the left of your optic range
sand sweet as grass, from red and blue cinnabar, rivalling
the Linnaean geocracy
    bright with dew and quick bees
all light burning, not damned or lost
    in th'imagined breath
to live in the flight of shy nervous origins
loving their origin
    (from the *'Iron Work'* section)

Evidently this is hard to paraphrase. In a sense, it cannot be paraphrased except in a version longer than the original text. The passage about bird dancers evokes the shamanism of Inner Asia – an ecstatic, irrational, practice, associated with wild dancing and repetitive drumming. Those shamans did wear iron pectorals, aimed to clink impressively as they danced. The theme is also nomadism – used by these poets to get away from rootedness and its mental consequences, and the equivalent in poetry of cosmic flight in rock. The realm of anthropology was expected at that time to switch on thoughts about the function of social institutions, the possibility of changing them. The relaxation of rational boundaries acts to release impulses – both Freud and anthropology are used as windows on a hidden inner self of metaphors, analogies, wishes, fantasies, and pictures. The self dissolves its contracts with the outside world, and finds a way of grasping what *reason* is. This unbearably rich formal world reminds us of the undisciplined sonic world opened up by the 'free' guitar solo. It is spontaneous, improvised, led by affect, constantly shifting. Reducing it to order damages something integral and perpetually moving. It serves as a "frame opener" to key the kind of free association we are supposed to carry out while reading the poem. It is there as a window, opened through convention to show our inner selves: *Now we are blue with the reflected coldness / of strangeness affecting us.* This is really the opposite of didactic writing – although it is very erudite and rich in ideas. *sand sweet as grass,[…] rivalling / the Linnaean geocracy / bright with dew and quick bees* : I suggest that geocracy, a rare word, can be translated as soil regime. This is the difference between soil and sand, as mineral grains. Dew and bees are relevant to soil, which holds moisture and has flowers, not to sand regions. The statement that this sand is sweet as grass is startling. The passage on "rich off dead strata" is repeated in a variant, elsewhere in the book. It is in collocation with *sand*, the infertile product of silicates by weathering or pounding, and is likely to refer to the accumulation in strata of humus in certain districts, allowing exploitation – by farming, which in turn allows a sedentary existence and so other forms of culture based on accumulation, such as writing. Writing is a stratum of dead language.

We have to mention Deleuze and Guattari, because they also wrote about nomadism, and because Thom's later career was as a translator of French psychoanalytical works – he was probably very early in reading avant-garde psychoanalysis, such as Guattari, in the early Seventies. So the breakthrough in connecting free association, vagrant thoughts, with nomadic wandering, may already come from *Traité de nomadologie: la machine de guerre.* But – it may come from *The English Intelligencer* circa 1966. *delirious in no-home* uses a keyword from Deleuze and Guattari, linking nomadism with the lack of rational constraint, and is a metaphor for the boundless expanses which the new poetry is going to gallop over; the jumps between personal experience in the now and the deep time of the ethnographical descriptions evoke this wildness and are the match of psychedelic disorientation.

Also floating around is the idea that the ecstatic religion is possible in societies that do not have fixed ideas about property, that is nomadic societies, but not in peasant or peasant-urban societies. The shaman's soul leaves his body and wanders. There is also a theory of Indo-European origins (a phase before the Saxon identity) among nomads north and east of the Black Sea. This was proposed by Otto Schrader in the late 19th century. The material of the poem is like soft sand – fit to record the finest ripples of the medium passing over it, passive to autosuggestion. The moment of "jet iron amber" takes us to Northern Europe, source of these raw materials – a very long way either from Mesopotamia (as cited by the poet) or from Central Asia, where it is dry enough for sand deserts to form. These regions are very far from each other.

Poetry sited boundlessness in the free reaches of Inner Asian space (or, the North Atlantic, or, the prairies of the mid-western USA) rather than in the space beyond the earth's atmosphere or under the ground. Yet the dry air and flat horizons make the stars perilously close: *A true / night of pale registrations / spread out coldly above / the nomadic line.* The line about blue and red cinnabar is curious. Red cinnabar is mercury sulfide, the main ore from which pure mercury was refined. It is also a pigment for painters, called cinnabar or vermilion. The sand is a decomposition from reefs of cinnabar. I am not convinced that blue cinnabar exists.

Because "German" and "Indus" occur together, it is likely that the reference is to the Indo-Germanic culture, so named by German scholars, who dominate the field.

In French or English you say *Indo-European.* The central Asian milieu is shown also as the homeland of the Indo-Europeans. They appear elsewhere, indirectly, through the citation of Émile Benveniste, who was an Indo-European scholar. He is quoted as saying "arbitrary, but only when seen from Sirius" – a contradiction of the famous statement by Ferdinand de Saussure about the link of sound and sense in language.

*Axe* is French for an axis, which in linguistics generates oppositions, and the *disappearing axe* may be an axis which goes away when a phonetic opposition is deleted. *the glass of the world does not speak* refers to a mirror, and as night falls it is the axis of reflection which is deleted.

We can bring alongside works by other poets who studied anthropology: Ted Hughes, David Wevill, Tom Lowenstein, David Barnett. We could mention the poem by Tom Harrisson included in his *Savage Civilisation* (1937), his only poem so far as I know. Revealingly, he came back from Melanesia to study English society – focusing on Bolton. The ethnographical gaze was always likely to be turned back on England and its neighbours.

Page 45 has "absolute property of this moment or else / stop writing". This may be a comment on how the book was written – how it retains its primary quality. There is a moment (the poem is called 'Messiaen') which runs "Ah skull your house / Is it an imagined house/ spouting flame / and the unthinkable / is it a / dark face / your own / thought too". This may be a gloss on the title of the whole volume – the shaking house is the skull. The title includes a pun which is methodically indicative – the poem likes double meanings. So, *shed* is both a partner of *house*, so a building – and an act of pouring, as in "bloodshed". But a "shed of blood" could be a head. Blood pours down from the head, back to the heart. But the word could also relate to *watershed* (where *headwaters* part)– the brain is a binary structure, the right cortex is functionally different from the left cortex. And – this asymmetry is arguably the origin of dualities of classification.

Most of the passages in the book are not "anthropological" but might be autobiographical myth, that is they are passages from the emotional life of a speaker, the poet, but written in primary, mythical form. That would require a review as lyric poetry, not as a fantasia about Central Asia or Lapland. The pre-final section starts "One ought not forget, however, that for this very reason a man as a person cannot limit her: he too will some time become an image of unities that lie beyond him". The ending of the poem is:

'Everyone and Everything
apart from you
is feminine'
              the trader
              in false

dualism, shrieked
and fell
singing the dissolution

: all earthly structures
in their airy reversed images find
comfort through Nerval
asleep beneath Sirius

Turn and return
distance is the last quietness
far from wish
ringing in the ear
everything is sewn to everything
is threadbare
not broken, coheres

This is likely to be a reliving of the experience of being loved and feeling guilt about the oppression of women, by men. The initial quote is, I think, the words of the "trader in false dualism", and that would imply that the passage is saying that there is a general humanity from which the male:female split is a false boundary, a property marker. As would follow, the experience of love involves identification with the other person so intense that the I:you division is erased – an axis falling silent. Empathy is so much part of our nature that male experience is largely made up of identification with female humans (and privatisation is a passing fantasy). The "airy reversed images" are a symbolic statement of this, a strange and beautiful utterance of a truth about humans. Sirius refers to the view from Sirius, the perspective in which the Earth is immensely clear and remote, which Benveniste invoked. From Sirius, gender differences are arbitrary, just as the associations of sound and sense are. A previous passage reached Nerval through a Tarot card and spoke about Lou Andreas-Salomé, possibly as a symbol of a woman whom men inevitably fall in love with; and the psychoanalyst Victor Tausk, who wrote about "influencing machines". 'El desdichado' deals with personal passions through archetypes, as perhaps Thom does. It is possible that the dualities referred to often in the text all point towards the male:female duality whose resolution is in course here. The *turn and return* possibly refer to the act of dividing space: field boundaries and city streets were mythically laid out by a priestly figure walking and *turning*, this is the primary division, but can be effaced and redrawn simply by the act of turning. The *last quietness far from wish* is a stillness when passionate impulses have stopped shouting, where the truth can be heard. The poet hears reconciliation in this quietness.

There is a specific sensation involved in reading Thom's poetry and it derives partly from his ability to set everything in primary terms, visual like a dream, and partly from his truly astonishing inventiveness, tapping into a source of images which is apparently inexhaustible and never repeats. But also, it has this directly human quality, a pattern of melodic moves which displays someone emotional, susceptible, and prone to exaltation. It has that sweetness and impulsiveness. And you never want it to stop.

# 20 Notions on Allen Fisher

*1.* Because literature is pushed ever more either into the area of saying 'this is my personality. you like me and I like me' or into the area of gardening and cookery, there is a need for a work which takes the opposite pole of endeavour and stands up for that. Craving drew the outline of a book which re-imagines society and in which all our thoughts about a different society are released from control and lived out on the broadest possible canvas. It would enact a heroic view of art which takes on all the political radicalism of the era of 1968, and which dissolves the downward weight of history by recounting the past and removing the illusion of inevitability from its open processes. For my generation this function was fulfilled by the work of Allen Fisher.

*2.* The artistic impact of 'Place' isn't the force of one theme or another but the stripiness, the alternation and recurrence, in the course of a page or a book, of many themes. So it's ABCD A1 B1 C1 E D1 A2 F B3 C3 and so on.

*3.* There was a conceptual art movement called Fluxus in the Sixties; Fisher was involved directly with its European wing, Fluxshoe, in the Seventies. By reconstruction, his main interest in the 1960s was in this conceptual art. This came before the start of the poetic project *Place*. He was more experienced in performance and visual art than in verbal art, and created verbal art, subsequently, using the practices developed for visual and performance art.

What was conceptual art? I don't really want to define it. A definition is beside the central point of a bolt of energy and of a social atmosphere – a number of people intensely involved with art working and whose capacity for violent enthusiasm or boredom was formative for other people caught up in that atmosphere. Defining just what made them bored or enthusiastic is a forlorn hope – they weren't that simple and the art works they were reacting to or in weren't simple either.

Generically, Allen is a conceptual artist and if, in going to exhibitions of conceptual art or reading books about it, you reach a state of understanding its motives and hearing its message, then you are just one step away from being a Fisher expert. Of course, the idea of conceptual art involves building a new concept and set of procedures for each new work.

The process of moving through radically unfamiliar art is a preparation or analogy for moving through a radically unfamiliar life.

In the USA, the conceptual art project began really as a reaction to Cold War propaganda, as an attempt to walk out of the conditioning apparatus and find empty ground. In Britain, conceptual art consisted of disengaging the rules of the middle class project and was linked to acquiring middle class values. Understanding capitalism at the level of firms, families, and individuals was the superordinate goal of an intellectual project. It was linked to a burst of class mobility, an exceptional phase, as it seems. Today this project may be over.

There is that strange dream in a Martin Thom poem about simultaneously being the chess player and being the piece on the board. The universities have that strange dual project of teaching students how to criticise society and teaching them how to become middle class adults.

4. We can imagine Fisher as beginning with the idea that William Blake was a great writer and cultural leader, and imagining what a writer in around 1970 who was like Blake would do. This included looking for an alternative physics.

The transition from hippie physics to experimentally based physics is one of the major processes causing Fisher's work to change, over decades. The word hippie is important. The notions of a transformation of everyday life and of radical opposition to values implicit in Western capitalism are basic to Allen's work. If you don't grasp that the whole project loses its meaning. His work takes place completely in a countercultural framework and is a form of living differently as part of a shared intent of changing the way we all live.

5. We can see all this question asking as being like the Parsifal legend. Someone comes out of the forest where they have lived all their life, having been kept away from society in order to protect them.

In the 1950s and 1960s, a branch of sociology called ethnomethodology tried to uncover the rules governing the generation of behaviour (the methodology) of ordinary people in their own view (this was the 'ethnic' bit) by asking the question 'why are you doing that' endlessly. The classic reply was 'you know I have to do that'. But you don't. There is a reason and you can unbury that reason and utter it. Subjects found this process very stressful.

Poets don't like this process. The answer comes to be, interminably, repeatedly, 'because it makes me sound more attractive'. 'I write poems showing myself taking moral decisions because it makes me sound attractive'. The need to bury the basic decisions is all-powerful. It is hard to switch it off even for five minutes. Fisher wrote poems in which explicit processes replace value-judgements. While doing this he opened the question of why society behaves in the way it does.

The conceptual art movement did succeed in explaining why society runs the way it does. But the results got buried.

6. One of the two lead sources underlying *Place* is Charles Olson's *Special Theory of History*. The process we see in the text is Fisher developing away from this stage.

This can be seen as a tracking of the main line of poetic modernism: Olson was visibly a disciple of Pound and was trying to develop on from him, Pound was visibly connected to Paris in 1914 and the fabled era of modernism. We can set *Gravity* and *Place* in a series of large-scale modernist works in which the *Cantos*, *Paterson*, and the *Maximus* poems are also episodes. Fisher writes about Lambeth in reaction to poems about Paterson, New Jersey, and Gloucester, Massachusetts.

7. The other main initial source of 'Place' was Raoul Vaneigem's *The Revolution in Daily Life*. Instantly, we get the feeling that Olson had written a history of a community and by extension of the whole of the West but had left out class conflict and the political process in general. The Situationist Vaneigem moves the aim of art resolutely back towards the transformation of everyday life. Everything in 'Place' starts with an individual who has a revolutionary attitude: this is the point of departure for the knowledge process.

*Place* reclaims the main line of revolutionary form from the figures who had compromised variously because of affluence, egoism, or even a belief in esoteric science, and combines it again with revolutionary politics.

Working out the overlaps or non-overlaps between hippies, counter-culture, Situationism, and New Left is probably key to grasping the state of mind of involved people in say 1968–73, including writers, and including Allen Fisher. We will point to this area without entering it. Surely bringing up facts like Ted Heath winning the 1970 general election does not amount to a refutation of revolutionary theses – as opposed to a setback or detour.

*8.* Conceptual artists published or made available documentation of the idea behind the works – the concept, in fact. The 'schema' of *Gravity* is in *Ideas of the Culture Dreamed of*. The concept of *Place* is at least partly in *Prosyncel* and various notes in the original publications (now reprinted in *Marvels of Lambeth*).

*9.* The original cover for *Stane* shows a map of part of London with an inset of a diagram which we find out is a drawing from a photograph of 'the micro-structure of material about to break'. Inside, an account of rick burning by dispossessed day labourers in a rural economy gripped by a crisis in about 1820. All of these images related to damaged fabric. The text also describes the poet's migraine, congestion of blood as a consequence of stress – a function perhaps of social damage in the map of London. Sometimes Fisher likes to line similar things up. Accumulating analogies is one rule for generating the text.

*10.* One principle (in the poems of 'Shorting Out') is based on the vitrines made popular by Francis Picabia in the years after the First World War, cases where objects are made into a mysterious new whole by being placed together. Collecting objects by analogy is complemented by a step of grouping objects which are dissimilar and unrelated: disengaging the power of association and freeing it from tradition. Associating is one of the fundamental acts of the mind. Fisher is starting here from objects, as one of the significant components of visual art, and their function as bearers of memory. Arranged in set groups, they instruct us to experience certain memories. But by creating new groupings one can return to the moment when coding is set up and so to a primal freedom.

This departs from the original rule of conceptual art, that is to create visual art which left no objects behind as commodities.

*11.* There are 'rules' for constructing a volume of verse. Fisher's ideas involve a shape of the imaginary surface on which the poem is written and a variety of transforms, bending, reconnection, distortion, etc. applied to the surface and so to the poem. The tomb of Bishop Elphinstone in Aberdeen has a poem on it written in Classical Gaelic (although composed in the early 20th century) which begins and ends with the same word (*lige*), an old practice known as *dunadh* or 'closing'. (A better translation might be *joining* – so castle is *dun* because the walls run right round and join.) Fisher sees the poem as a physical shape on an imaginary object.

If you look at the development of writing, at the spirals, ribbons, etc. on which very early inscriptions run, it emerges that a set-up in which the containing space is a rectangle, lines are all straight, all letters are the same size and colour, the page has straight sides and is always the same size, is the most monotonous and schematic of all possible patterns. The variation of form became sharply reduced in the Iron Age – from roughly 300 BC. Writing became bound to an imaginary grid, homogeneous and universal. The realm of scrawl and spiral survived in the service of magic.

*Spanner* is a theoretical magazine which has always explored the suppressed variants at every level of the production of sound and written sound. Allen is the editor. *Spanner* represents the core of theoretical activity in an English poetry scene where most poets refuse theory. Related to this is the sound work *Art of Flight* (there is a tape version of this) which starts out, obviously, from the idea that reproducing a single voice with fidelity to its accidentally present sound characteristics is not compulsory. *The Art of Flight* disassembles the idea of attention by positing the idea of a space in which meaning is three-dimensional and distributed universally.

Consciousness shows up as a line in a world made of volumes. Momentary flooding gives us the idea of a border which seals consciousness off from unconsciousness – where clarity and suppression are inextricably related. The idea of erasing that line invokes subversion, infinity, transcendence.

*12.* 'Gravity' has a title which starts out with an invisible truth: a body which has its centre of gravity at the centre of an imaginary sphere has 'down' and gravity, whereas a body of the same mass arranged in a different way would not have a centre of attraction at its centre. The earth really is a near-sphere – but $n$ variant arrangements of mass can be imagined and modelled. The title detourns a familiar sentence, that the shape of an organism is the consequence of gravity. This is an example of detourning as an aesthetic gesture: the loss of an owned concept as the moment of liberation – the step into an unknown territory.

Society has a certain shape because we imagine what we are familiar with. Someone could write a long poem whose theme was to re-imagine the social process.

Fisher was impressed, early on, by research disengaging numerical patterns as part of the rules by which *The Faerie Queene* was written. Such patterns recur throughout his work – though not based on the movement of constellations and seasons, as in Spenser.

*13.* The process preceding the written text of Fisher's work is one of conceptual interrogation. The text describes the answers and so points back to the questions – which were the structural principle of the work, we can say. It would be pointless to look at this interrogation without emphasizing the process hidden within it, of moving from 'why is it like this' to 'whose interests does this arrangement serve' and 'how can we arrange it to better serve the interests of every other living human being'. The initial challenge to arranging a text in regular characters in regular lines on an exactly quadrilateral page is part of a project for overthrowing the ruling class. The ruling class relies on acquired attitudes and it is the people who shed those acquired attitudes who will change society. The point of codifying processes in conceptual art was also and from the very start an attempt to expose and make conscious patterns sunk into the unconscious of society and economy. Recovering how we acquired the rules of capitalist society demonstrates how we could acquire the rules of a completely different society.

*14.* The exceptional feature of Fisher's work is after all the scale of the structures. The initial questions displace or suppress an area of acquired knowledge, creating a gap. The course of the work is to fill this gap by answering the questions. This involves a movement in depth which makes the domestic lyric poem seem quite trivial. The small-scale structure of the poetry has to be light enough so that when huge quantities of it are built into an architectonic structure it does not put unbearable stresses on the individual parts. To put this another way: the exercise of those stresses has pressed the local design into the pattern, rigorous and buoyant, which it actually possesses.

A Fisher reader has to anthologise the large-scale structures – the ones which represent themselves at actual size.

*15.* A good deal of Fisher's work involves evaluating objects. His approach is more like art history than literary criticism. The piece in *Unpolished Mirrors* ('Morale Confusion') on a decorated ceiling is a good example of this: "Spurt of Juno's milk into night sky / silver coins/ Milky Way in idealised universe // visible equinoctial colure / celestial north south connected / uninterrupted broad Watling Street / intersecting eclipses' field / equatorial crossroads/ axes uniting galactic avenues / centring noble embraces". He lacks the background of classroom literary criticism in which most English poets developed their idea of the poem and what its limits are. Gazing at the means of traditional poetry so intently made it impossible for people to see that poetry could have quite other *ends*.

I think we have to say that a great deal of poetry written in England in the late 20th century is very similar. Also that, after the first 15,000 pages or so of this English standard, the effects are convergent, converging specifically on losing any effect at all.

Language is built on norms. A phoneme is a statistical norm, and pronouncing the sound short a in an eccentric way hinders understanding. Words have conventional sound shapes and conventional values. But we can doubt that this normality was equally good when it was applied to the construction of poems and the presentation of the self speaking them. Talking in a certain way signalled, rather accurately, that the speaker was educated and belonged to a certain social spectrum. At maximum the operation of literature was to signal the presence of someone bearing certain forms of prestige – a photograph of someone recognisable. People were led to discount the value of this proposed good by the observation that it went along with apathy and unwillingness to carry out more energetic operations such as dealing with the *unknown*. The more the writer and engaged readers desired the educated or insider role, the less interest they had in anything else. The present of the text was squeezed out by the past of acquired and licensed knowledge. The self was reduced to the boundaries of a social role. We can see this question of convergence as a mathematical problem – in which the information value of new texts slowly sinks to zero and is replaced by recognition and recurrence.

At some boundary in artistic space there is a shift whereby predictability ceases to be a source of clarity and starts to be a source of dullness and dankness. The exact location of this boundary is of great interest.

*16.* In part 4 of *Place* we hear an 18thC story set in a wood in Lambeth (Norwood) where a man, Samuel Matthews, eccentric and possibly with learning difficulties of some kind, lives alone in a hut in the wood and makes a living by gardening. Matthews has cognitive difficulties; the story is told in his language, incomplete but expressive, retained as an act of respect to him. It tells that the owners of the wood had an argument with him about the right to firewood: 'And College Warden come / ask how I dare to sell wood / I don' know it is your wood'. (That is, Dulwich College.) A few years later, in 1802, he was murdered, possibly by people who thought he had money. This is a point where Fisher overlaps with a

wider area of English writing, because we can imagine quite a few writers
telling this story. It is there because it is part of the history of Lambeth,
which is the overarching subject of *Place*, but it is also thematic because
it is a degree zero: it shows how someone can live as a drop-out, in a hut
of furze and branches, and almost outside the exchange system. It is a
fable about how space becomes property: the wanderer has no notion
that the land on which he lives also belongs to someone. The whole
history of appropriation is profoundly unequal and is threadbare in its
claim to be consensual. It is fundamental to the recorded and hoarded
knowledge of society, and the project of acquiring great knowledge is
threatened by the possibility of excessively internalising, in doing so,
the ascriptions of property and the rights of the powerful. The theme
of *Place* is also how artificial divisions of time bind people into acquired
patterns of anxiety, energy, and exhaustion; and how artificial divisions
of space bind people into rigid patterns of movement. Through all the
detail we glimpse a pristine and blank field underlying everything,
something infinitely permissive, boundless, undamaged. Another story
in *Place* is that of Roger Pike (parts 42 and 44), confined in a home as a
child perhaps around 1820:

> Roger Pike 'housed' in Elder Road
>        for breaking church music
>            misspelling 'guard'
>
> 'Clean up the centre…
> 'Sugar dust the page…
> 'Move out the feeble…
>
> Herbert Spencer, Malthus, Cyril Burt
> Rockefeller debudding minor blooms in the rosary

– seen as a victim of classification – humans bound into rigid patterns
as objects of knowledge just as property titles bind the originally blank
land into plots. Roger was placed in the House of Industry for the
Infant Poor in Elder Road. The thinkers named were fans of eugenics,
the restriction of births, the hereditary nature of intelligence.

17. Mainstream poetry has been reformed. The old middle class has
become less fanatical about the boundaries of its territory. Yet a work

like *Gravity* is as divergent from the literary norms of 2012 as it was when being designed around 1981. It gives us a vision of what poetry is by denying the rules, which are exposed as we remember, in this wholly new, wholly designed, linguistic space, what they were. Through *ostranenie* (making strange) we detect the rules of literary endeavour – as a preliminary to uncovering the rules by which society is composed. In this outside, we see the negative outline of the mainstream; the edge of what always presents itself as inevitable.

*18.* An alternative to lyric, the biography of sentiments, is constructivism. In this, rather than reproducing situations from ordinary experience, the artist creates situations from constructed rules and then reacts to the unexpected circumstances brought about by the hidden possibilities of those rules. Fisher's theme might be said to be the power of rules to generate the unforeseen, and the animating force of his work is the moment when a new and strange pattern becomes visible as the dice come to a halt. Part of the definition of a game is that it can be run multiple times and that it can be reset to the starting point, unaltered, after being played. But games are just a subset of rule-driven behaviour, for example language can also be defined as the repeated application of a finite set of rules.

This is distinct from the notion of authenticity whereby the poem reproduces the poet's personality, the documentary view. It seems to have more potential. Many people don't have very interesting personalities. Things that actually happen might reveal principles or they might make them invisible because they are so familiar. If you look at a large amount of contemporary poetry based on 'domestic anecdote' principles you may well conclude that they are ineffective and worn out. Whereas using preset rules immediately makes social rules visible by breaking them. Why should something be significant just because you walked into it? Or how is it that so many thousands of poets lead such boring lives? why make a record of this?

*Place* describes the old roads leading through Lambeth (mainly). This is a melody on reiteration – the road was not originally different from the rest of the land surface, but was worn into a road by being walked on many times by travellers. Tiny initial differences become the features dividing the world into substances, over millions of iterations. The journey reinforces the route.

*19.* As a critic, I know of poets who can be described economically because they have a small set of procedures and recycle them multiple times. If you describe the procedures you get to a vast number of poems in a brief prose statement. This only works for poets who are obstinate about their procedures. Someone like Fisher has made the rules as flexible as the instances. He does not want to depress the procedures to the unconscious level, where they are reliable and just keep cycling.

*20.* I was searching for analogies to Allen Fisher. J.H. Prynne & Iain Sinclair spring to mind. This just foregrounds the problem of analogy – and so of literary terminology, which presupposes valid analogies supporting its units of meaning and distinction. A comparison with visual artists of the same generation might be more productive.

I have a copy of *intermediate spirit receiver*, an A4 stapled object on yellow paper, published by Zunne Heft (undated, but 1980). It is credited to Ulli McCarthy but is actually Allen writing in Ulli's style, a sort of tribute. This is just an example of how prolific Allen was and of how natural his writing was. There is a specific aura, affecting my whole state of being, about A4 photocopied work of the 1970s. They sum up what I miss. The problems with distributing such products – bookshops never displayed them, they really just sold on stalls I think – give an outline justification for reprinting the work in more robust form. Also – the sheer fluency of Fisher's output, a productivity rooted in 'flow', in a whole state of mind. Piling up many of these works suggests an excuse for not being complete – we can afford to leave stuff out. One thing about *Spirit Receiver* is that it lets the social language around Allen break in for a while – suggesting, for me anyway, that the whole of these projects is a social thing, that their energy is that of a conversation and that it is what everyone was thinking (and not just Allen). It works as a history of ideas – flows in a shared intellectual life. This is more accurate than a description as 'autobiographical'. Fisher essentially does not believe that intelligence is also property. Did I say everyone – no, just the people who found their way to certain rooms and read those stapled photocopied books.

# Nomenklatura:
# Rod Mengham

In dealing with this poet I am going ahead to a time after the end of the Seventies – as with Paul Brown. Indeed, Mengham is the youngest of the poets included here and is a window on moods changing and so the end of an era. Yet he did get two pamphlets out during the decade, and their content is also part of the achievement of the time, although this might take the form of a rejection of what came before it. I will mention the word *reinforcement* and quote –

> Full of purpose the glistening orange like now on this land
> where rain has shot down the flock sawed in half
> with haywire. That failing parliament is shifting hold
>
> in the word hit and run his helmet bears the blood
> decimal. She repairs the wick to blaze in the lamp.
>
> Bodies of some are the wand with its weight behind
> a remnant in the harbour. To the throne room he climbs
>
> bent. And met each convoy shaking on the rock
> wet and soft. Have no part of glamour mud.
> (from Polyalbum, published 1977)

It is clear that a feature is missing – the words do not form patterns that would confirm the words. The gratification of divining the poet's state of mind (and perhaps sharing it) is absent. If we are to succeed in reading the poetry, we have to abandon this project. Because identification is the main source of behaviour learning, programming happens in face to face interactions and deprogramming is *primarily* to do with unstitching human relationships. Clearly the norm in poetry is a kind of tautology in which phrases reinforce each other and objects in the world express, by repeating, the state of mind of the poet. The poem mimics this within a small scale, and so the idea of deprogramming shows up in poetics as a suspension of gratification and reinforcement. I believe that this sparseness is the foreground feature of the poem. This empties out the poetic space, but what this means is that the overall landscape can be a psychological equivalent. The atmosphere is what the emptiness carries – a rejection of the social environment so radical that pleasure slips right out of the perceptible world, and the poem reproduces the surface of that vacancy. The language does not offer any literal description of that landscape, but it may be that we are seeing a whole series of proverbial phrases which evoke a political atmosphere (and an emotional state). If you imagine a journalistic report on some eastern European country (or a north-west European one, in fact), and that report being cut up so that all the figurative language is preserved but the logical argument is snipped out, we might have a plan of what *Polyalbum* is. So the language about a fleet coming to harbour (whose bottom is perhaps filled with glamour mud) might refer to a *ship of state* – success is not expected and this is very clear even if the poem could be called obscure. The orange, in collocation with rain, might be the sun; it defines now because it is the source of time. The parts are crushed and impacted but highly subjective. There are no facts here, no literal equivalents of objects in space. The connectives have been eliminated. The names of the country and the period are something we have to work out.

A key factor is that reinforcement/emphasis would take the misery to an unacceptable level. Raising the speed is a necessary step on the way to conceptual clarity. It generates an excess momentum which takes us beyond realism. The background argument is likely to include the breakdown of the post-war settlement during the mid-70s, and the suspicion (expressed by various critical prose writers) that the warmth of art relaxed people and made them less aware of political abuses and the need to work for change. In the Seventies, the expectation of a classless and de-repressed society was the content of much poetry and music and could itself be regarded as a narcotic drug. *Polyalbum* is peculiarly disconsoling, although its very asperity leads to a new acuity, and the elimination of foreground cognitive clutter allows glimpses of larger and less humanised shapes. Perhaps this attenuation of the physical is the first moment of abstract thought. It feels like an illness during its first onset.

So, society is the product of history. This was apparently a moment when we realised that we had been inside a programming box all our lives and we were now being shown a way out of it. Something else it exposed was that poetry was based on the human voice and that the poet was setting us the task of understanding them, and that the gratification part of poetry came from recognising the signs and the patterns and doing what the poet asked us. So, if you had an artistic experience (or field, should I say) in which there was no approval, no reward, the experiencer could feel miserable, desolate, unwanted, pointless. In fact this was the most likely outcome. These experiments did highlight how much of traditional art consisted of cognitive rewards (and, inseparably, of very symmetrical, unambiguous, patterns).

Both the gratification and the pattern strength could fit under the heading of reinforcement.

I mentioned the theme of didactic wilderness, earlier on. This continues a Christian figure and is related to narratives about penances and pilgrimages. These were expressed visually as mazes. Related terms would include deprogramming, depatterning, and alienation effect. The fascination with uncoded landscapes could hardly avoid landscapes without paths, and gratification is part of the coding.

It is reasonable to speak of foregrounding what is absent, here. As the poem continues without reassuring us, all the conventions of art become conscious. The more they are not there, the more clearly we can see them. Playing with the idea of attachment brings on scene two theses: that attachment and reinforcement trap us in a social order which may be malign, and that our psychological inclination to develop attachments is a free energy which could "naturalise" us in a new society.

*Equofinality*, edited by Mengham (first issue, 1981, last 1991 perhaps) was a radical break with the poetry showcased in *A Various Art*. Arguably, this was the start of the 1980s and would require a new book. One part of this new atmosphere was an awareness that the socialist utopia was not an imminent event – the poets knew that there was a swing to the Right, and indeed 1979 saw the start of eighteen years of Conservative rule. Optimism was, at that point, a form of ignorance. The editorial decision not to include any poets from the older generation summed up the sight of a breach.

For me, Mengham's first two pamphlets did not unite disillusion and the flash of awareness. His poetry acquired much more depth and confidence at a point recorded in Paul Green's anthology *Ten British Poets* (1993, and itself a definition of the generation born in the 1950s, so the disillusioned). The 1970s pamphlets are a breakthrough, but too acerb to give pleasure. The later poetry takes more pleasure in furnishing its scenes of citizen powerlessness and political corruption, and is correspondingly rewarding in its alignment of serenity and anguish. Take the poem 'Nomenclature':

For whom the great Atlantic cables in a black outflow
Twist in their beds within great load-bearing veins

Launching men into perdition; far to the west
Flotsam begins combusting, flames and sparks carried off

At this moment they have touched
The prow-lit tunnel. He or she speaks

It is eve-of-election
Maple leaves fall over shining elements

The French are painting their front doors and they
Hang their jackets like champions

One shop window is filled with mutes
Less and less makes it more

Transcaucasia like a burning wheel, 27 languages
On the verge of saying 'cosa nostra'
                (circa 1986? quoted from the book *Unsung*, 1996)

Mengham spent much time in Poland during the 1980s. The Soviet system relied on promotion via lists of people suitable to hold power, which implied suitable to abuse power and unlikely to cause trouble for anyone else abusing power. These lists of names had the innocent name nomenklatura, and the term came to be used by dissidents as a label for the Soviet elite – and, by extension, for a system in which over 90% of the population had no power whatsoever. The label could be extended to Poland, where the Stalinist system had reproduced itself in the 1950s without much popular enthusiasm. The poem is likely to be describing the collapse of communism and predicting the rise of a state/corporate mafia, a "cosa nostra". The nomenclature word is likely to mean something like, democracy in name only. Prosperity in name only. Liberation in name only. The transatlantic cables are likely to be carrying instructions from the financial centre in New York, business decisions which meant loss, *perdition*, for many and profit or asset acquisition for the few.

    Outflow applies normally to sewer outlets, something else which uses trenches (and involves the sea a lot). There is something exhilarating about the zest and scorn of Mengham's rapid panoramic scan through a landscape where every object is an allegory of a new politics and every moment is startling before it resolves into a startling new framework. It is a philosophy of everyday life. This is a great poem and it was followed by others. The poems require to be read from a very specific emotional stance, but the stance is plainly pointed out and mirrored by the poems, which by now carry an impressive weight.

> The ink fades on the escudos bill in its journey ever westward; ever backward, through gold standard, silver, copper, tin, faïence, hide, bone. The notes for general circulation become detached from each other and float off on tiny currents, all bobbing in dactylic rhythm for a moment before they decompose. The separate meanings disinflate as they touch the same horizon, a narrow ridge between precipices.
>
> (from 'The Dog Star')

# Afterword

Events have intervened, and since the election of December 2019 the blithe Corbynism with which I opened the book now looks like a historical backwater. This must affect the asset value of the poets, born roughly 1947 to 1950, who had pursued the long route of radicalism in the Seventies and forever after. What the effect will be, it is too soon to say. People don't agree about anything and so what I remember is not a collective thing. Do poets of 2020 even know about the Seventies? Is there a continuity of technique? I doubt it, since after all it doesn't sound right that someone could own what doesn't exist yet. If nobody owns it, the function of legacy and ancestors almost vanishes. There are two ways of looking at the continuity between the 1970s and now. First, you could see it as a broad river reaching a rich delta. The heroic figures of the Seventies were excluded from view by malevolent conservative critics, stood out heroically in the wilderness, issued junk bonds which cost pennies to acquire but which appreciated thousand-fold, came into their own, and begot a world of younger poets in their image, who gave them the accolade and learnt everything of value from their example. As a result, every small press poet of the Seventies is now famous and widely loved. I guess this is what you would put in someone's obituary. It conserves prestige and self-esteem.

But, secondly, you can see the Underground as a river that breaks up into dozens of shallow streams and finally runs into the sand. It blossoms as dozens of oases but never reaches the sea and a haven. Old papyri are preserved where a fertile soil turns into abiotic sand as water ceases to flow into it. The papyri are dug up from a town that was abandoned – they didn't survive unless the ground dried up. Sand as the substance of memory, as much as stone, stable because forbidding the cycles of life. This raises the question of whether the Underground is an organism. How can you have an organism without organs?

There is a whole world of alternative poets today. However, this may be because mainstream and dumbed-down poems are unattractive rather than because there is any memory of the Underground. An awareness of alternative possibilities might come from the visual arts or from literary theorists – these are available in a way which British modernist poetry is not. In fact, the possibility of a "vertical transmission" was deleted because the industry really did cut the British innovators out of the libraries, magazines, and shops, and the Underground really was persistently invisible. What this means is that there is a regenerative revolt whose breeding sites are *inside* the festering anatomy of the mainstream, and are even a nameless part of that anatomy. We are looking at some Mendelian law of the reproduction of norms whereby the outcome is regularly 70% conventional poets and 30% outlaws.

This is the context in which I set out to document the poetry of the Seventies, to rescue things that have never been written down and which are threatened with forgetfulness and decay. I have been describing what people said and wrote in the 1970s, but this sets aside the whole area of what people in 2020 think about the time and what selective memory processes have been set in motion to cover up deception. That is, any kind of marketing is better than total oblivion. I suspect that discontinuity is the key. I think what we are seeing is a whole theme park of abandoned poetic projects, exotic because no path runs to them, staggering in their numbers and diversity. A desert landscape full of incomplete but beautiful structures.

# Bibliography

**Generalisations**
General surveys of the period in:
Booth, Martin, *British Poetry 1964–1984: Driving Through the Barricades* (London: Routledge and Kegan Paul, 1985)
chapters in Andrew Duncan, *The Failure of Conservatism* (2nd ed., Shearsman Books, 2016), pp.168–237.
Ginsberg interview in *Second Aeon* (periodical: Cardiff, 1972)
Mottram, Eric, 'The British Poetry Revival 1960–74' in 'Catalogue' of PCL poetry weekend, 1974
Raban, Jonathan, *The Society of the Poem* (London: Harrap & Co., 1971)
Stevenson, Randall, *The Last of England?* (Oxford; Oxford University Press, 2004) pp.165–270;
Thwaite, Anthony, 'The Two Poetries', in Abse, Dannie, ed. *Poetry Dimension 2* (London: Abacus, 1974)

**Crave That Hurting Thing**
Grigson, Geoffrey, *Blessings, Kicks, and Curses* (London: Allison and Busby, 1982)
Kneale, Trevor, ed. *Contemporary Women Poets* (Liverpool: Rondo Publications, 1975)
Perlstein, Rick, *Nixonland* (London: Scribner, 2008)

**Speaking Volumes**
Gardiner, S.T., ed., *The Poet's Yearbook 1977* (London: Poet's Yearbook Ltd, 1977)

***Sounds surround the icy waters underground*: Psychedelic Coding**
Whiteley, Sheila, *The Space Between the Notes* (London: Routledge, 1992)

**Short Poems of the 1970s**
Porter, Peter, *Collected Poems* (Oxford: Oxford University Press, 1983)
Raban, Jonathan, *The Society of the Poem* (*ut supra*)

**Post-Western?**
Gibbs in Michael Gibbs, *All or Nothing and Other Pages*, see below
*Joe Di Maggio* (magazine, Bexleyheath, 1971–), #11
Levy, G.R., *The Gate of Horn* (London: Faber and Faber, 1948)
Michell, John, *Flying Saucer Vision* (London: Abacus, 1974)
Mottram, Eric, *Local Movement* (London: Writers Forum, 1974)
Sinclair, Iain, *Lud Heat* (London: Albion Village Press, 1975)

**Rite- and Fore-time: the Liminal as a Form of the Sublime**

Fisher, Allen, *Shorting Out* (reprint in *future exiles*, London: Paladin Books, 1992)

Mottram, Eric, *1922 Earth Raids* (London: New London Pride, 1976*)*

Turner, Victor, and Turner, Edith, *Image and Pilgrimage in Christian Culture* (New York, NY: Columbia University Press, 2011)

Turner, Victor, *Dramas, Fields, and Metaphors* (Ithaca, NY: Cornell University Press, 1974)


**Blink and It's There**

Raban, Jonathan, *Soft City* (2nd edition, London: Fontana/Collins, 1975)


**Spaced Out: Long Poems of the 1970s**

Beeching, Jack, *Myth of Myself* (in: *Penguin Modern Poets 16*, Harmondsworth: Penguin, 1970)

Bowen, Euros, *Siâp ryw brofiad* in *Cylch o gerddi* (Liverpool: Gwasg y Brython, 1970)

Casey, Gerard, *South Wales Echo* (London: Enitharmon, 1973)

Crozier, Andrew, *High Zero* (Cambridge: Street Editions, 1978)
    Crozier interview is in *Don't Start Me Talking* (Tim Allen and Andrew Duncan, eds., Cambridge; Salt Publications, 2005*)*.

Fisher, Allen, *Sicily* (London: Aloes Books, 1973); *Paxton's Beacon* (Todmorden: Arc Publications, 1976)

Fisher, Roy, *The Cut Pages* (London: Fulcrum Press, 1970; 2nd edition, containing title poem only, London: Oasis Books/Shearsman Books, 1986)

Flintoff, Eddie, *Sarmatians (no publisher,* 1978*)*

Graham, W.S., *Dark Dialogues* (in: *Penguin Modern Poets 17*, Harmondsworth: Penguin, 1970)

Guest, Harry, *Elegies* (in: *Lost and Found. Poems 1975–82*, London: Anvil, 1983; republished separately, Shearsman Books, 2018)

Jenkins, Phil, *Cairo* (in: Tony Frazer, ed., *A State of Independence*, Exeter; Stride Publications, 1998)

Jones, David, *The Sleeping Lord and Other Fragments* (London: Faber, 1974)

Lopez, Antony, *Change. A Prospectus* (London: New London Pride, 1978)

MacBeth, George, *The Orlando Poems* (London: Macmillan, 1971); *A Poet's Life* (in: *Collected Poems*, London: Hutchinson, 1989)

MacLean, Sorley, *Uamha 'n Oir / The Cave of Gold* in: *From Wood to Ridge* (London: Vintage, 1991)

MacLean: Sorley, in Ross, Raymond, and Hendry, Joy, eds., *Sorley MacLean: Critical Essays* (Edinburgh: Scottish Academic Press, 1986); *Tocher*, (periodical, Edinburgh), issue 47. Westwood, Jennifer, and Kingshill, Sophia, *Scottish Lore* (London: Arrow Books, 2011). *Béaloideas* (periodical, Dublin), Iml. 57 (1989).

Morgan, Edwin, *Memories of Earth* (in: *The New Divan*, Manchester: Carcanet Press, 1977)

Mottram, Eric, *Tunis* (Sheffield: Rivelin, 1977)

Kathleen Raine, *On a Deserted Shore* (London: Hamilton, 1973)

Reed, Jeremy, *The Isthmus of Samuel Greenberg*, (London: Trigram, 1976; 2nd edition, Shearsman Books, 2018)

Smith, Iain Crichton, *From the Notebooks of Robinson Crusoe* (London: Gollancz, 1975); *The White Air of March* (in *Collected Poems*, Manchester: Carcanet Press, 1992; *New Collected Poems,* Manchester: Carcanet Press, 2011)

Turnbull, Gael, *Residues* in: *A Gathering of Poems* (London: Anvil, 1983); and in *There Are Words… : Collected Poems* (Exeter: Shearsman Books, 2006)

Wain, John, *Feng* (London: Macmillan, 1975)

*Long poems discussed in previous works by the author:*
'Notes for Joachim', *Fishermen with Ploughs, Marimarusa, Crow,* 'Bargain Basement Sonnets', 'Lamentation for the Children', *Dry-points of the Hasidim, Lud Heat, Where the Arrow Falls,* in *Silent Rules.*
*Place* in *Marvels of Lambeth.*
'For Man and Islands', 'Ancestor Worship', 'Clytemnestra', 'Pancakes for the Queen of Babylon', 'Stratton Elegy', in *The Long 1950s.*
'Black Torch' in Paul Batchelor, ed., *Reading Barry MacSweeney.*
'Czargrad' in *Origins of the Underground.*
*Tristan Crazy, Apocrypha from the Western Kingdom, Referendum, Thomas 'Müntzer'* in *The Failure of Conservatism.*
*New Confessions* in *Heresy.*

### The Little Magazine World

Brown, Paul, *Meetings and Pursuits* (London: Skyline, 1978)

— *Masker* (Newcastle: Galloping Dog Press, 1982)

— *A Cabin In the Mountains* (Hastings: Reality Street, 2012)

### Open Field In the Badlands: Simms

DeVoto, Bernard, *Westward the Course of Empire* (London: Eyre and Spottiswoode, 1954)

Simms, Colin, *The American Poems* (Exeter: Shearsman Books, 2005)

More on Simms in *Silent Rules* and *Centre and Periphery.*

### News of Warring Clans

Text in J.H. Prynne, *Poems* (Newcastle: Bloodaxe Books, 2005)

**Conceptual Art**

Cork, Richard, ed., *Sviluppi alternativi*, vol 2. of catalogue of British Council show of English Art 1960–76 at Milan in the year 1976 (Milan: Electa Editrice, 1976). Volume 1 was the non-alternative.

—*Everything Was Possible: Art of the 70s* (New York, NY: Columbia University Press, 2003)

Felipe Ehrenberg interview online.

Sigi Krauss interview online.

Chapter, 'Critique of the individual', in *A Poetry Boom*. 'Primer of the avant-garde', in *Council of Heresy*.

**Two Conceptual Poets**

Gibbs, Michael, *All or Nothing and Other Pages* (eds. Gerrit Jan de Rook and Andrew Wilson; a retrospective which includes work and essays on Gibbs) (Axminster: Uniformbooks, 2016)

— *Selected Pages* (Amsterdam: Kontexts, 1976)

— *SomevolumesfromtheLibraryofBabel* (2005 reprint, Cromford: RGAP, 2005)

Ward, John Powell, *From Alphabet to Logos* (Cardiff: 2nd Aeon, 1973)

**Suicide Bridge**

Redford, Donald B., ed., *The Oxford Essential Guide to Egyptian Mythology* (New York: Berkley Books, 2003), *s.v.* Atum

Sinclair, Iain, *Suicide Bridge* (Cheltenham: Skylight Press, 2013)

AD in *Origins*

There is a list of the sources of *Suicide Bridge* on my website at www.angelexhaust.blogspot.com

**Ideas about Time**

Smith, Ken, 'Fox Running' in *The Poet Reclining* (Newcastle: Bloodaxe, 1982)

**The Sphere of Intimacy, 1.**

Evans, Paul, *February* (London: Fulcrum Press, 1970)

Evans, Paul, *The Door of Taldir* (Exeter: Shearsman Books, 2009)

**The Sphere of Intimacy, 2: New Magical Earth**

Hawkins, Ralph, *soft in the brains* (in *Spanner* magazine, London, 1981)

Jackowska, Nicki, *The House that Manda Built* (London: Menard Press, 1981)

McCarthy, Ulli, *sonnet brushes* (London: Bonefold Imprint, 1976)

Pordage quoted in van den Broek, Roelof, and Hanegraaff, Wouter, eds., *Gnosticism and Hermeticism* (Albany, NY: State University of New York Press, 1998)

Sinclair, Iain, *Red Eye 1973–2013* (London: Test Centre, 2013)

**20 Notions on Allen Fisher**
Fisher, Allen, *The Marvels of Lambeth* (Exeter: Shearsman Books, 2013)

**The Bloodshed, the Shaking House**
Thom, Martin, *The Bloodshed, the Shaking House* (London: X Press, 1977)

**Nomenklatura**
Mengham, Rod, *Unsung* (Cambridge: Folio/Salt, 1996)

# Acknowledgements

Thanks are due to the following for permission to quote from the works mentioned. Where no specific approval is listed, a quotation falls under fair-usage rules.

Euros Bowen, excerpts from *Cylch o gerddi* (Liverpool: Gwasg y Brython, 1970). All attempts to trace who is responsible for the author's estate have proved fruitless, and we would welcome any information that would help us to resolve this.

Paul Brown for excerpts from 'Memorandum to all field-staff' in *Meetings and Pursuits* (Skyline, 1978), 'May 22nd' in *Masker* (Newcastle-upon-Tyne: Galloping Dog Press, 1982), and from the uncollected 'Work Areas'.

Carcanet Press for two excerpts from *High Zero* by Andrew Crozier, collected in *An Andrew Crozier Reader*, edited by Ian Brinton (Manchester: Carcanet Press, 2012).

Nathalie Blondel for the Estate of Paul Evans for excerpts from 'We Are the Instruments of Adoration' and '1st Imaginary Love Poem', in *February* (London: Fulcrum Press, 1970) and an excerpt from 'Extempore' in *The Manual for the Perfect Organisation of Tourneys* (London: Oasis Books, 1979); the second and third poems were republished in *The Door of Taldir: Selected Poems*, edited by Robert Sheppard (Exeter: Shearsman Books, 2009).

Allen Fisher for 'Erase Muse' from 'Shorting Out' in *Poetry for Schools* (London: Aloes Books 1980).

Ralph Hawkins for an excerpt from *soft in the brains* (London: Spanner, 1981);

Nicki Jackowska for excerpts from 'The King Rises' and 'Rose House' in *The House That Manda Built* (London: Menard Press, 1981).

Brian Marley for excerpts from 'Bargain Basement Sonnets #5', from *Springtime in the Rockies* (London: Trigram Press, 1978).

Ulli Freer for an excerpt from Poem 9, by Ulli McCarthy, in *Sonnet Brushes* by Ulli McCarthy & Bernard Kelly (London: Bonefold, 1973).

Rod Mengham for excerpts from 'Polyalbum' and 'Nomenclature' collected in *Unsung: New and Selected Poems* (Cambridge: Folio/Salt, 1996).

King's College London, for The Estate of Eric Mottram, for excerpts from 'A Book of Herne', in *A Book of Herne 1975–1981* (Colne: Arrowspire Press, 1981); from 'Homage to Denis Saurat'; from '1922 Earth Raids', in *1922 Earth Raids and other poems 1973–1975* (London: New London Pride Editions, 1976) and two excerpts from *Tunis* (Sheffield: Rivelin Press, 1977).

Colin Simms for excerpts from *Rushmore Inhabitation* and *No Northwestern Passage*, collected in *The American Poems* (Exeter: Shearsman Books, 2005).

J.H. Prynne and Bloodaxe Books for excerpts from 'A New Tax on the Counter-Earth', originally published in *Brass* (Ferry Press, 1971), and excerpts from *News of Warring Clans* (London: Trigram Press, 1977), all now collected in *Poems*, 3rd edition (Hexham: Bloodaxe Books, 2015).

Jeremy Reed for excerpts from *The Isthmus of Samuel Greenberg* (London: Trigram Press, 1976; 2nd edition, Bristol: Shearsman Books, 2018), and for excerpts from 'Junky Tango Outside Boots, Piccadilly' (an elegy for Paula Stratton), collected in *Black Russian – Out-Takes from the Airmen's Club 1978–79* (Brighton: Waterloo Press, 2011).

Iain Sinclair and Skylight Press for excerpts from *Suicide Bridge* (London: Albion Village Press, 1979; 2nd, expanded edition, Cheltenham: Skylight Press, 2013); Iain Sinclair and Prototype Publishing for an excerpt from *Red Eye* (London: Test Centre, 2015).

Carcanet Press for excerpts from 'The Notebooks of Robinson Crusoe' from *The Notebooks of Robinson Crusoe and other poems* (London: Gollancz, 1975) by Iain Crichton Smith, and 'The White Air of March' from *Penguin Modern Poets 21* (Harmondsworth: Penguin Books, 1972), all collected in Iain Crichton Smith, *New Collected Poems* (Manchester: Carcanet Press, 2011).

Martin Thom for excerpts from 'Iron Work' in *The Bloodshed, the Shaking House* (London: X Press, 1977).

The Estate of Gael Turnbull for excerpts from *Residues* (Pensnett: Grosseteste Press, 1976), collected in *There Are Words… : Collected Poems* (Exeter: Shearsman Books, 2006).

The Estate of John Wain for excerpts from *Feng* (London: Viking Press, 1975), and from *Letters to Five Artists* (London: Macmillan, 1969).

# The Author

Andrew Duncan was born in 1956 and brought up in the Midlands. He worked as a labourer in England and Germany after leaving school, and subsequently as a project planner with a telecoms manufacturer (1978–87), and as a programmer for the Stock Exchange (1988–91). He has been publishing poetry since his Cambridge days in the late '70s, including *Threads of Iron, Anxiety Before Entering a Room, Skeleton Looking at Chinese Pictures, Savage Survivals* and, in 2018, a selected poems titled *On the Margins of Great Empires*. He is one of the editors of *Angel Exhaust* and has translated a lot of modern German poetry, most recently Thomas Kling's Selected Poems, *zerodrifter* (Shearsman Books, 2019). Over the past dozen years he has also published a substantial amount of literary criticism: *The Failure of Conservatism in Modern British Poetry* (2006, rev. ed. 2016); *Origins of the Underground: The Occlusion of British Poetry, 1932–77, Centre and Periphery* (2005, rev. ed. 2016), *The Council of Heresy* (2009), *The Long 1950s* (2012), *A Poetry Boom 1990–2010* (2015), and *Fulfilling the Silent Rules* (2018), as well as the current volume.

Milton Keynes UK
Ingram Content Group UK Ltd.
UKHW041502021224
3327UKWH00050B/898